Abuse and Cover-Up

ABUSE AND COVER-UP

*Refounding the Catholic Church
in Trauma*

Gerald A. Arbuckle, SM

ORBIS BOOKS
Maryknoll, New York 10545

ORBIS BOOKS
Maryknoll, New York 10545

Fathers and Brothers
MARYKNOLL™

Founded in 1970, Orbis Books endeavors to publish works that enlighten the mind, nourish the spirit, and challenge the conscience. The publishing arm of the Maryknoll Fathers and Brothers, Orbis seeks to explore the global dimensions of the Christian faith and mission, to invite dialogue with diverse cultures and religious traditions, and to serve the cause of reconciliation and peace. The books published reflect the views of their authors and do not represent the official position of the Maryknoll Society. To learn more about Maryknoll and Orbis Books, please visit our website at www.maryknollsociety.org.

Names: Arbuckle, Gerald A., author.
Title: Abuse and cover-up : refounding the Catholic Church in trauma / Gerald A. Arbuckle.
Description: Maryknoll : Orbis Books, 2019. | Includes bibliographical references and index.
Identifiers: LCCN 2019008951 (print) | LCCN 2019019679 (ebook) | ISBN 9781608338030 (e-book) | ISBN 9781626983397 (print)
Subjects: LCSH: Child sexual abuse by clergy. | Catholic Church—Clergy—Sexual behavior. | Catholic Church—Discipline. | Catholic Church—History—21st century.
Classification: LCC BX1912.9 (ebook) | LCC BX1912.9 .A73 2019 (print) | DDC 282.09/051—dc23
LC record available at https://lccn.loc.gov/2019008951

For Francis Sullivan

Contents

Acknowledgments

My particular thanks to Robert Ellsberg and Jill O'Brien for accepting this book for publication on behalf of Orbis Books; Maria Angelini, production coordinator; members of the community at Campion Hall, Oxford University, for providing me with a congenial environment where the planning and research for this book first began; and Anthony Maher, Thomas Ryan, SM, Michael Mullins, SM, Peter Steane, MSC, and Brian Cummings, SM, who patiently read the text and offered astute comments. These people, however, are in no way responsible for any shortcomings of the book.

Introduction

The culture of abuse and cover-up is incompatible with the logic of the Gospel. The "never again" to the culture of abuse and the system of cover-up that allows it to be perpetuated demands working among everyone in order to generate a culture of care.
> —Pope Francis, *Letter to the Church in Chile,*
> May 31, 2018

Clericalism is a perversion and is the root of many evils in the church.
> —Pope Francis, Opening Address to Synod on Youth,
> October 3, 2018

Judging from the public outcry by Catholics throughout the Western world . . . the abuse problem by clergy, and the response to the abuse by the Church hierarchy and the Vatican, is one that will be settled only by structural reform, a new more critical theology and a new ecclesiology.
> —Marie Keenan, *Child Sexual Abuse*
> *and the Catholic Church: Gender, Power,*
> *and Organizational Culture,* 2012

Instead of seeking easy answers and scapegoats, it's time . . . to . . . identify the real problem and the true villains. . . . Sooner or later each of us has to accept . . . that complexity is here to stay and that order begins out of chaos.
> —Warren Bennis, *Why Leaders Can't Lead:*
> *The Unconscious Conspiracy Continues,* 1990

The global Catholic Church is in a paralyzing state of cultural and personal trauma, its most challenging condition since the

Reformation. Once we were a "strong mountain" (Ps 30:7) of great prosperity. Now the power and prestige previously granted to us have all but disintegrated. We People of God are not sure what to do. With the psalmist we cry to God: "What profit is there in my death, if I go down to the Pit? . . . Hear, O Lord, and be gracious to me! O Lord, be my helper!" (Ps 30:9, 10). This praxis-oriented book focuses on the cultural reasons for this trauma and how, as People of God, we can and must move forward. Written for readers deeply concerned for the future of the church, it seeks to answer two questions:

- Why is the culture of the Catholic Church, despite Vatican II's emphasis on collegiality and transparency, still prone to covering up abuses of power?
- How can this culture change in order for the Church to move forward?

Many hierarchies, priests, and religious, as a consequence of the overwhelmingly revelations of appalling sexual abuse scandals and cover-ups, have finally been largely discredited and demoralized. Lay people feel betrayed, disillusioned, and angry, their trust in their leaders destroyed. Many are leaving the church in disgust. As the media identifies yet another scandal somewhere in the world, we in our hearts may identify with the poignant feelings of the shamed psalmist: "I am the scorn of all my adversaries, a horror to my neighbors, an object of dread to my acquaintances; those who see me in the street flee from me" (Ps 31:11). Pope Francis rightly declares that these cultures of sexual abuse and cover-ups must be identified and changed, the survivors[1] compassionately listened to and supported.

---

[1] The word "survivor" means: "Someone who has experienced harm or abuse whether sexually, physically or emotionally, and has survived this abuse. It is thought that this term might be more empowering than 'victim.' . . . For some the term 'victim' suggests that they are defined and restricted by the experience." *The McLellan Commission: A Review of the Current Safeguarding Policies, Procedures and Practice within the Catholic Church in Scotland* 2015, 83, www. mclellancommission.co.uk.

Silenced voices, muffled cries in the darkness, unacknowl-
edged tears, the tyranny of invisible suffering, the never-heard
pleas of tortured souls, bewildered by an indifference to the
unthinkable theft of their innocence. . . . Why was their trust
betrayed? Why did those who know cover it up? Why were
the cries of children and parents ignored? Why has it taken
so long to act? Why were other things more important than
this, the care of innocent children? Why didn't we believe?[2]

Rhetoric over Reality

Yet this chaotic state of systemic corruption cannot be considered in isolation from what has also been occurring culturally
in the church universally and locally over the past sixty years
since Vatican II. The fact is that the church has become discon-
nected—with tragic consequences—from its primary task: the
mission of Jesus Christ.

The People of God have for decades been experiencing an
overload of accumulated and unarticulated grief, as they have
observed with growing resentment and sadness the widening gap
between Vatican II rhetoric and reality. The fact is that "the program of Vatican II, which envisaged a more collegial Church with
active lay participation and a better balance of power between
the papacy and local churches or branches, has not for the most
part been realised."[3] Secrecy, not transparency, has intensified, a
fact that Pope Francis frequently deplores and struggles to change.
Youthful energy for the mission of Christ has been constantly
suffocated (see Chapter 2).

Our efforts to process this grief publicly have too often been
forbidden by hierarchical officials who have sought to maintain
pre–Vatican II order at all costs. But the suppression of this grief
has only intensified the sadness and rage in their hearts. Unless
this amassed grief is allowed to be openly and ritually named,
any attempts to move forward will ultimately be frustrated. As

---

[2] Australian Prime Minister Scott Morrison, *National Apology to Those Who
Have Been Abused Delivered at House of Representatives* (October 22, 2018).

[3] Marie Keenan, *Child Sexual Abuse and the Catholic Church: Gender, Power,
and Organizational Culture* (Oxford: Oxford University Press, 2012), 267.

Mary, sister of the deceased Lazarus, was weeping at his tomb (Jn 11:31), "Jesus was greatly disturbed in spirit and deeply moved . . . [and he] began to weep" (Jn 11:33, 35). As Jesus lamented over the loss of Lazarus and the sadness of his sisters, so must we. Without lament over abuses of power in the church, and the sufferings of survivors, we cannot be open to reform and the cultural changes necessary to facilitate this. Indeed the very foundations and existing governance structures of the church must be reexamined: "Blessed are you who weep now, for you will laugh" (Lk 6:21).[4] Yes, we need to weep now, acknowledging countless cultures of abuse over generations. Only then can we collectively begin to journey forward with the faith-based laughter of converting hearts (see Chapters 3 and 6).

Cultures of Abuse and Cover-Up

The revelations in the 1980s and 1990s of sexual abuse by clergy and religious were at first generally denied by church authorities. Then questions began to be asked: Has there been a conspiracy among bishops, clergy, and religious to conceal this abuse in the past? Is there something in the church's culture that has encouraged a cover-up for so long? It is important in seeking answers to these questions that we do not confine ourselves only to tragic cases of sexual abuse.[5] Until recent times, for example, authoritarian behavior and the alcoholism of clergy and religious have also been repeatedly hushed up. In fact, argues Philip Jenkins, "Catholic clergy are not necessarily represented in the sexual abuse phenomenon at a rate higher than or even equal to their numbers in the clerical profession as a whole."[6]

Why then the dramatic spotlight on the Catholic Church? A significant factor is the past attempts at concealment, something

---

[4]The importance of lamentation over loss as the condition for moving forward is more fully explained in Gerald A. Arbuckle, *The Francis Factor and the People of God: New Life for the Church* (Maryknoll, NY: Orbis Books, 2015).

[5]See Jason Berry, *Lead Us Not into Temptation: Catholic Priests and the Sexual Abuse of Children* (Urbana: University of Illinois Press, 2000), 5–168.

[6]Philip Jenkins, *Pedophiles and Priests: Anatomy of a Contemporary Crisis* (Oxford: Oxford University Press, 1996), 8. See Gerald A. Arbuckle, *Violence, Society, and the Church: A Cultural Approach* (Collegeville, MN: Liturgical Press, 2004), 91–92.

the Church has been prone to do for centuries. As the "modernist" George Tyrrell wrote in 1907: "The short-sighted fear of scandal has been, and is, the curse of the Church. . . . Because it is an easily and much used cover for cowardice, it exploits the future in the interests of the present, preferring scandal of millions to come to that of hundreds now."[7] In the case of sexual abuse, the actual acts "have been magnified for the victims by the extent to which the brotherhood of priests and bishops has closed ranks in denial, cover-up, and protection for the offenders."[8] All this is abuse of power.

What does "the culture of abuse *and* the system of cover-up" that Pope Francis and others have spoken of mean, exactly? Corruption is systemic whenever it becomes an essential element or pattern in an institutional culture (see Chapter 1). Philip Zimbardo, emeritus professor of Stanford University, says that the evil of corruption can occur at one of three levels: (1) people are just "bad apples" because they are personally so disposed;[9] (2) they act corruptly because the "barrel" they are in happens to be unethical; that is, the situation people are in disposes them to act in evil ways; or (3) people act in evil ways because the system, supported by the culture, causes the "barrel" to be corrupt. Sexual abuse cover-ups are systemic institutional evil because the culture of the church in this matter is corrupt. It is thus this third form of corruption we are particularly concerned about in this book. Since the crisis is a systemic cultural issue, then the solutions to this evil must be culturally based. The tragedy is that the disappearance of evil as a concept and a reality is one of the most extraordinary qualities of contemporary society.

We as People of God are committed, writes Pope Francis, "to create a culture where each person has the right to breathe an air free of every kind of abuse. A culture free of the cover-ups, which end up vitiating all our relationships. A culture which in the face

---

[7] Letter of George Tyrrell to Baron Friedrich von Hugel, 27 June 1903 and 19 November 1905, cited by Anthony Maher, *The Forgotten Jesuit of Catholic Modernism* (Minneapolis: Fortress Press, 2018), 9.

[8] Joanna Manning, *Take Back the Truth: Confronting Papal Power and the Religious Right* (New York: Crossroad, 2002), 126–27.

[9] See Philip Zimbardo, "The Psychology of Evil," TED Lecture (September 23, 2008).

of sin creates a dynamic of repentance, mercy and forgiveness, and in the face of crime, accusation, judgment and sanction."[10] That is, to be a church of repentance, mercy, and forgiveness there *must* be major culture changes. But we have a problem! What do the words "culture," "culture change," and "cultural systems" mean? Uninformed use of these words endangers reforms. Organizational analyst David Wilson's warning is timely:

> "Change the culture and the majority of current organizational problems will be solved" has become something of a recurrent theme from many students of management, theorists and consultants alike. The phrase (like the term "culture") is a useful catch-all, incorporating broad aspects of organization. . . . Despite a growing empirical research base which testifies to the difficulty in defining, let alone managing, organizational culture, it has remained a seductive concept, imbued with a seemingly elixir-like quality for facilitating corporate change and renewal.[11]

There are literally hundreds of different definitions of culture. Books on leadership, for example, commonly either ignore culture or define it simplistically as "what we do around here," yet culture is far more complicated than this (see Chapter 4). Sustained cultural change is fraught with many complex difficulties, especially in massive and highly multifaceted organizations such as the Church. In culture analysis there is no room for simplification. As anthropologist Clifford Geertz writes, cultural analysis is always inherently incomplete: "And, worse than that, the more deeply it goes the less complete it is."[12] Consequently, inaccurate perceptions of and defective attitudes toward cultures invariably result in bad theology as well as defective pastoral policies and practices.

One fundamental truth that would-be change agents or reformers must accept is this: culture, as difficult as it is to define and analyze, is stronger and more resistant to change than the walls

---

[10]Pope Francis, *Letter to the Church in Chile*, May 31, 2018.

[11]David C. Wilson, *A Strategy of Change* (London: Routledge, 1992), 69.

[12]Clifford Geertz, *The Interpretation of Cultures: Selected Essays* (New York: Basic Books, 1973), 29.

of St. Peter's Basilica.[13] We need to turn to cultural anthropologists for help because the specific task of cultural anthropology is to unravel the complex meanings of culture and apply them to the themes of this book (see Chapter 1).[14] This cultural analysis gives the book its uniqueness.

Refounding the Church

The trauma of the church, which is a culture in emotional overload, can be the catalyst for an immense surge of faith-inspired evangelization both of ourselves and the world around us (see Chapter 3). For this to happen we desperately need inner conversion, new structures, and methods of evangelizing; we need a Copernican revolution in our mind-sets as well as new patterns of action. But the problem is that deeply entrenched cultures, such as we find in the church, are like formidable inertial systems. So enormous are the task and the risks involved that no longer is the phrase "renewal of the church" sufficient to convey the immensity of the challenge confronting us. It is no longer a question of simple culture change, but rather the building of a radically new culture in the church. Hence, we speak of *refounding the church*[15] (Chapter 4). This is more akin to the phoenix—a rebirth—than the gentle, refreshing wind that "renewal" has come to mean.

Refounding means going to the very cultural roots of corruption to begin healing. All the structures and ministries must be measured by, and openly accountable to, the mission of Jesus Christ. What business consultant Peter Drucker says of secular organizations applies equally to the leadership and managerial poverty of the church at this time: "Any government, whether

---

[13]Research finds that "90 percent of all desired organizational change initiatives fail because organizational culture is not sufficiently taken into account." Rasmus Hougaard and Jacqueline Carter, *The Mind of the Leader* (Boston: Harvard Business Review Press, 2018), 161. See also Nate Boaz and Erica A. Fox, "Change Leader, Change Thyself," *McKinsey Quarterly* (March 2014), www.mckinsey.com/.

[14]See Gerald A. Arbuckle, *Culture, Inculturation, and Theologians: A Postmodern Critique* (Collegeville, MN: Liturgical Press, 2010), passim.

[15]In 1993 I wrote *Refounding the Church: Dissent for Leadership* (London: Geoffrey Chapman), which went through several editions and translations. This present book radically revises and updates the anthropological theory of that earlier work.

that of a company or of a nation, degenerates into mediocrity and malperformance if it is not clearly accountable for results and not clearly accountable to someone."[16] The "someone" for us is Jesus Christ and his mission.

Reform cannot be confined to structural change, as Pope Francis reminds us: "Changing structures without generating new convictions and attitudes will only ensure that those same structures will become, sooner or later, corrupt, oppressive and ineffectual."[17] Structural change without conversion ends in more corruption and oppression: "There are ecclesial structures which can hamper efforts at evangelisation, yet even good structures are only helpful when *there is a life constantly driving, sustaining and assessing them*."[18]

Thus, refounding must always involve a journey into an interior silence, a solitude that gives inner space for our souls to wait to hear the Spirit speaking to us: "Therefore, I will lure her, and bring her into the wilderness, and speak tenderly to her" (Hos 2:14). The waiting in faith may be painful. With Isaiah we may cry: "Truly, you are a God who hides himself" (Is 45:15), or with the psalmist: "My God, my God, why have you forsaken me? Why are you so far from helping me, from the words of my groaning?" (Ps 22:1). Yet all the while in the waiting and listening we will be people of hope: "Why are you cast down, O my soul, and why are you disquieted within me? Hope in God; for I shall again praise him, my help and my God" (Ps 42:6). Refounding is a hope-filled journey into the paschal mystery for mission under the inspiration of the Holy Spirit.

Overview of the Book

In this book I draw particularly on the insights of cultural anthropology and scripture; however, no previous knowledge of these subjects is needed. A major mission of cultural anthropology[19] is to heighten our awareness of culture—its power and

---

[16]Peter Drucker, *Post-Capitalist Society* (New York: HarperBusiness, 1993), 71.

[17]Pope Francis, "The Joy of the Gospel" (*Evangelii Gaudium*) (Strathfield: St. Pauls Publications, 2013), para. 189.

[18]Pope Francis, ibid., para. 26. Italics added.

[19]In British Commonwealth countries cultural anthropology is commonly

complexity. When complicated cultural situations are naïvely interpreted, people will inevitably be hurt. We need the help of cultural anthropology to prevent this from happening.

Anthropology "is probably among the most challenging disciplines in the entire academic curriculum. It ruthlessly excavates and exposes the preconceptions by means of which we comfortably order our [cultural] lives, and turns every certainty into a question. This is not a subject for the faint-hearted, but for those who embark in a spirit of adventure, the potential rewards are immense."[20] Applied cultural anthropology does not tell us what we want to know; rather, it unsettles the foundations of what we thought we knew already. My hope is that readers will, when finishing this book, agree with this. In the process they will be wiser than before about the church's contemporary trauma and how to move forward. What anthropologist Ruth Benedict argued in 1934 is just as relevant today:

> There has never been a time when civilization stood more in need of individuals who are genuinely culture-conscious, who can see objectively the socially conditioned behavior of other peoples without fear and recrimination.[21]

We need culture-conscious individuals in the church, who can objectively see how the church becomes trapped in cultural forces that foster abuse of power and cover-ups, thus suffocating the Gospel message.

In studying cultures, Clifford Geertz distinguishes between "thin description" and "thick description." The first approach simply concentrates on what is merely observable and a simple detailing of facts. Thick description, however, seeks to delve deep into cultures to uncover meanings behind behaviors. Within a culture there is "a multiplicity of complex conceptual structures, many of them superimposed or knotted into one another, which are at once strange, irregular, and inexplicit, and which we must

---

referred to as *social anthropology*, but the difference is of little consequence.

[20]Tim Ingold, foreword to Alan Barnard, *Social Anthropology: Investigating Human Social Life* (Abergele, UK: Studymates, 2006), xii.

[21]Ruth Benedict, *Patterns of Culture* (New York: Houghton Mifflin Harcourt, 1934), 10–11.

continue somehow to grasp and then to render."[22] The anthropological observer looking for meanings becomes as it were a translator for others of what is happening. In this book I am using this "thick description" method in the study of church cultures. To help readers I do this particularly through culture models adapted to the themes of this book. A culture model aims to explain complex realities by stressing emphases and downplaying details that might interfere with the clarifying process.

The following summarizes the themes of the chapters. In 2017 the Australian government released the final report of a five-year study into *Institutional Responses to Child Sexual Abuse*,[23] the most extensive review of this kind ever made anywhere. Included in the study is the in-depth analysis of the Catholic Church's responses over recent decades to the sexual abuse of minors and vulnerable people. Because the analysis is so thorough and globally relevant, the chapters draw at times on its findings and recommendations[24] to illustrate theoretical points. The first three chapters of this book seek to respond to this question: "What moral blindness has made a church so renowned for its benevolence so reluctant to root out and punish all the child abusers in its midst, and even willing—as the evidence clearly shows—to move them on to greener pastures with unsuspecting flock?"[25] The remaining three chapters answer the question: What practical steps must be taken to make the church refocus on the mission of Christ and become more transparent and accountable in its governance?

Chapter 1: Covering Up Power Abuse: Cultural Dynamics

This foundational chapter explains in a series of axioms key words such as culture, authority, power, cover-up, corruption, systems, revolutionary cultural change, and scandals. The axioms

---

[22]Clifford Geertz, *Local Knowledge* (New York: Basic Books, 1973), 10.

[23]See *Final Report of the Royal Commission into Institutional Responses to Child Sexual Abuse* (Barton, ACT: Commonwealth of Australia, 2017), vol. 16, bk. 1.

[24]Of the 189 recommendations in the final report of the commission, twenty relate directly to the Australian Catholic Church and many have an indirect effect; thirteen of those twenty recommendations involve the Holy See.

[25]Geoffrey Robertson, *The Case of the Pope: Vatican Accountability for Human Rights Abuse* (London: Penguin Books, 2010), 5. Robertson is an internationally distinguished human rights lawyer and judge.

will be referred to, and further explained, at relevant points in subsequent chapters. The chapter answers such questions as: Why are cultures inherently resistant to change? What happens when authority is confused with power? Why do cultures become secretive? Why are cultures prone to cover-up movements? What do we mean by culture systems? What are the catalysts that break open cultures of cover-up? Secular and contemporary ecclesial examples illustrate the material.

Chapter 2: Why Is the Church Culture Prone to Cultural Cover-Ups?

We cannot move forward unless we accurately diagnose the nature and causes of the cultural disease in the church. Failure to do so will only further exacerbate the abuse of power in the church. This chapter describes why certain types of cultures, for example, hierarchical (including the church), are especially secretive and self-protective. Such cultures, such as clericalism, are particularly resistant to outside scrutiny and to change. The more they feel their identity, security, power, and privilege are threatened, the more secretive they become. Unless the clerical culture is radically changed, the church's proneness to cover-up behavior will continue.

Chapter 3: The Grieving Church in Focus

The culture of the church is in trauma. The People of God feel overwhelmed with grief: angry, paralyzed, shamed, leaderless. Yet paradoxically the public revelation of the scandals by the media, government inquiries, and the courts is able to do what efforts at internal renewal have been unable to achieve: these revelations are forcing the church to admit to the institutional evil in its midst.

Chapter 4: Leadership for Refounding the Church

The trauma in the church has many causes, for example, clericalism and catastrophic failures of leadership.[26] To grasp what is

---

[26] "We have concluded that there were catastrophic failures of leadership of

happening a model of cultural disintegration is explained and then applied to the contemporary church; among the possible reactions is the call for the refounding of the church. Only through refounding can the necessary revolutionary cultural change occur in the church according to Vatican II values. One sign that refounding is beginning to happen is when abused survivors receive justice and the vulnerable are safeguarded.

Chapter 5: Structural Reform in the Church

Chapter 5 lists the reforms required in light of previous chapters. For example, for theological and administrative reasons lay people—men and women—can no longer be excluded from involvement in the governance of the church.[27] In important ministries of the church, for example, education and health care, lay people are now in the forefront of leadership and management.

Chapter 6: Refounding the Church: Action Plans and Strategies

This chapter offers sixteen action plans and strategies for reforming the church culture to ensure collegiality, transparency, and accountability. It responds to questions such as: What are the drivers in cultural change? How is the church to reconnect with its primary mission? How is refounding leadership to engage in the tasks of reforming the church? How are we to move to a new model of church, that is, the pilgrim model? How are we to involve laity in governance positions? How is trust to be restored? What does Scripture tell us about *how* reform and refounding are to take place?

Catholic Church authorities over many decades. . . . The powers of governance held by individual bishops and provincials are not subject to adequate checks and balances." *Final Report of the Royal Commission,* 36. Reports from other countries indicate a similar conclusion.

[27]See the Anglican–Roman Catholic International Commission (ARCICIII) (2018), *Walking Together on the Way.*

1

Covering Up Power Abuse

Cultural Dynamics

Never make any claims for yourself or cover up the truth
with lies—the principles of this kind are not wisdom that
comes down from above: they are only earthly, animal
and devilish.

—James 3:14–15, *Jerusalem Bible,* 1966

The powers of governance held by individual diocesan
bishops and provincials are not subject to adequate checks
and balances.

—Australian Royal Commission, *Final Report of the
Royal Commission into Institutional Responses to Child
Sexual Abuse: Religious Institutions*

By force of habit we no longer stand up to evil.

—Pope Francis, "Rejoice and Exult"
(*Gaudete et Exsultate*), 2018

This chapter explains that:
- Culture and cultural change are complex realities.
- Cultures resist change because order is threatened.
- Power is an integral quality of cultures.
- Hierarchical cultures are prone to power abuse.

Reformers agree: The culture of the church must change. Pope
Francis in his pastoral letter to the Catholics of Chile wrote that

"the culture of abuse, and the system of cover-up that allowed it to be perpetuated"[1] must be eliminated. Yet elimination of cultural aberrations anywhere may be difficult, if not impossible, at times. Cultures resist change. And the cultures of the church are *no* exception; any reforms in the church that ignore this will fail. By defining key words, such as "culture" and "cultural cover-up," this foundational chapter explains why this is so.

Reflecting on the American business world, David Callahan wisely cautions that "the cheating culture [of cover-ups] will not be dismantled easily. In many places the root causes of cheating have receded into the background and self-perpetuating dynamics have taken hold, generating their own imperatives for dishonesty. When cheating becomes so pervasive that the perception is that 'everybody does it,' new ethical calculus emerges."[2]

The fact is that cultures are more complex, messy, and inherently paradoxical than many commentators think. A culture may be several things simultaneously: homogenous, divided into a multiplicity of subcultures, an array of identities that evoke complex contradictions, making it difficult, even impossible at times, to alter cultures. Indeed, a culture can be a multifaceted matrix of interacting and often conflicting powers. The culture of the Catholic Church is no exception. Hence, the need to clarify in this opening chapter the meaning of the slippery word "culture" and associated terms. *Inaccurate insights and faulty attitudes about culture will invariably result in flawed reform policies and practices.*

Cultural historian Raymond Williams is right: "Culture is one of the two or three most complicated words in the English language . . . mainly because it has now come to be used for important concepts in several . . . disciplines, and in several distinct and incompatible systems of thought."[3] Although this confusion exists about culture's meaning, there is nothing nebulous about it. Nonetheless, the problem of clarity remains. Authors differ in defining "culture." For example, one sees culture as "what

---

[1]Pope Francis, "Letter to Chilean Catholics," May 31, 2018.

[2]David Callahan, *The Cheating Culture: Why More Americans Are Doing Wrong to Get Ahead* (New York: Harcourt, 2004), 25.

[3]Raymond Williams, *Keywords: A Vocabulary of Culture and Society* (New York: Oxford University Press, 1985), 87.

we do around here"; another sees it as "the tacit social order of an organization. It shapes attitudes and behaviors in wide-ranging and durable ways. . . . [Yet agreements] on specifics is sparse across definitions."[4] Another describes characteristics of cultures: "culture is learned; culture is transmissible; culture is dynamic; culture is selective; the facets of culture are interrelated, and culture is ethnocentric."[5] Although these descriptions of what culture means are helpful, they do not sufficiently define its complexity. We must dig deeper.

Since anthropological literature is not readily available to the general reader, it will be helpful to summarize our clarifications in a series of guiding axioms.[6] In subsequent chapters readers will be directed back to these axioms. But a word of warning. No matter how clear the definition of culture to be used in this chapter may be, the culture of any institution, including the church, is, in fact, very hard to interpret, a point I will be repeating in different ways throughout this book. It is my hope that by the book's end readers will be wary of claims that instant cultural changes in the church are possible.

Cultural Cover-Ups

Cultural cover-ups are attempts to prevent people from finding out the truth about a serious mistake or crime. They are all too common in the business world. Here are several examples:

---

[4]Boris Groysberg, Jeremiah Lee, Jesse Price, and J. O-Jud Cheng, "The Leader's Guide to Corporate Culture," *Harvard Business Review* 96 (January–February 2018): 46. In 1952, two anthropologists—Kluckholn and Kroeber—gathered 156 different definitions of culture! Over fifty years later, in view of the mushrooming interest in culture one can imagine that the number of definitions has increased dramatically in many different disciplines. See Alfred Kroeber and Clyde Kluckhohn, "Culture: A Critical Review of Concepts and Definitions," in *Papers of the Peabody Museum of American Archaeology and Ethnology*, no. 47 (Cambridge, MA: Harvard University Press, 1952), 5.
[5]Richard E. Porter and Larry A. Samovar, "An Introduction to Intercultural Communication," ed. Larry A. Samovar and Richard E. Porter, 7th ed., *Intercultural Communication: A Reader* (Belmont, CA: Wadsworth, 1994), 12.
[6]The meaning of culture is more fully explained in Gerald A. Arbuckle, *Culture, Inculturation, and Theologians: A Postmodern Critique* (Collegeville, MN: Liturgical Press, 2010).

- In the early 2000s in the United States, telecommunications giant WorldCom was forced into bankruptcy as a consequence of massive accounting frauds and attempted cover-ups: "WorldCom cooked its books and leading pension funds lost billions."[7] Enron, the giant American energy company, declared bankruptcy in 2001, after having attempted to cover up unethical actions within its organizational culture. Its cover-up culture reflected "the leading moral toxins of the 90s—extreme individualism, money obsession, and social Darwinism."[8]

- In 2018 the Australian government initiated an independent inquiry into the behavior of banks and other financial institutions. Revelations of serious cover-ups by several institutions rapidly emerged. Customers, for example, had been charged for services that they had never received; one bank was still charging fees to clients knowing that they had died years before; and banks continued to employ financial advisers whom they knew were ill-qualified for their task. It was revealed that in the largest Australian bank staff were depositing small amounts into children's inactive accounts to make them appear active, because the more active and numerous the accounts the more employees were rewarded for their initiatives. Cultural factors, such as complacency and hiding unethical practices, were said to lie at the heart of the cover-ups.

Church Cover-Ups

These examples illustrate that the church is far from being alone in its efforts to conceal serious unethical behavior, such as the sexual abuse of children. *But the difference is that the church, not business institutions, claims to be society's guardian of morality.* And the sexual abuse of innocent victims has been

---

[7]David Callahan, *The Cheating Culture: Why Americans Are Doing Wrong to Get Ahead* (Orlando: Harcourt, 2004), 25.

[8]Ibid., 126–27. Social Darwinism assumes that individuals and societies are by nature destined to compete; only the strongest will survive. See Gerald A. Arbuckle, *Violence, Society, and the Church: A Cultural Approach* (Collegeville, MN: Liturgical Press, 2004), 104–5.

accompanied by spiritual abuse. They have been denied Gospel instruction *and* example. Not only have their personal growth and self-worth been placed at risk but their capacity for faith has been damaged. Why was sacred trust betrayed? Why did those who knew what was happening cover up these abuses? Why were the lost cries of blameless children and their guardians ignored? Can this happen again? We now seek cultural answers.

Cultural Resistance

Axiom 1. A Culture Is a Response to a Fundamental Need. A culture responds to our need for consistency and order because we fear the uncertainties of change and chaos; this need for order can obstruct cultural change.[9]

Within each human person, there is an unlimited yearning for liberty, but this desire competes with a longing for order and the familiar. Ultimately, it is the latter that most often wins. We may even put up with persecution provided it is predictable. As Peter Berger writes, culture protects people from the awesome insecurities and meaninglessness of chaos (*anomy*). Culture (*nomos*) is "an area of meaning carved out of a vast mass of meaninglessness, a small clearing of lucidity in a formless, dark, almost ominous jungle."[10] Chaos is feared. Order must prevail. Anthropologist Clifford Geertz agrees:

> Man [*sic*] depends upon symbols and symbol systems with a dependence so great as to be decisive for his creatural viability and, as a result, his sensitivity to even the remotest indication that they may prove unable to cope with one or another aspect of experience raises within him the gravest sort of anxiety.[11]

---

[9]Dianne Waddell and Amrik S. Sohal caution that resistance in certain circumstances is necessary. It can have an essential role in emphasizing inappropriate aspects in what is proposed, thus acting as a catalyst for new alternatives to emerge. "Resistance: A Constructive Tool for Change," *Management Decisions* 36, no. 8 (1998): 543–48.

[10]Peter Berger, *The Sacred Canopy: Elements of a Sociological Theory of Religion* (New York: Doubleday, 1969), 23.

[11]Clifford Geertz, *The Interpretation of Cultures* (Columbus: Free Press, 1963), 99.

It is not surprising, therefore, that anyone who questions the cultural status quo, for example, an innovator, a whistle-blower (see *Axiom 14*, below), can become the object of violence such as scapegoating or marginalization: "The individual who strays seriously from the socially defined programs can be considered not only a fool or a knave but a madman."[12] This is one reason why survivors of sexual abuse find it difficult to be heard: because they dare to question an existing cover-up culture.

Change, in brief, even on occasion the faintest whisper of it, substitutes ambiguity and uncertainty for the familiar, and we hanker after the predictable, for order. Cultures begin like tender, fragile cobwebs but rapidly become grim prisons, eventually smothering innovative attempts, unless appropriate active moves are made. It is estimated that the number of changes that fail due to the neglect of cultural issues "ranges from as high as 70 or 80 percent of all [culture change] initiatives."[13] The word "change" causes emotional reactions because it is not a neutral word. For many people the word "conjures up visions of a revolutionary, a dissatisfied idealist, a trouble-maker, a malcontent."[14] Pope Francis is conscious that cultural change evokes resistance and that reform consequently is bound to be laboriously slow and with uncertain results. He jokingly referred to his efforts to reform the Roman Curia to be like trying to clean the Egyptian sphinx with a toothbrush.[15] Some examples of cultural resistance include the following:

---

[12]Berger, *Sacred Canopy, 23.*

[13]Mike Oram and Richard S. Wellins, *Re-Engineering's Missing Ingredient: The Human Factor* (London: Institute of Personnel and Development, 1995), 4.

[14]Dorwin Cartwright, "Achieving Change in People: Some Applications of Group Dynamics Theory," *Human Relations* 4 (1966): 381.

[15]Pope Francis cited by Christopher Lamb, "Reviving the Spirit of Reform," *The Tablet*, March 10, 2018, 4. Pope Adrian VI (1522–1523) declared in 1523: "We know well that even in this Holy See . . . abominable things have happened. . . . We intend to use all diligence to reform the Roman Curia, where all these evils began; then the recovery and renewal will start where the sickness had its origin. . . . The sickness is, in fact, deeply rooted and has many symptoms. Consequently, it is necessary to proceed step by step, first applying the appropriate medicine to the more serious and more dangerous evils, in order not to cause even greater confusion by a hasty reform." Cited by Luigi Accattoli, *When a Pope Asks for Forgiveness* (New York: Alba House, 1998), 7.

- *Failure to stop sexual harassment.* It is reported that in the early 1990s in two Chicago plants of Ford, one of America's most storied companies, "Bosses and fellow laborers treated [female workers] as property or prey. . . . [For example] supervisors traded better assignments for sex and punished those who refused." Twenty-five years later, despite efforts to change the culture, "women at those plants say they have been subjected to many of the same abuses. And like those who complained before them, they say they were mocked, dismissed, threatened and ostracized. . . . At the moment when so many people are demanding that sexual harassment no longer be tolerated, the story of the Ford plants shows the challenges of transforming a culture."[16]

- *Hand washing in the healthcare industry.* The washing of hands by all involved in the care of patients in hospitals "is the simplest, most effective measure for preventing [hospital-acquired] infection."[17] In 2006 the public hospital authorities in the state of New South Wales, Australia, at significant financial cost, initiated a hand hygiene campaign: "Clean Hands Save Lives." It was found that the highest rate of compliance, following the campaign, was that of nurses with 76 percent, but the lowest rate was 36.9 percent for doctors.[18] Peter Garling, in his lengthy report on the condition of the state's public hospitals, expressed his frustration at the deplorable example set even by senior clinicians who were among the worst to conform. "I am truly staggered at how few hospital staff wash their hands before and after patients. The culture . . . which does not insist on a high level of compliance . . . is bordering on the scandalous."[19] Given the urgency

---

[16]Susan Chira and Catrin Einhorn, "How Tough Is It to Change a Culture of Harassment? Ask Women at Ford," *New York Times* (December 19, 2017), https://nyt.ms/2oMtVRY.

[17]Didier Pittet, "Improving Adherence to Hand Hygiene Practice: A Multidisciplinary Approach," *Emerging Infectious Diseases* 7, no. 2 (2001): 234.

[18]See Peter Garling, *Final Report of the Special Commission of Inquiry: Acute Care Services in NSW Public Hospitals, Volume 2* (November 27, 2008) (Sydney: NSW State Government, 2008), 686.

[19]Ibid., 684.

of hand hygiene, reinforced by a year-long campaign, the refusal by highly educated doctors to do so aptly illustrates the power of culture to resist change. In addition, prior to the publication of the audit's negative findings, many of the state's Health Services claimed that the hand hygiene campaign had been successful, contrary to the evidence.[20]

- *The Japanese work culture,* dating from the end of the Second World War, is still resisting change despite the fact that the culture is harmful to workers and that both the government and employers agree something must be done. *The Economist* notes:

Twelve-hour days are common. Holidays are stingy. . . . The model holds Japan back. It is miserable for male workers. . . . It is even worse for women. . . . Government and businesses increasingly acknowledge a problem, but struggle to deal with it. . . . Yet too many of Japan's politicians and corporate titans are male, hidebound and timid. Many workers are undemanding. Conformism remains powerful.[21]

In summary:
- People are likely to resist change for one of two reasons: loss of the familiar or concern over personal loss. Changes substitute ambiguity and uncertainty for the known.
- The level of people's opposition to change very much depends on the type of change in question and how well it is understood: "what people resist is not change but loss, or the possibility of loss."[22] The cultures that oppose change the most are those where long-standing core values in myths or widely accepted rituals or practices are endangered (see *Axiom 3*, below).

---

[20]*Independent Panel: Caring Together: The Health Action Plan for NSW: Stage 1 Progress Report,* October 2009 (Sydney: NSW Health, 2009), 201. The author was a member of this panel.

[21]"No One Is Happy with Japan's Workstyle, but It Is Proving Hard to Change," *The Economist* (August 4, 2018), 21.

[22]W. Warner Burke, *Organizational Development: Principles and Practices* (Boston: Little, Brown, 1982), 52.

Most planned change is directed at the visible structures of a culture. What is hidden in a culture resists significant changes. As it is said: "Most of what is important in a culture is below the surface. It is like the moon—we observe the front, which appears flat and one-dimensional, but there is another side and dimensions we cannot see."[23] So often I have witnessed planning sessions for executives of organizations in which they wholeheartedly agree about new strategies, for example, to stop bullying, but on their return to their offices nothing eventuates. As it has been said: "Culture eats strategy for breakfast."[24] The fact is that "it takes a lot of effort to turn concepts into behavioral realities and to embed them into all the daily routines. Thus, experienced change managers talk in terms of five to ten years for any substantial change projects."[25] In her conclusion to her study of cultures, Shirley P. Lowry writes: "Most mythic systems agree on this basic point: What promotes cosmic order, harmony, and life is good, and what promotes chaos, disintegration, and death is evil."[26]

Symbols

Axiom 2: Cultures and the Power of Feelings. A culture, including that of the church, consists of countless symbols that evoke positive or negative feeling reactions; when people and their cultures emotionally react negatively to symbols, they resist change.

A symbol "is any reality that by its very dynamism or power leads to (that is, makes one think about, imagine, get into contact with, or reach out to) another deeper (and often mysterious) reality through a sharing in the dynamism that the symbol itself offers (and not merely by verbal or additional explanations)."[27]

There are three essential elements to any symbol: the meaning, the emotive, and the directive. The *meaning* aspect is its thought

---

[23] Porter and Samovar, "An Introduction to Intercultural Communication," 13.

[24] Groysberg et al., "The Leader's Guide to Corporate Culture," 46. A strategy describes the process of defining how an institution's resources can best be positioned for peak organizational success.

[25] Edgar H. Schein, *Organizational Culture and Leadership* (San Francisco: Jossey-Bass, 1987), 291. I believe this figure to be overly optimistic.

[26] Shirley P. Lowry, *Familiar Mysteries: The Truth in Myth* (New York: Oxford University Press, 1982), 131.

[27] Definition by Adolfo Nicolas, SJ (personal communication).

element; the symbol makes a statement about something that the mind is able to grasp, for example, that a McDonald's cheeseburger provides quick food. Second, a symbol has an *emotive* element that affects the hearts and imaginations of people, evoking in them positive or negative feelings. For example, I can have positive or negative feelings about cheeseburgers. This emotive aspect of a symbol *re*-presents the object. Cheeseburgers become present to me. Third, a symbol has a *directive* quality. As a result of its cognitive *and* emotional impact I am directed to act in a certain way.[28] I either refuse the cheeseburger that is *re*-presented to me because I do not like them or enthusiastically buy one.

Of the three elements of a symbol the emotive power is the most significant. *Symbols tug at the heart!* In 1990 I was in a disastrous rail accident in which several passengers in my coach, including the driver, were killed. It occurred as the train was leaving a tunnel on the side of a small mountain outside Sydney, Australia. Ever since, when I pass through this tunnel I relive the haunting scene. *More haunting than this is the experience of a sexually abused survivor whenever they see a symbol that reminds them of what has occurred.* One survivor of sexual abuse by clergy in Australia feels "hatred . . . for men who dress up in the name of clergy."[29] The clerical clothes are horrific reminders for the survivor of what has occurred.

The Australian Royal Commission of Inquiry into Institutional Responses to Child Sexual Abuse uses a definition of culture that is adequate in many ways but that fails to emphasize the feeling qualities of symbols. The inquiry "understands culture to consist of content and form. Cultural content includes assumptions (most importantly, presumptions of fact regarding people's attitudes and behaviours), values and beliefs (most importantly, understandings regarding the virtue of alternative ways to think and act) and norms (expectations regarding how people should think and behave)."[30] The definition fails to explicitly highlight the all-important *affective* aspects of a culture; it is too "heady,"

---

[28]For a fuller explanation see Arbuckle, *Culture, Inculturation, and Theologians,* 22–29.

[29]*Final Report of the Royal Commission,* 501.

[30]Donald Palmer and Gemma McKibbin, *Final Report: The Role of Organisational Culture in Child Sexual Abuse in Institutional Contexts* (December 2016), 6.

neglecting the emotional power of symbols. Remember, sexual abuse is a form of violence that affects not the just the mind of a victim but especially their feelings, their inner spiritual life, and their self-worth. Many survivors are haunted for their entire lives by their memories of their maltreatment.

A symbol has multiple meanings. This makes it difficult to identify the meaning people even within the same culture are giving to a symbol at a particular time. For example, Cambridge in England calls to mind a beautiful medieval town, but it also reminds me of the university and of Christ College, my alma mater, of freezing winters and slippery roads. I could go on. At the same time the word "Cambridge" may evoke quite different meanings for other people, even my former colleagues. So it is hazardous to think that when I use the word people will immediately understand what I am saying. This also illustrates just how risky it is to assign meanings to symbols that belong not just to my own culture but, even more difficult, to other cultures.

For example, for Irish Catholic immigrants to England prior to Vatican II, the Friday abstinence had generally ceased to symbolize its original meaning, that is, as a form of mortification; rather it had become a proud symbol of identity for immigrants in a world of prejudice and discrimination. It linked them to their cultural roots in Ireland and to "a glorious tradition in Rome." Not surprisingly, therefore, the sudden removal of the abstinence requirement by the English bishops deeply distressed them; the bishops failed to grasp that the abstinence law gave these immigrants a sense of identity and security in what they considered a hostile land.[31]

Myths Cement Culture

Axiom 3: Myths Cement a Culture. A culture more or less coheres because of symbols, myths, and rituals; myths are narrative symbols that legitimize the cultural status quo, even if this legitimation may historically contradict reality and morality.

I have defined culture as "a pattern of meanings, encased in

---

[31]See Mary Douglas, *Natural Symbols: Explorations in Cosmology* (New York: Pantheon Books, 1970), 37–53.

a network of symbols, narrative symbols, that is, myths and rituals, created over time by dominant groups, subcultures and individuals, as they struggle to achieve their identities in the midst of the competitive pressures of power and limited resources in a rapidly globalizing and fragmenting postmodern world, and instructing its adherents about what is considered to be the correct and orderly way to *feel, think, and behave.*"[32]

This definition has several particular benefits. It emphasizes the power influences within cultures of dominant groups, subcultures, and individuals. The term "subculture" defines and honors the particular design and identity of different interests or of a group of people within a larger collectivity. The term is a reminder that cultures are not homogenous, but commonly significantly fragmented.[33] In every subculture there is always an aspect, sometimes intensely obvious, of protest against the dominant culture of which it is a part. The more people of the subculture feel threatened by the dominant group, the stronger and more vivid will be their symbols of protest and resistance. For example, following Vatican II the Roman Curia felt its dominant authority/power was being threatened by the growing authority/ power of the local churches, the subcultures of the church. The curia sought to resist this move to legitimate subsidiarity by again seeking to recentralize authority/power in key areas such as liturgical reform. This evoked growing tensions between the curia and the local churches until the election of Pope Francis (see Chapter 2).

The definition also highlights the fact that a culture (and its subcultures) through its symbols, myths, and rituals shapes people's *emotional* responses to the world around them. Through a culture people feel an affective sense of belonging, but depending on the context, they may also feel other emotions, such as shame or anger. In organizational cultures where bullying is tolerated or encouraged, individuals will likely feel shame, humiliation, and/or anger. The following comment by psychoanalyst Erich

---

[32]Arbuckle, *Culture, Inculturation, and Theologians*, 17.

[33]For more description see Peter Brooker, *A Concise Glossary of Cultural Theory* (London: Arnold, 1999), 208–9.

Fromm is thus particularly incisive: The "fact that ideas have an emotional matrix" is "of the utmost importance" as this is "the key to understanding . . . the spirit of a culture."[34]

Myths as narrative symbols form the heart of every culture that gives meaning to people's lives; emotionally embedded in the myths are a culture's fundamental values and assumptions about life.[35] They claim to reveal in an imaginative and symbolic way fundamental truths about the world and human life;[36] they are efforts to explain what usually is beyond empirical observation. No matter how hard we seek to deepen our grasp of the meaning of myths, they still remain somewhat ambiguous and mysterious because they attempt to articulate what cannot be fully articulated. As they are stories that mold a people's behavior, they can inspire people, energize them to act, to make sacrifices beyond the normal. For example, at the football World Cup in 2018 huge crowds of Latin Americans, despite the enormous financial costs, packed the stadiums in deepest Russia. Why this devotion?

> For European fans, club [membership] often comes before country. For Latin Americans it is the reverse. However much they may despair at their countries' problems, Latin American patriotism is strong and uncomplicated. . . . [For example], grown men burst into tears when singing "Contigo Peru," an unofficial national anthem, before the match against Denmark that marked [Peru's] return to the final stages of a World Cup for the first time since 1982.[37]

Players became national heroes overnight. The game is a ritual revealing the depth of the national mythology: "Rituals are repetitive sequences of activities that express and reinforce the

---

[34]Erich Fromm, *The Fear of Freedom* (London: Routledge & Kegan Paul, 1960), 240.

[35]See Percy S. Cohen, "Theories of Myth," *Man: Journal of the Anthropological Institute* 4, no. 3 (1969): 337–53; William G. Dotty, *Mythography: The Study of Myths and Rituals* (Montgomery: University of Alabama Press, 1986), 41–71.

[36]See Arbuckle, *Earthing the Gospel: An Inculturation Handbook for Pastoral Workers* (Maryknoll, NY: Orbis Books, 1990), 26–43, and *Culture, Inculturation, and Theologians*, 19–42.

[37]"Closed because of Football," *The Economist* (June 23, 2018), 42.

key values [inherent in myths] of the organization, what goals are most important, which people are important and which are expendable."[38]

In brief, myths constitute the emotional adhesive that affectively cements people together at the deepest level of their group life; myths radiate power because every "society is held together by a myth system, a complex of dominating forms that determines and sustains all its activities."[39] Myths are like invisible blueprints that shape the way people see the world. The psychologist Rollo May says that "myths are like the beams in a house: not exposed to outside view, they are the structure which holds the house together so people can live in it."[40] They can be likened to knowledge concealed in the DNA of a cell, or the program technology of a computer. Myths are the cultural DNA, the software or invisible blueprints of the heart and mind, the programs that sculpt the way we view the world and how we must act accordingly.[41] Myths are stories branded large with social acceptance. Hence, another way of defining culture is: *"the collective programming of the heart and mind that distinguishes the members of one group or category of people from another."*[42]

Structures and Myths

Frequently comments are made that there must be structural reforms in the church today if it is to recover from the present crises, but rarely is the word "structure" defined. Structures exist not *outside* but *within* cultures. They are of two types: *Visible*

---

[38]Stephen P. Robbins, *Organizational Behavior: Concepts, Controversies, and Applications,* 4th ed. (London: Prentice-Hall, 1989), 480.

[39]Robert M. MacIver, *The Web of Government* (London: Macmillan, 1947), 4.

[40]Rollo May, *The Cry for Myth* (New York: Delta, 1991), 15.

[41]See description by Sam Keen, "The Stories We Live By," *Psychology Today* (December 1988), 10.

[42]Geert Hofstede, *Cultures and Organizations* (London: HarperCollins, 1994), 5. Italics in original. Hofstede notes that this emphasis on "collective programming" resembles the notion of *"habitus,"* an insight of the French sociologist Pierre Bourdieu: "Certain conditions of existence produce a habitus, a system of permanent and transferable dispositions. A habitus . . . functions as the basis for practices and images . . . which are collectively orchestrated without an actual conductor." Pierre Bourdieu, *Le sens practique* (Paris: Editions de Minuit, 1980). Translation by Hofstede, *Cultures and Organizations,* 18.

structures are what can be seen and touched, for example, an organizational chart or printed regulations that describe how individuals must relate to one another; *invisible* structures, however, are the symbols and myths or "webs of significance," as Clifford Geertz[43] describes them, that, though hidden from view, give meaning, identity, and shape to an organization, which is its cultural DNA. Visible structures are easily changed, but invisible structures are not (see Chapter 6).

Residual Myths and Cover-Ups

The emotional quality of myths is especially evident in "residual myths." A residual myth is one with little or no daily impact on a group's life, but at times it can surface to become a powerful operative myth. Residual myths lurk in the culture's unconscious, always waiting to reemerge. For example, racist mythology that oppressed African Americans and native Indians in the founding of the United States has resurfaced, encouraged by the words and actions of President Donald Trump.[44]

Likewise, pre–Vatican II culture, with its mythology of covering up abuses of power, still lurks within the contemporary culture of the church, despite proclamations to the contrary. Residual myths, for example, clericalism (see Chapter 2), resist change unless rigorous active efforts are made to articulate *and* remove them (see Chapter 6).

Myths and History

The purposes of myth and history differ; myth is concerned not so much with a series of events as with the moral significance of these happenings. A myth is a "religious" commentary on the beliefs and values of a culture. Rollo May describes it this way: "The myth is a drama which begins as a historical event and takes on its special character as a way of orienting

---

[43]Clifford Geertz, *The Interpretation of Cultures* (New York: Basic Books, 1973), 5.

[44]See Gerald A. Arbuckle, *Loneliness: Insights for Healing in a Fragmented World* (Maryknoll, NY: Orbis Books, 2018), 70–82.

people to reality."[45] Barack Obama can be viewed in historical or mythological terms. As seen from the historical perspective, he is portrayed as belonging to a definite time period, influencing and being influenced by events around him. If, however, he is judged as one who exemplifies virtues of compassionate and courageous leadership in establishing health care insurance systems for people who are poor, then we are measuring him by Gospel mythology. Ultimately, a story that becomes a myth can be true or false, historical or unhistorical, but what is important is not the story itself but the purpose it serves in the life of an individual, a group, or a whole society. History and myths relate to facts from different standpoints: that is, history observes facts from the "outer physical side, myth from the inner spiritual side."[46] Myths simply allow people of different societies and subcultures to understand themselves and their world;[47] they are not some kind of mixed-up history.

Myths, therefore, tell those who believe them what reality is and what it should be.[48] But myths, however, can be a mixture of remembering, forgetting, interpreting, and inventing historical events. That is, myths can discard historical facts, particularly if they may be detrimental to the dominant social group in power. This is the reason that Erica Schoenberger warns that myths can "provide a comforting—if false—sense of continuity and stability in the face of uncertainty and external turmoil. . . . They tend to blind people to the need for change."[49] The following examples of cultural amnesia illustrate this conclusion:

- The Slavery Abolition Act abolished slavery throughout the British Empire in 1833, but the Holy Office stated in 1866 that "Slavery itself . . . is not contrary to the natu-

---

[45]May, Cry of Myth, 26.

[46]Morton T. Kelsey, Myth, History, and Faith: The Demythologizing of Christianity (New York: Paulist Press, 1974), 5.

[47]Arbuckle, Culture, Inculturation, and Theologians, 29–30.

[48]See Bruce Lincoln, Discourse and the Construction of Society: Comparative Studies of Myth, Ritual, and Classification (Oxford: Oxford University Press, 1989), 24.

[49]Erica Schoenberger, The Cultural Crisis of the Firm (Oxford: Basil Blackwell, 1997), 132.

ral and divine law."[50] This fact is quietly forgotten in the church's mythology.

- Mythology tells us that the church is not a democracy, never has been, and never will be. Since it is assumed to be integral to the founding myth of the church, no argument to the contrary is possible. In accordance with this myth, it is correct for Rome to appoint bishops without any consultation with local churches.

Yet this behavior ignores not only the values of participative and consultative leadership fundamental to Vatican II, but also the custom during a significant period of history. The choice of bishops by clergy and laity was normal until the twelfth century. Indeed, as late as the beginning of the twentieth century, fewer than half of the world's bishops were chosen by the pope.[51] The fact is that in early New Testament times the church was very much a decentralized network of communities. Over time, the church's administrative structures began to mirror secular ones, for example, those of the Roman emperors, Byzantine suzerains, feudal lords, or the courts of medieval kings (see Chapter 2).[52] The monarchical structure of the church that emerged over the centuries is an example of mythological development; the founding myth emphasized hierarchical roots with simultaneously a notable emphasis on democratic principles.

Manipulation of Myths

Axiom 4: Manipulation of Myths. Myths are able to be manipulated in ways that exploit and oppress people without them being aware of what is happening.

---

[50]Cited by Maureen Fiedler and Linda Rabben, eds., *Rome Has Spoken* (New York: Crossroad, 1998), 84.

[51]See Leonard Swidler, "Democracy, Dissent, and Dialogue," in *The Church in Anguish*, ed. Hans Küng and Leonard Swidler (San Francisco: Harper & Row, 1986), 310; Eugene C. Bianchi and Rosemary Radford Ruether, eds., *A Democratic Catholic Church: The Reconstruction of Roman Catholicism* (New York: Crossroad, 1992), passim.

[52]See Terrence L. Nichols, *That All May Be One: Hierarchy and Participation in the Church* (Collegeville, MN: Liturgical Press, 1997), 95–170.

Culture operates as a form of normative control beyond the volition of the individual. . . . While cultures might control people, it is almost unthinkable that people could control culture.[53]

Pope Francis is particularly sensitive to the hidden and resistant mythological forces that can lurk in cultures. For example, he writes: "The message that we proclaim always has a certain cultural dress, but we in the Church can sometimes fall into a needless hallowing of our own culture, and thus show more fanaticism than true evangelising zeal."[54] Francis is referring to the "culture unconscious,"[55] that is, because symbols and myths are so much part of our inner lives, their existence and influence are apt to escape our conscious awareness. We may think we are preaching the Gospel, when in fact we are unconsciously imposing our own culture on others.

In our daily lives we do so many things without conscious deliberation, for example, we drive on the correct side of the road, we sit automatically, as it were, in our favorite chair. Anthropologist Edward Hall adds this caution: "The cultural unconscious, like Freud's unconscious, not only controls man's actions but can be understood only by painstaking processes of detailed analysis."[56] Hence, the importance of this present analysis of abuse in church cultures. Psychologist Max Lerner, in a moving passage composed as Hitler was preparing for war, was extremely disturbed by the unquestioning support evoked by the führer, and prophetically warned that while the power of dictators derives from the "symbols that they manipulate, the symbols depend in turn upon the entire range of associations that they evoke. Men

---

[53]S. R. Barley, G. W. Meyer, and D. C. Gash, "Cultures of Culture: Academics, Practitioners, and the Pragmatics of Normative Control," *Administrative Science Quarterly*, no. 33 (1988): 44.

[54]Pope Francis, "The Joy of the Gospel" (*Evangelii Gaudium*) (Sydney: St. Pauls Publications, 2013), para. 117.

[55]See Terry Eagleton, *Culture* (New Haven, CT: Yale University Press, 2016), 49–95.

[56]Edward Hall, *Beyond Culture* (Garden City, NY: Anchor Press/Doubleday, 1977), 43.

possess thoughts, but symbols possess men."[57] The following are two further examples of the seductive influence of myths:

- *Abuse cover-ups:* The symbols and myths of clerical superiority unconsciously and insidiously influenced for several hundred years the behavior of people. This is the power of the "culture unconscious." Similarly, incidents of sexual abuse of minors have been concealed simply because "this is the way things have always been done in this culture." Rational reasoning is suppressed. Cultures can lull people into not thinking or questioning what has always been done. Remember: "[Myths] provide a comforting—if false—sense of continuity and stability in the face of uncertainty and external turmoil. . . . They tend to blind people to the need for change."[58]

- *Health service cover-ups:* The National Health Service in England (NHS) "is the most popular institution in the country." Mythologically, it is viewed as "an embodiment of British values at their best; compassion and decency." Although the NHS has certainly been an immense blessing for the health needs of the population, the myths of perfection surrounding the NHS have discouraged the service "from learning from other countries"; they "may even have allowed scandals to go uncovered because nobody can bring themselves to blow the whistle on saintly NHS workers." *The Economist* continues: "Britain is right to celebrate a [health] service that provides all Britons with free health care. . . . But they are wrong to treat the NHS as an object of awe rather than a human institution with all the imperfections that being human entails."[59]

---

[57]Max Lerner, *The Ideas of the Ice Age* (New York: Viking, 1941), 235. See comments by David I. Kertzer, *Ritual, Politics, and Power* (New Haven, CT: Yale University Press, 1988), 5–6.

[58]Schoenberger, *Cultural Crisis*, 132.

[59]"The National Health Service Is a Great Institution. It Is Also the Subject of Fairy Tales," *The Economist* (June 30, 2018), 48.

Culture and Power

Axiom 5: Culture and Power. "*Culture is very much about power.*"[60] *The church culture is no exception.*

Sexual abuse is an exploitation of power. Though power permeates "our thoughts, our ambitions, our social interactions, and our society, . . . it is curious how little we know about it."[61] Since power is a word that has succeeded in meaning very different things to different people, we need to look closely at what the term stands for.[62] Power is not necessarily malevolent. It is the darker aspect, the abuse of power, which gives power its bad press. Thus, most commonly power is assumed to mean the exercise of force over individuals or particular cultural or social groups by other individuals or agencies. For example, the nineteenth-century philosopher Friedrich Nietzsche believed that all life sought to increase its hold on power; all identities were the result of relations of force.[63] Celebrated sociologist Anthony Giddens defines power "as generated in and through the reproduction of structures of domination."[64] This is unfortunate since it makes power synonymous with only one form of its expression, namely *coercive power*. Rather, *power is simply the potential that a person, institution, or group has to influence.*[65] Two types are identifiable: positive power seeks to empower,

---

[60]Schoenberger, *Cultural Crisis*, 121.

[61]Annette Y. Lee-Chai and John A. Bargh, preface to *The Use and Abuse of Power: Multiple Perspectives on the Causes of Corruption*, ed. Annette Y. Lee-Chai and John A. Bargh (Philadelphia: Psychology Press, 2001), xiii.

[62]See Nigel Rapport and Joanna Overing, *Social and Cultural Anthropology* (London: Routledge, 2007), 337–45.

[63]See Friedrich Nietzsche, *The Will to Power*, trans. Walter Kaufmann (New York: Vintage, 1968).

[64]Anthony Giddens, *A Contemporary Critique of Historical Materialism* (Berkeley: University of California Press, 1981), 1:4. See also Lars Bo Kaspersen, *Anthony Giddens: An Introduction to a Social Theorist* (Oxford: Blackwell, 2000), 40–41.

[65]Rollo May has a similar understanding of power; it is "the ability to cause or prevent change." *Power and Innocence: A Search for the Sources of Violence* (New York: W. W. Norton, 1972), 99. But for Max Weber (1864–1920), power is "the possibility of imposing one's will upon the behavior of other persons." *Max Weber on Law in Economy and Society* (Cambridge, MA: Harvard University Press, 1954), 323.

not only oneself, but also others; negative power is about the domination of others. "Leadership" is an *effort* to influence, but "power" is a leader's *potential* to influence; "authority" is the legitimacy to exercise power.

Unfortunately power is commonly assumed to belong only to individuals. Long-established cultures can be said to have lives of their own that are independent of the individuals that belong to them. I am born into an existing culture; when I die, it remains. Therefore, cultures contain power and authority independent of individuals. The incontrovertible fact is: "Culture is very much about power."[66] The following authors insist that cultures have inherent power.

Clericalism and Power

Clericalism "is the idealization of the priesthood, and by extension, the idealization of the Catholic Church . . . linked to a sense of entitlement, superiority and exclusion, and abuse of power."[67] Clerics and others who become entangled in clericalism assume they have the specialized status and knowledge to *subjugate* laity for their own status advantage. They gravely misunderstand their authority and use power inappropriately and unjustly. John Kenneth Galbraith's, Roland Barthes's, and Michel Foucault's insights help explain the power dynamics of the clerical culture.

John Kenneth Galbraith (1908–2006) significantly draws attention to the historical roots of clerical power. In "the Middle Ages there could have been little talk or thought of power. It was massively possessed only by the prince, the baron, and the priest. For the citizenry in general, submission to it was natural, automatic, and complete. . . . [It] was not something that the ordinary individual ever expected to exercise. Nor, after the rise of capitalism, was the situation much changed. . . . For the silent masses, powerlessness was the natural order of things. Power was not discussed because only a tiny minority of people exercised it."[68] The prince, the baron, and the priest assumed that by rea-

---

[66]Erica Schoenberger, *Cultural Crisis*, 121.

[67]*Final Report of the Royal Commission*, 36.

[68]John Kenneth Galbraith, *The Anatomy of Power* (London: Hamish Hamilton, 1984), 181–82.

son of their cultural status and associated expertise they had the authority *and* power to dominate the powerless.

Roland Barthes (1915–1980) highlights the immeasurable power that symbols and myths possess within popular culture to seduce people's attitudes and behavior.[69] He shows how racism, sexism, and colonialism hide behind seemingly harmless advertisements. The power of myth is to be found, he argues, in its potential to make an arbitrary system of values appear as a system of facts. Use this brand of hair tonic and you will surely feel younger! Barthes's view of the power of myth to subtly mold people's attitudes and actions contributes to our understanding of the priesthood as it developed in church culture from the Council of Trent (1545–63) to Vatican II; the mythology of the priesthood came to overemphasize its exclusive and unique cultic role to the detriment of its pastoral role.

Michel Foucault (1926–1984) insists that coercive power seductively infuses every aspect of a culture and is psychologically invasive and oppressive.[70] The communication of knowledge for Foucault is central to culture and is never linear. Rather it is connected to power that is devious, patchy, and ubiquitous; and it rises above national and ethnic boundaries. Power is the pattern of texts, the specialized languages and networks of power relations operating in and defining a particular field. For him power and knowledge are really the same thing, and he is a master of revealing vested power interests. People who control specialized disciplines, for example, government officials, mass media moguls, and religious leaders, hold extraordinary power in society, power that can rarely be questioned by outsiders. To illustrate his theory, Foucault examines the discourses of madness and sexuality, both of which he concludes are socially constructed.

> There is no such thing as madness or sexuality except ideas about them that are formed through discourse. The disciplines of medicine, psychiatry, biology, economics and linguistics have through history inflexibly defined their

---

[69]See Roland Barthes, *Mythologies* (St. Albans: Paladin, 1973).
[70]See Michel Foucault, *The Order of Things: An Archaeology of the Human Sciences* (New York: Vintage Books, 1974).

"proper" subjects, dividing the world into ordered, controllable entities. Thus, once people are socially defined as mad then they must be controlled accordingly. People who control specialized disciplines hold extraordinary power in society, power that can rarely be challenged by outsiders because they lack the expert knowledge.[71]

Such is the case with clericalism, which assumes that only the clergy, with specialized knowledge, are able to decide what is good for the People of God and how they should behave.[72] An overemphasis on the priest as *alter Christus* ("another Christ") means he has secret knowledge that cannot be questioned and powers to define his superiority over lay people and to control them.[73] This led to the popular view that the clergy *are* the church.[74]

Though power and authority are intimately linked, power is not synonymous with authority. For example, down through the ages bullies have terrorized their victims, believing that might give them the authority to act. Consider the case of Jesus Christ. The Jewish court has sentenced him to death (Jn 11:53). Then the chief priests and the Pharisees, members of the court, bring Jesus to Pilate, the official representative of the Roman occupiers, to implement the death sentence. Pilate said to him: "Do you not know that I have the power to release you, and the power to crucify you?" (Jn 19:10). Pilate assumes that because he has the power to coerce people, even to kill them, he has authority to do so. But Jesus replied: "You have no power over me unless it had

---

[71]Arbuckle, *Culture, Inculturation, and Theologians*, 11.

[72]Richard R. Gaillardetz enlighteningly applies Foucault's notion of power as domination and control to "the harmful structures and habits of power enacted in the Catholic Church, past and present." "Power and Authority in the Church: Emerging Issues," in *A Church with Open Doors: Catholic Ecclesiology for the Third Millennium*, ed. Richard R. Gaillardetz and Edward P. Hannenberg (Collegeville, MN: Liturgical Press, 2015), 91.

[73]The Australian Royal Commission concluded that: "The theological notion that the priest undergoes an 'ontological change' at ordination, so that he is different from ordinary human beings . . . is a dangerous component of the culture of clericalism. The notion that the priest is a sacred person contributed to exaggerated levels of unregulated power and trust, which perpetrators of child sexual abuse were able to exploit." *Final Report of the Royal Commission*, 68.

[74]See William R. Burrows, *New Ministries: The Global Context* (Maryknoll, NY: Orbis Books, 1980), 105–12.

been given you from above" (Jn 19:11). That is, Pilate's use of power lacks the legalizing authority that only comes from God. In the book of Revelation we also read that "You are worthy, our Lord . . . to receive power," but this is possible because the authority of God to possess this power comes from the fact that God had "created all things" (Rev 4:11).

Authority, therefore, simply means legitimacy to exercise power. One can have the authority to influence others, but for various reasons have no power to act. On the other hand, one can have the power to affect others' behavior yet possess no authority for doing so. Clerical perpetrators of sexual abuse assume because they have the power to exploit their victims they automatically have the authority to do so.

Abuse of Authority

Several types of authority can be distinguished. First, *position* authority is the legitimacy to use power flowing from the status one has within an organization or culture. For example, the president of the United States has position authority derived from his office as legitimized in the Constitution. The pope has position authority legitimized by Christ's founding of the church. Of the various kinds of position authority, *coercive* authority permits people to force others to act through fear of punishment;[75] *reward* authority encourages a response by offering or refusing benefits. When power is wielded exploitatively or manipulatively it is done so illegitimately—that is, without authority. President Richard Nixon (in office 1969–74) abused his position authority when he berated members of Congress who sought to expose his cover-up of the Watergate affair.

In child sexual abuse cases, approximately one-third of offenders are relatives of the victim; that is, the offenders have used their authority in the family tragically and unjustly to dominate the victims.[76] Social workers, counselors, and ministers

---

[75]Max Weber defines coercive power as "the chance of a man or a number of men to realise their own will in a communal action even against the resistance of others who are participants in the action." Hans H. Gerth and C. Wright Mills, *From Max Weber: Essays in Sociology* (London: Routledge & Kegan Paul, 1948), 180.

[76]See J. N. Lam, "Child Sexual Abuse," in *Violence in Intimate Relationships*,

of religion who sexually abuse children similarly use their position authority negatively; that is, they abuse their authority. The Australian inquiry into child sexual abuse "revealed numerous cases where senior officials of Catholic Church authorities knew about allegations of child sexual abuse in Catholic institutions but failed to take effective action." And it adds: "It is also evident that other priests, religious . . . and lay members of the Catholic community were aware either of specific abuse or of rumours or gossip about certain priests or religious." The inquiry sees these not only as cover-ups but as the abuse of authority. "While the knowledge and understanding of child sexual abuse may have developed and deepened in the last two decades of the twentieth century, it is clear that Catholic Church leaders were aware of the problem well before that time."[77]

The second broad category of authority is termed *personal.* This is legitimacy to influence others because of the personal gifts that one has; for example, *expert* authority may allow one to influence others as a result of one's skills at animation; *information* authority comes from one's knowledge of a subject; *referent* authority is a result of one's attractive personal qualities that draw people to listen and act. Expert and referent authority combined would be equivalent to what we popularly call charismatic authority. Jesus taught "as one having authority" (Mk 1:22), healed with "authority" (Mk 1:27), encouraged people to "follow" him (Jn 10:27), and had "authority on earth to forgive sins" (Mk 2:10). What is this authority? Where does it come from? It is certainly not coercive authority, but the way he teaches and acts is personal/referent. He exemplified the unswerving qualities of compassion, charity, and justice, which legitimized his claim to speak and act with authority. The Father confirmed this authority (Mt 28:18).

Rollo May distinguishes between *nutritive* and *integrative* authority/power (both can be part of position or personal authority/power categories); the former is used for or on behalf of another and the latter *with* another. For example, one who fosters a collaborative form of government is exercising an inte-

---

ed. N. A. Jackson and G. C. Oates (Boston: Butterworth-Heinemann, 1998), 51.
[77] *Final Report of the Royal Commission,* 35–36.

grative gift; one who acts for the welfare of another person but without their involvement is using nutritive authority/power.[78] Minors and vulnerable adults who are sexually abused have the right to experience positive nutritive or integrative power; the abuse destroys this growing encounter, with long-term tragic consequences.

Coercive Power in Toxic Cultures

Authority and power to constrain individuals reside in individuals and in cultures. Social theorist Steve Lukes clarifies this when he distinguishes two dimensions of coercive power.[79] The first is when power is used overtly and deliberately to coerce preferences of one group over those of others. Thus immigration officers exercise this power, as authorized by their culture, when they refuse entrance of people legally excluded by the state.

Lukes's second dimension of power is "more subtle than the use of direct force and refers to the ability to not only make decisions but to also control the political agenda. Control of the agenda negates the necessity of direct force by its capacity to ensure that potential issues of conflict, either as express policy preferences or as grievances, are kept out of the political process."[80] For example:

- For over a century the Vatican, the dominant authority in the church culture, maintained that it alone had the right to discipline pedophiliac priests, not the state. So, in 1997 the Catholic bishops of Ireland were warned by the papal nuncio that "if they adopted the policy of automatically reporting pederasts to the police, they would be breaking canon law."[81] Thus the issue of pederasts was to be firmly

---

[78]See May, *Power and Innocence*, 105–9.

[79]See Steve Lukes, *Power: A Radical View* (Basingstoke: Palgrave Macmillan, 1974).

[80]Daphne Habibis and Maggie Walter, *Social Inequality in Australia: Discourses, Realities, and Futures* (South Melbourne: Oxford University Press, 2015), 92–93.

[81]Roy Hattersley, *The Catholics: The Church and Its People in Britain and Ireland, from the Reformation to the Present Day* (London: Chatto & Windus, 2017), 542. Canon law required that any credible allegation of clerical sexual abuse had to be reported to the Congregation for the Doctrine of the Faith (CDF) to be dealt with either by the CDF itself or the relevant local bishop. Any

kept out of the secular political process. Shortly after this intervention by the nuncio the Vatican reiterated the policy that allegations against priests must be dealt with by its own procedures in secret. However, this dimension of power ceases to be effective when "a public issue gains voice in the public sphere."[82] And that is precisely what has happened. The global outcry following the publication in the secular press of pederasts among the clergy effectively undermined this highly secretive Vatican process.

- President Donald Trump's "system of power is his contempt for the truth," believing that "his power means he can get away with a great deal. . . . When power dominates truth, criticism becomes betrayal." By this misuse of authority he sets the political agenda for his followers.[83]

Axiom 6: Hierarchal Governance and Abusive Power. *Hierarchical governance cultures, for example the Catholic Church, are prone to abuse coercive power through bullying and lack of accountability; such cultures are "toxic."*

There are many occasions when coercive power permits people legitimately to force others to act, such as when police have to use force to arrest a robber. However, bullying is a misuse of coercive power. Bullying is persistent unwelcome action or verbal, psychological, or physical aggression that is knowingly or unknowingly directed by an individual or group against people who normally are not in a position to defend themselves. It evokes strong emotions in both bully and victim. In brief, bullies wish to force people to do what they want them to do and will try all kinds of intimidation to achieve this. The victim feels helpless, especially when, as is commonly the case, the bully has seniority over the victim.[84] The sexual abuse crisis is an example of bul-

---

investigation had to be handled covertly with all parties and witnesses sworn to secrecy. In 2010 a limited form of reporting to civil authorities was allowed but only if the civil law demanded it. For a detailed explanation of canon law regarding clerical abuse see Geoffrey Robinson, *The Case of the Pope: Vatican Accountability for Human Rights Abuse* (London: Penguin, 2010), 42–62.

[82]Habibis and Walter, *Social Inequality*, 93.

[83]"What Has Become of the Republican Party?" *The Economist* (April 21, 2018), 9.

[84]See Gerald A. Arbuckle, *Confronting the Demon: A Gospel Response to*

lying; the perpetrators misuse power to subjugate for their own advantage those who are vulnerable and defenseless.

In hierarchical cultures such as business firms, the army, hospitals,[85] and the Catholic Church, there is considerable potential for top-down bullying, especially when the "power distance" between superiors and subordinates is notably marked. In such cases, a small number of people with position authority are able to control the avenues of communication and hence to cover up any perceived or real abuse of power.[86] People who complain become cynical about ever being listened to impartially and, consequently, feel oppressed. They feel demeaned, of little importance in the system, powerless, unable to do anything to rectify problems. The bully who is a superior, for example, a bishop, a parish priest, a principal of a school, a CEO of business firm, can act with little or no organizational restraints or accountability.[87]

Cultures that foster bullying are *toxic* cultures. Favoring secrecy and displaying poor internal and external communications, such cultures encourage an environment that can damage the emotional and physical well-being of people who do not have the power to call superiors to account for their behavior. Toxic cultures stifle the energy of people who want change. Since hierarchical organizations are modeled on traditional patriarchal family systems in which males dominate, they can reinforce aggressive male-dominant behavior patterns.[88] Marie Keenan writes of her experience of the toxic Catholic Church culture in Ireland:

Adult Bullying (Collegeville, MN: Liturgical Press, 2003), 17–63.

[85]See Gerald A. Arbuckle, *Humanizing Healthcare Reforms* (London: Jessica Kingsley, 2013), 131–60.

[86]Rasmus Hougaard and Jacqueline Carter report "that neuroscience seems to find that power, if not managed well, structurally changes the brain, leaving leaders with a deficit of empathy and an inability to put themselves in others' shoes." *The Mind of the Leader* (Boston: Harvard Business Review Press, 2018), 143. See also J. Hogeveen, M. Inzlcht, and S. S. Obhi, "Power Changes How the Brain Responds to Others," *Journal of Experimental Psychology: General* 143, no. 2 (2014): 755–62.

[87]See Angela Ishmael, *Harassment, Bullying, and Violence at Work* (London: Industrial Society, 1999), 131–32.

[88]See Gareth Morgan, *Images of Organization* (Beverly Hills: Sage, 1986), 210–12.

Accountability is expected to function in a bottom-up fashion. The laity and lower-ranking clergy are accountable to the hierarchical leadership and the bishops are accountable to the pope, but there is no accountability the other way round.... Rigidly hierarchical models of accountability that are accompanied by rigid hierarchies of power foster by their very nature mechanisms of denial and structural secrecy.[89]

And the Australian inquiry into the sexual abuse of minors is equally concerned:

> The powers of governance held by individual diocesan bishops and provincials are not subject to adequate checks and balances. There is no separation of powers, and the executive, legislative and judicial aspects of governance are combined.... Diocesan bishops have not been sufficiently accountable to any body for decision-making in the handling of allegations of child sexual abuse or alleged perpetrators. ...The hierarchical structure of the Catholic Church created a culture of deferential obedience in which poor responses to child sexual abuse went unchallenged.[90]

Cultural Change and Grief

Axiom 7: Cultural Change Evokes Grief and Resistance. Many changes, even if intellectually agreed to, necessitate loss, and loss evokes the sadness of grief in individuals and cultures. Unless this grief can be publicly articulated in mourning rituals,[91] it will haunt the living and lead to dysfunctional behavior and resistance to culture change.

Profound cultural change is a messy and painful process. It takes quite a while for individuals to get their heads and hearts

---

[89]Marie Keenan, *Child Sexual Abuse and the Catholic Church: Gender, Power, and Organizational Culture* (London: Oxford University Press, 2012), 39.

[90]*Final Report of the Royal Commission*, 36.

[91]"Ritual, a form of storytelling, is the repetitive spontaneous or prescribed symbolic act of bodily movement and gesture to express and articulate meaning within a social context in which there is possible or real tension/conflict and a need to resolve or hide it." See Arbuckle, *Culture, Inculturation, and Theologians*, 83.

adjusted to the fact that the world has changed and they may have to change also. Grief or grieving is the internal experience of sadness, sorrow, anger, loneliness, anguish, confusion, shame, guilt, and fear, in individuals and cultures as a consequence of experiencing loss. Unless this grief is allowed to be openly expressed, individuals and cultures become increasingly depressed and resistant to change: "Suppressed grief suffocates" (Ovid).[92] The term *mourning*, in contrast, refers to formal or informal rituals and internal processes of transformation that the bereaved undertake to deal with grieving. Grieving is very much an automatic reaction to loss, but mourning is the decision to relate to grief in constructive ways, that is, a willingness to acknowledge publicly that grief has occurred, to let it go, and then to be open to the world ahead. This is further explained in Chapter 3, and in *Action Plan 3*, Chapter 6.[93]

Cultures and Social Systems

Axiom 8: Cultural Change and Systems. A culture, for example the Catholic Church, is a "social system," that is, it contains many interrelated parts; touch one part and all other parts are affected.

Cultures are complex systems. If one part of a culture is touched, then everything else in the culture is affected in some way or other in a domino effect.[94] For example, the introduction of railways as the means of transport in England and North America in the nineteenth century led to dramatic economic and social changes in cities and rural communities. A *system* may

---

[92]Ovid, *Tristia*, book 5, eleg. 1, line 63.

[93]For a fuller explanation of grief and mourning see Gerald A. Arbuckle, *The Francis Factor and the People of God: New Life for the Church* (Maryknoll, NY: Orbis Books, 2015), 59–124.

[94]Marie Keenan writes: "It is always important that organizations take extreme care in managing systemic change, as change in one part of the system will produce changes in all others, raising the potential for unforeseen problems in the attempt to resolve the original problem. This is exactly what is happening now in the Catholic Church." Keenan notes that the new "superstructures for child protection" in Ireland and the United States have negatively affected "the relationships between bishops and priests and the rights of Catholic clergy who are falsely accused." *Child Sexual Abuse*, 229.

be defined literally as "an organized or complex whole; an assemblage or combination of things or parts forming a complex or unitary whole."[95] How parts of a social system relate to one another in an ordered way is determined and supported by its culture. So, when Pope Francis speaks of the "culture of abuse, and the system of cover-up that allowed it to be perpetuated" in the church of Chile, he is saying that in the culture of the Chilean church there is a definite organizational pattern to the abuse and that the culture supports it. That is, the Chilean system of abuse exists because it is intimately connected to its supportive cultural elements—symbols, myths, and rituals. The abuse crisis, however, is not restricted to Chile. The pattern of abuse is globally systemic because it is supported by a universal culture of clericalism (see Chapter 2).

In summary, a social system is an entity with interconnected parts that relate to one another in regularized ways; each part affects the others and each depends on the whole.[96] For example, the #MeToo crusade began as a movement against the sexual harassment particularly of women, chiefly because Hollywood notable Harvey Weinstein was found to be a predator in 2017. However, no longer is it a movement only about sexual harassment. It has morphed into a crusade to change the unequal distribution of power in society between women and men: "Thanks to #MeToo, women's testimony is at last being taken more seriously. For too

---

[95]David L. Cleland and William R. King, *Systems Analysis and Project Management* (New York: McGraw-Hill, 1983), 19–20. Nano McCaughan and Barry Palmer write: "So systems thinking is a way of describing and explaining the patterns of behaviour that we encounter in the life of organizations: the regularities of individual behaviour, which we describe as a role, the characteristic ways of doing things in organizations which we refer to as their culture." *Systems Thinking for Harassed Managers* (London: Karnac Books, 1994), 12.

[96]Mary Jo Hatch describes the origin of General Systems Theory: "In the 1950s, German biophysiologist Ludwig von Bertalanffy presented a theory intended to explain in all scientific phenomena across both natural and social sciences from the atom and molecule . . . all the way up to the level of individuals, groups, and societies. He recognized that all these phenomena were related—societies contain groups, groups contain individuals. . . . [He] sought the essential laws and principles that would explain all systems." *Organization Theory: Modern, Symbolic, and Postmodern Perspectives* (Oxford: Oxford University Press, 1997), 34–35. See also W. Buckley, "Systems," in *Organizations as Systems*, ed. Martin Lockett and Roger Spear (Milton Keynes: Open University, 1983), 34–45.

long, when a woman spoke out against a man, the suspicion was turned back on her."[97]

So it is also in the Catholic Church today. The ripple effects of the sexual abuse by clerics and religious are raising all kinds of cultural and theological questions about the unequal distribution of power in the church, for example, between Rome and local churches, between laity and hierarchies, between men and women (see further clarifications in *Axiom 10: Culture and Corruption*).

Types of Culture Change

Axiom 9: Institutional Change Demands Alteration of the Essential Character of Institutions. *Efforts to change institutional cultures, such as we find in the Catholic Church, and overcome resistances, have uncertain consequences, as radical change demands alterations of the institution's symbols, myths, and rituals.*[98]

Pope Francis and others frequently call for culture change in the church so that abuse and cover-ups will cease. However, radical change in an institutional culture, particularly a culture as complex as the Catholic Church, is intensely difficult because of the resistances already noted. At the deepest levels, a cultural change demands alteration of the fundamental assumptions of the institution's essential character inherent in its symbols, myths, and rituals. Two examples will help illustrate why this is so:

- Consider that New York State has the most segregated public schools in the United States. Attempts at significant desegregation "reforms have met fierce opposition. There have been videos of white parents angrily arguing that changing the schools will unfairly harm their children; politicians who backed reforms and then waffled after public pressure; and protests outside the city's Education

---

[97]*The Economist*, "#MeToo, One Year On," September 29, 2018, 13.

[98]William G. Dyer comments: "Changing an organization's culture is considerably more dramatic than modifying parts of a system. . . . [At] the deepest level, a cultural change requires alteration of the basic assumptions of the organization and its essential character." *Strategies for Managing Change* (Reading, PA: Addison-Wesley, 1984), 163.

Department punctuated by chants of 'Save our Schools.' "[99] Desegregation demands massive fundamental cultural changes among white parents; despite years of efforts there has been little success.

- Recently, less dramatically in Sydney, Australia, there was what became known as the "plastic bag rage." Two major supermarkets had freely decided for ostensibly ecological reasons that they would no longer provide customers with free small-sized single-use plastic bags for purchases. The public became enraged, and the proprietors could not understand why. They had, they said, brought in the cultural change to help save the environment, and they believed customers understood this and would willingly bring their own bags to collect groceries. The public outcry was so great that the managers had to rethink their decision. What had gone wrong?

Pasquale Gagliardi's[100] insights provide important distinctions that help explain why there has been a public backlash against a small change by management in the shopping culture for the right ecological reasons. Moreover, his clarifications have important implications for the major theme of this book, namely, how we are to proceed in refounding the church in trauma. Gagliardi distinguishes three types of change: apparent, incremental, and revolutionary.

- *Apparent* cultural change is superficial because the identity of the institutional culture, that is, its symbols, myths, and rituals, remain substantially intact. For example, a business firm may change its name to make its products appear more relevant.
- In *incremental* change the symbols, myths, and rituals of a culture absorb over time other symbols, myths, and

---

[99]Adam Harris, "Can Richard Carranza Integrate the Most Segregated School System in the Country?" *The Atlantic* (July 23, 2018), 2.

[100]See Pasquale Gagliardi, "The Creation and Change of Organizational Cultures: A Conceptual Framework," *Organizational Studies* 7, no. 2 (1986): 117–34, and *Symbols and Artifacts: Views of the Corporate Landscape* (New York: Aldine de Gruyter, 1990).

rituals from outside, so that there is substantial but not disruptive change. For example, the founding fathers of the American Constitution gave limited executive powers to the president, but over many years due to challenges of security and the complexities of administering public services these powers have slowly and significantly expanded. That is, there has been incremental cultural change. Another example is when a hospital develops several new medical specialty departments over the space of a few years; there is change, but the hospital's founding mythology and identity remain the same.

- However, if the hospital changes from providing general services to the public and becomes instead open *only* to children, there is a *revolutionary* mythological change in its identity and purpose. *Revolutionary* change thus connotes the destruction of one culture and its replacement by a drastically different one. This involves a major cultural upheaval capable of causing intense pain, anxiety, even trauma, to people the hospital once served.

Now back to the simple plastic bags! The supermarket managers failed to see that the decision to cease supplying single-use bags involved neither apparent nor incremental change. It was a revolutionary change demanding of the customers a radical change in the way they shopped; they had now to develop profoundly new symbols, myths, and rituals in order to do their weekly shopping. The management had provided a logically rational, ecological argument for why they would cease providing plastic bags, thinking that culture change can simply occur as a consequence of heady reasoning. On the contrary, especially for revolutionary change, cultural change demands emotionally charged mythological conversion, the outcome of which is always uncertain. One further lesson: the management assumed that the bags were used by customers *only* for carrying groceries. However, customers wanted the bags also for all kinds of home use, for example, as bin-liners, packaging kitchen items, picnic lunches. The lesson? Culture analysis and culture change are tricky and time-consuming tasks. If the managers had listened to their customers, they could have saved themselves a lot of needless frustration.

How does this apply to a key theme of this book? The Holy Office was officially known between 1908 and 1965 as the Supreme Sacred Congregation of the Holy Office, but in 1965 it changed its name to the Congregation for the Doctrine of the Faith. This was an *apparent* change since its method of investigating and judging theologians remained in practice the same—for example, informants remained anonymous. However, Vatican II called for *revolutionary* change, neither *apparent* nor *incremental* change. In its documents the council radically changed the model of the church from "fortress" to "pilgrim." The council called for the mythological rupture or breakup of one cultural model and its substitution with a radically different one. However, as will be explained in Chapter 2, Rome, supported by the curia, in practice predominantly held to the former model. Changes were to be superficial. The rhetoric proclaimed that there was substantial change when, in fact, cultural change became more apparent than real. Clericalism and other significant power systems remained fundamentally intact. The revolutionary change that the council and now Pope Francis calls for has not occurred. The pre–Vatican II culture remains. Change to a Vatican II culture is going to require revolutionary mythological change, particularly in the thinking and acting of hierarchical authorities (see Chapters 4 and 6).

Culture, Corruption, Cover-Ups, and Shame

Axiom 10: Culture and Corruption. Not only individuals, but also cultures, can use power corruptly and seek to cover up its consequences; sexual abuse of minors in the church is due to systemic corruption of power.

There are many definitions of corruption.[101] However, for our purposes, corruption can be defined as "the misuse of public power for private gain"[102] of individuals and/or institutions. When people who are in authority supported by organizational cultures bypass the law, then power is corrupted. This power corruption involves two fundamental elements, writes Cambridge sociolo-

---

[101]See Eric M. Uslaner, *The Historical Roots of Corruption* (Cambridge: Cambridge University Press, 2017), 4.

[102]Susan Rose-Ackerman, *Corruption and Government: Causes, Consequences, and Reform* (Cambridge: Cambridge University Press, 1999), 91.

gist John Thompson: "(1) the infringement of rules, conventions or laws concerning the proper exercise of public duties for the purposes of private, pecuniary or personal gain; and (2) the perversion or undermining of the standards of integrity associated with public office."[103] Corruption can be of two kinds: petty and grand. *Petty* corruption, for example, occurred in the 1990s when some minor members of the International Olympic Committee involved in choosing venues for the Olympic Games accepted bribes; their primary aim was to enrich themselves.[104] *Grand* corruption occurs when those in high office influence government policies for the sake of private gain *or* to protect their own government institutions.[105] For example, in March 1968 dozens of innocent Vietnamese were slaughtered in cold blood by U.S. troops—the My Lai Massacre.[106] President Richard Nixon, supported by his subcultural team, sought to hide the truth from the American public in a cover-up operation through a campaign to sabotage the trials so that no American soldier would be convicted of war crimes.[107]

The hierarchical officials in the church who sought to cover up sexual abuse of minors were involved in *grand* corruption, though they may not have thought their actions were necessarily morally wrong. They were acting, their ecclesiastical culture assured them, to protect the reputation of the church and even the welfare of perpetrators. It was taken for granted that the end justified breaking ethical principles. But in fact their actions were an infringement of moral and often civil laws; their actions ran contrary to the standards of gospel integrity. It can happen that

---

[103]John B. Thompson, *Political Scandal: Power and Visibility in the Media Age* (Cambridge: Polity, 2000), 28.

[104]See Nihal Jayawickrama, "Transparency International: Combating Corruption through Institutional Reform," in *The Use and Abuse of Power: Multiple Perspectives on the Causes of Corruption*, ed. Annette Y. Lee-Chai and John A. Bargh (Philadelphia: Psychology Press, 2001), 281.

[105]See George Moody-Stuart, *Grand Corruption* (Oxford: Worldview, 1997), 1.

[106]See Herbert C. Kelman and V. Lee Hamilton, "The My Lai Massacre: Crimes of Obedience and Sanctioned Massacres," in *Corporate and Governmental Deviance: Problems of Organizational Behavior in Contemporary Society*, ed. M. David Ermann and Richard J. Lundman (New York: Oxford University Press, 1996), 180–206; Stanley Cohen, *States of Denial: Knowing about Atrocities and Suffering* (Cambridge: Polity, 2001), 261–66.

[107]See Thompson, *Political Scandal,* 200–218.

power is misused "by those who do not realize they are doing so, who at a conscious level believe that they are acting in an objective and fair-minded manner and in the best interests of their subordinates"[108] because the culture of power abuse has never been challenged. Such has been the case in the church, where the culture of cover-up remained unchallenged until recently. It was tragically considered to be the normal way of acting.[109]

Eric Uslaner and others in their analyses of corruption argue that it "stems from inequality and reinforces it." People with limited political, economic, and social power are voiceless in the presence of the powerful; they see "the system as stacked against them. . . . [Inequality distorts] the key institutions of fairness in a society."[110] Donatella Della Porta and Alberto Vannucci argue that ubiquitous corruption makes it difficult for people to denounce it as immoral.[111] Such was the case in the church. Survivors of sexual abuse became voiceless because the ubiquitous culture of clericalism and cover-up was "stacked against them."

Systemic Cover-Up Culture in the Church

Corruption is *systemic* whenever it becomes an essential element or pattern in an institutional culture. As noted in the introduction, Philip Zimbardo asserts that the evil of corruption can occur at one of three levels: People are just "bad apples" because they are so disposed. Or they act corruptly because the "barrel" they are in happens to be corrupt, which is situational

---

[108]John A. Bargh and Jeannette Alvarez, "The Road to Hell: Good Intention in the Face of Nonconscious Tendencies to Misuse Power," in *The Use and Abuse of Power*, ed. Annette Y. Lee-Chai and John A. Bargh, 45.

[109]Louise F. Fitzgerald found in her study of the sexual harassment case literature, in 1993, that three out of four perpetrators simply did not understand that they were guilty of harassing. Nor did they see that they caused the victim any anguish, "and instead [ascribed] their behaviour, which they [acknowledged], to some more acceptable motive." "The Last Great Open Secret: The Sexual Harassment of Women in the Workplace and Academia." This is an edited transcript of a Science and Public Policy Seminar presented by the Federation of Behavioral, Psychological, and Cognitive Sciences, Washington, DC (1993), cited by Bargh and Alvarez, "Road to Hell," 45.

[110]Uslaner, *Historical Roots*, 6, 7.

[111]Donatella Della Porta and Alberto Vannucci, *Corrupt Exchanges* (New York: Aldine, 1999), 146.

corruption. Or people act in evil ways because the system, supported by the culture, causes the "barrel" to be corrupt. That
is, the wider culture causes the barrel to be corrupt.[112] Sexual
abuse cover-ups are systemic because the culture of the church in
this matter is corrupt. In Australia it was found that "individual
pathology on its own is insufficient to explain child sexual abuse
perpetrated by Catholic clergy and religious. Rather, a heightened
risk of child sexual abuse arises when specific factors in relation
to an individual's psychosexual dysfunction combine with a range
of *situational and institutional factors* [i.e., cultural factors]."[113]

Axiom 11: Culture and Cover-Ups. *Organizational cultures, not
only individuals, may deny that corrupt cover-ups are occurring;
such has been the case in the Catholic Church.*

Denial is "the need to be innocent of a troubling recognition.
. . . [We] seem to have access to reality, but choose to ignore it
because it proves convenient to do so."[114] There may even be
a vague recognition "that we choose not to look at the facts
without being conscious of what it is we are evading."[115] Denial
can be *active*, which is the deliberate rejection of reality. Such
is the case, for example, when the Turkish nation chooses not
to acknowledge their Armenian genocide. Denial can also be
passive, which is denial by directing one's attention elsewhere.[116]

Cultures, not just individuals, can conveniently deny, that is,
whole cultures can "turn a blind eye" to reality. Stanley Cohen
quotes the Protestant theologian Adolph Visser 't Hooft's reflections on the churches' knowledge of the Holocaust: "People could
find no place in their consciousness for such an unimaginable
horror . . . and they did not have the courage to face it. It is possible to live in a twilight between knowing and not knowing."[117]
Ervin Staub observes that passivity "in the face of others' suf-

---

[112]See Philip Zimbardo, "The Psychology of Evil," TED Lecture (September
23, 2008).

[113]*Final Report of the Royal Commission*, 42. Italics added.

[114]John Steiner, "Turning a Blind Eye: The Cover-Up for Oedipus," *International
Review of Psycho-Analysis* 17 (1985): 163.

[115]Ibid., 161.

[116]See Stanley Cohen, *States of Denial: Knowing about Atrocities and Suffering*
(Cambridge: Polity Press, 2001), 32.

[117]Ibid., frontispiece.

fering makes it difficult to remain in internal opposition to the perpetrators and to feel empathy for the victims." He writes that to lessen "their own feelings of empathic distress and guilt, passive bystanders will distance themselves from victims" and consider "victims as deserving of their fate, and to devalue them."[118]

People who collude with their culture are also in passive denial, turning a blind eye, and conveniently sidelining facts, "allowing something to be both known and not known."[119] We know what is happening, but we do not want to examine the disturbing implications; there is "a respect and fear of the truth and it is this fear which leads to the collusion and cover-up."[120] The reality of sexual abuse in the church would have been known by particular bishops and congregational leaders, but most would have ignored the ethical implications of concealing the perpetrators. The good name of the church had to be preserved at all costs; a blind eye was turned to wider moral and legal implications.

What happened in Australia was typical of the reactions of other local churches:

> It is apparent that the avoidance of public scandal, the maintenance of the reputation of the Catholic Church and loyalty to priests and religious largely determined the responses of Catholic Church authorities when allegations of child sexual abuse arose.[121]

The ecclesiastical culture approved of the fact that those in responsible positions would do their utmost to conceal what was happening as "corruption thrives on secrecy."[122] Others may have been vaguely aware of what was occurring, but the less they knew the easier it was for them to turn a blind eye.

---

[118]Ervin Staub, *The Psychology of Good and Evil: Why Children, Adults, and Groups Help and Harm Others* (Cambridge: Cambridge University Press, 2003), 305–6.

[119]Cohen, *States of Denial*, 34.

[120]Steiner, "Turning a Blind Eye," 233.

[121]*Final Report of the Royal Commission*, 36.

[122]Nihal Jayawickrama, "Transparency International: Combating Corruption through Institutional Reform," in *Use and Abuse of Power*, ed. Lee-Chai and Bargh, 290.

[Thus complaints] of child abuse were not reported to police or other civil authorities, contributing to the Catholic
Church being able to keep such matters "in-house" and out
of the public gaze. . . . When the priest or religious left [i.e.,
from a particular ministry], sometimes hurriedly, untrue or
misleading reasons were sometimes given for their departure.
On occasions, the move was timed to avoid raising suspicion. In some cases, no warning, or no effective warning,
was given to the new parish or school of the risk posed by
the incoming priest or religious.[123]

Fear and Shame Motivate Coverp-Ups

*Axiom 12: Fear Motivates Cover-Ups. The fear of being publicly
shamed motivates corruption cover-ups in the church.*[124]

To have a "sense of shame" simply means that we behave in
ways that society expects of us. This can be a good thing if what
is expected of us is just. To feel shame, however, can be a trau-
matizing experience. Elizabeth Horst writes: "At its most basic,
shame is a feeling that interrupts other, positive feelings, and in
doing so produces a global, negative evaluation of the self."[125]
This feeling of shame occurs when a person or a culture concludes
that they are negatively judged by others (and even by themselves
as assessed by their own personal standards), expressing itself
in behavior such as speech disruption, lowered or averted gaze,
blushing, scarcely audible speech, or the desire to hide.[126] "To
feel shame" means that the mocking or disapproval has struck
a raw nerve. It is that piercing feeling of humiliation that public

---

[123]*Final Report of the Royal Commission*, 36, 37.

[124]For a fuller explanation of shame and honor see Thomas Ryan, "The Positive
Function of Shame: Moral and Spiritual Perspectives," in *The Value of Shame:
Exploring a Health Resource in Cultural Contexts*, ed. Elizabeth Vanderheiden
and Claude-Helene Mayer (Cham: Springer International Publishing, 2017),
87–105; Arbuckle, *Violence, Society, and the Church*, 79–93; Jayson Georges
and Mark D. Baker, *Ministering in Honor-Shame Cultures* (Downers Grove,
IL: InterVarsity Press, 2016).

[125]Elizabeth A. Horst, *Recovering the Lost Self: Shame-Healing for Victims of
Clergy Sexual Abuse* (Collegeville, MN: Liturgical Press, 1998), 14.

[126]See Thomas J. Scheff, "Shame and Conformity: The Difference-Emotion
System," *American Sociological Review*, no. 53 (1988): 395–405.

exposure causes, something far worse than feeling embarrassed, which is a short-lived experience of discomfort because some social norm has been ignored. Little wonder that individuals and cultures will do anything to avoid having their failings exposed to society. Brene Brown perceptively comments that:

> When the culture of any organization mandates that it is more important to protect the reputation of a system and those in power than it is to protect the basic dignity of the individuals who serve that system or who are served by that system, you can be certain that the shame is systemic, the money is driving ethics, and the accountability is all but dead.[127]

The honor of the institution must be safeguarded at all costs. This, Brown says, is true of all kinds of cultures, including faith communities. It is this fear of being publicly shamed, of not being the "perfect church," as Catholic pre–Vatican II mythology has long asserted, that has been a major cause of the cover-up of power abuses in the church for generations, including the sexual abuse of minors by clerics and religious: "Like a terrorist, [the fear of being shamed] strikes fear to expose our vulnerabilities and remind us of our weaknesses. When shame terrorizes and taunts, our hearts fear what shame might do."[128]

Shame differs from guilt. "Guilt is the inner experience of having broken a moral norm; shame is the inner feeling of being looked down upon by a social group. Guilt is something that can be expiated, for example, a person is imprisoned following conviction for a crime, but the shame of having been a prisoner is socially impossible to erase."[129]

> Shaming can lead to a false sense of guilt in the victim. Thus victims of abuse are often made to feel that they, not the violators, are the guilty party. In instances of sexual abuse the victim can be judged by the community to be the guilty

---

[127]Brene Brown, *Braving the Wilderness: The Quest for True Belonging and the Courage to Stand Alone* (London: Vermilion, 2017), 78.

[128]Georges and Baker, *Ministering in Honor-Shame*, 127.

[129]Arbuckle, *Violence, Society, and the Church*, 81–82.

one. This is common in cases of sexual abuse by the clergy and congregational members: people assume a priori that the minister or priest could not possibly be at fault because of the moral authority of the culture to which they belong, so the victim is branded as the perpetrator. The victim is made to feel guilty, in addition to shame—a twice-bitter experience of being violated.[130]

For example, in Australia, because of the assumed credibility of the churches, "Police often refused to believe children [abused in institutions conducted by religious congregations]. They refused to investigate their complaints. . . . Child protection agencies did not listen to children."[131] Moreover, it did not help that "the prevailing culture that 'children should be seen and not heard' resonated throughout residential care, religious institutions, schools. . . . Their complaints of abuse ignored and rejected, many children lost faith in adults and society's institutions."[132]

Uncovering Sexual Abuse Scandals

Axiom 13: Types of Scandals. The sexual abuse scandals in the church are of two types: "secular" and "theological."
Scandals can be defined in the secular world as "actions or events involving certain kinds of transgressions which become known to others and are sufficiently serious to elicit a public response."[133] That is, a "scandal can arise if and only if the veil of secrecy is lifted and the corrupt activities become known to others or become the focus of a public investigation."[134] The sexual abuse scandals and their cover-up in the church belong to the category of "power scandals," because they reveal how the church exploited that power it held publicly and politically.[135] Those in

---

[130]Ibid., 82; Horst, *Recovering the Lost Self*, 21.
[131]Royal Commission into Institutional Responses to Child Sexual Abuse, *Final Report*, 5.
[132]Ibid., 6.
[133]Thompson, *Political Scandal*, 13.
[134]Ibid., 29.
[135]"Political power is concerned with the co-ordination of individuals and the regulation of their patterns of interaction." Ibid., 97.

authority sought to hide the actions of sexual perpetrators from the publicly approved civil authorities of the state.

But "scandal" has also a far more serious meaning, derived from the Greek word *skandalon,* translated as a "stumbling block." Theologically, scandal means causing someone to stumble in their faith.[136] Thus, St. Thomas Aquinas writes that scandal is an "offense, downfall, or a stumbling against something."[137] He explains that it is a form of *spiritual abuse* because a person "may be disposed to a spiritual downfall by another's word or deed . . . as one man by his order, inducement or example, moves another to sin."[138] The focus here is on the deleterious faith impact on another, whereas in the secular meaning of scandal the emphasis is on the damaging appearance of the person or group doing a scandalous action.[139] Jesus is referring to the theological meaning of scandal when he says: "If any of you put a stumbling block before one of these little ones who believe in me, it would be better for you if a great millstone were fastened around your neck and you were drowned in the depths of the sea" (Mt 18:6). It is in this theological sense that Pope Francis acknowledged that "sins of clerical abuse against minors have a toxic effect on faith and hope in God."[140] By hiding this abuse the church "has caused scandal in a theological sense both to the victims of abuse for whom justice and truth were denied, and to the wider Catholic population."[141]

---

[136]"Scandal is an attitude or behavior which leads another to do evil. The person who gives scandal becomes his neighbor's tempter. He damages virtue and integrity; he may even draw his brother into spiritual death. . . . Scandal can be provoked by laws or institutions, by fashion or opinion." *Catechism of the Catholic Church,* 2nd ed. (Strathfield: St. Pauls Publications, 1994), paras. 2284, 2286.

[137]Thomas Aquinas, *Summa Theologiae,* Part 2 of Part 2, Article 1, Reply to Question 43, Objection 1.

[138]Ibid., Part 2 of Part 2, Art. 1, Reply to Obj. 4. "Spiritual abuse" is further explained in *Action-Plan 16,* Chapter 6.

[139]See Nathaniel Blanton Hibner, "Scandal: Delving into Popular versus Theological Definitions," *Health Progress: Journal of the Catholic Health Association of the United States* 99, no. 6 (2018): 71–72.

[140]Pope Francis, homily at a Mass with a group of clergy sex abuse victims (July 7, 2014), quoted by *The McLellan Commission,* vii.

[141]*McLellan Commission,* 9.

The Role of Whistleblowers

Axiom 14: The Role of Whistleblowers. Whistleblowers, that is, people who publicly name cultural cover-ups, become objects of gossip and shaming.[142] *The media often play a crucial role either in revealing corruption, for example, in the church, and/or in supporting whistleblowers.*[143]

Whistleblowers who dare to expose corruption within institutions face an arduous task. They are often branded with such "dishonorable" titles as "rat," "squealer," "whistleblower,"[144] "rebels," "deviants," "traitors to tradition."[145] The saying "blowing the whistle" is too trite to express the anguishes that people experience who risk identifying and reporting the offenses of others or their dramatic effects. Organizations will go to great lengths to discredit whistleblowers to prevent revelation of corruption.[146] Employees, for example, are commonly threatened with dismissal if they dare to reveal corruption, or they are given secret payments in return for their silence.[147] The media have a powerful role in revealing the truth and in protecting whistleblowers. Without the efforts of *Washington Post* journalists Carl Bernstein and Bob Woodward, it is doubtful that the corruption of Richard Nixon would have been revealed.[148]

---

[142]See Arbuckle, *Violence, Society, and the Church*, 95–98.

[143]"Since corruption thrives on secrecy, a diligent and professional media, operating within a legal framework that enables it to convey information freely, and responsibly, has an important role to play both in exposing corruption and in building support for efforts to combat." See Jayawickrama, "Transparency International," 290.

[144]For an example from the Australian police force, see Janet C. L. Chan, *Changing Police Culture: Policing in a Multicultural Society* (Cambridge: Cambridge University Press, 1997), 80.

[145]See Myron P. Glazer, "Ten Whistleblowers," in *Corporate and Governmental Deviance*, ed. M. David Erman and Richard J. Lundman (New York: Oxford University Press, 1996), 257–77.

[146]See Sheila O'Donnell, "Private Spooks: Washkenhut vs. Whistleblowers," ed. Eveline Lubbers, *Battling Big Business* (Melbourne: Scribe, 2002), 107–13. For a description of the stark sufferings of the biblical prophets as "God's whistleblowers," see Arbuckle, *Violence, Society, and the Church*, 95–96.

[147]See, for example, *Final Report of the Royal Commission*, 501.

[148]See Carl Bernstein and Bob Woodward, *All the President's Men* (New York: Touchstone, 1994).

The struggles of victims of sexual abuse in the church are increasingly being revealed by the media. For example, the *Boston Globe* released its expose of the cover-up by the Boston Catholic archdiocese in January 2002.[149] However, church officials were at first reluctant to listen. In the same year, it was reported that "many church officials, in the United States and Rome, continue to view the scandal as media-driven, even media-manufactured."[150] Later, in 2010, Pope Benedict XVI in his "Pastoral Letter to the Catholics of Ireland" admitted that victims of sexual abuse had had their trust betrayed and their dignity violated, and many found that "no one would listen."[151] It would take the media, having listened to victims, to reveal the scandals (see Chapter 3).

Moral Panics

Axiom 15: Ethnocentrism and Moral Panics. People are apt to see their own culture as clean or pure, while people of other cultures are viewed as dirty, polluting, or impure, and therefore threatening—to be excluded or eliminated.[152] In relating to people of clerical cultures, these dehumanizing attitudes must be avoided.

This axiom helps explain the tragic widespread and sometimes violent reaction to migrants in contemporary Western countries. Mary Douglas writes, "In short, our pollution behaviour is the reaction which condemns any object or idea likely to confuse or contradict cherished classifications."[153] Remember: culture is

---

[149]See the Investigative Staff of the *Boston Globe*, *Betrayal: The Crisis in the Catholic Church* (London: Profile Books, 2016).

[150]Peter Steinfels, "Abused by the Media," *The Tablet*, September 14, 2002, 9. The Truth, Justice, and Healing Council, established by the Australian Bishops Conference, recommended "that all Church authorities should have an operational whistle blower policy. Such a policy should apply both to child protection matters and more broadly, and operate to protect those who make complaints or reports in good faith." *The Truth Justice Healing Council*, vol. 1 (April 2018), 46.

[151]Pope Benedict XVI, "Pastoral Letter to the Catholics of Ireland" (March 19, 2010), para. 6.

[152]This axiom is more fully developed by the author in *Fundamentalism at Home and Abroad: Analysis and Pastoral Responses* (Collegeville, MN: Liturgical Press, 2017), 43-48.

[153]Mary Douglas, *Purity and Danger: An Analysis of the Concepts of Pollution and Taboo* (London: Routledge and Kegan Paul, 1966), 36.

about order; whatever endangers order threatens what we most like, that is, a world of the predictable (see *Axioms 1, 2,* and *4*). Douglas's definition does not denote the intrinsic hygienic qualities of things but rather their symbolic aspects. The more tribal or closed-in cultures become, the more they fear other cultures as polluting dangers. Each cultural tribal group takes the position of "thinking and feeling that anyone whose behaviour is not predictable or is peculiar in any way is slightly out of his mind, improperly brought up, irresponsible, psychopathic, politically motivated to a point beyond redemption, or just plain inferior."[154]

A *moral panic* is a specific type of contemporary ethnocentrism. In a moral panic, a particular individual or group of people is defined, especially through extensive mass media publicity, as a threat to the values and interests of the dominant society. A moral panic is an experience of widespread anxiety or hysteria; social deviants must be identified, bullied, and punished and then moral values will once again be restored to society. "Evil ones" are stigmatized and socially excluded, so that life can get back to "normal." Moral panics deflect attention away from more serious structural and social issues.[155] The word *panic* "implies not only fear but fear that is wildly exaggerated and wrongly directed."[156] President Donald Trump's border ban on Muslims and his vilification of illegal immigrants as rapists and murderers have fostered a moral panic against specific groups of people, scapegoating them for "stealing our jobs."[157] The contemporary widespread publicity about sexual abuse by members of the clergy and religious congregations, while invaluable in drawing attention to the crisis, is at risk at times of becoming a moral panic both outside and within the church with unfortunate consequences for survivors and others.[158] Thousands of innocent priests and

---

[154]Hall, *Beyond Culture*, 43.

[155]See Arbuckle, *Violence, Society, and the Church*, 141–44; Stanley Cohen, *Folk Devils and Moral Panics: The Creation of Mods and Rockers* (Oxford: Martin Robertson, 1980); Erich Goode and Nachman Ben-Yehuda, *Moral Panics: The Social Control of Deviance* (Oxford: Blackwell, 1994).

[156]Philip Jenkins, *Moral Panic: Changing Concepts of the Child Molester in Modern America* (New Haven, CT: Yale University Press, 1998), 6–7.

[157]See Arbuckle, *Loneliness*, 75.

[158]See comments by Philip Jenkins, *Pedophiles and Priests: Anatomy of a Contemporary Crisis* (Oxford: Oxford University Press, 1996), 169–71.

religious are in danger of being branded and shunned as possible sexual deviates, their credibility and integrity questioned. A moral panic within the church also diverts leaders from facing up to the real cultural causes and pastoral implications of the abuse crisis as highlighted in this book: identify and punish offenders, then the moral standards and authority structures in the church will again return to normal!

This axiom and its explanation, therefore, represent a warning. Thus while we condemn clerical cultures because they have fostered the abuse of innocent children, we must not ourselves fall into the trap of marginalizing, dehumanizing, and demonizing people who adhere to clerical cultures. Our task is to understand the *nature of these cultures, why they have developed and how we can respectfully work to change them.* Franklin D. Roosevelt remarked that "it has always seemed to me that the best symbol of common sense was a bridge."[159] A fine statement, but maintaining common sense when confronted with challengingly different cultures, such as clericalism, is far from easy in practice. Robert Benchley's comment will encourage readers to proceed: "It seems to me that the most difficult part of building a bridge would be the start."[160] Chapter 1 has provided readers with the technical instruments to begin constructing a bridge to understand the complexity and causes of clericalism, the subject of the next chapter.

Summary

- Institutional cultures, like individuals, are creatures of habit, and as useful as habits may be,[161] they are also the main obstruction to cultural change; people fear the comforting loss of the familiar.
- A culture consists of symbols, myths, and rituals; they bind the culture together in varying degrees of intensity. The stronger the bonding the stronger the resistance to change. "Culture operates as a set of implicit and silent

---

[159]Franklin D. Roosevelt quoted by Gerald I. Nierenberg, *Fundamentals of Negotiating* (New York: Harper and Row, 1973), 22.

[160]Robert Benchley quoted by Nierenberg, ibid., 22.

[161]See Charles Duhigg, *The Power of Habit* (London: Random House, 2013).

assumptions, which cannot change unless they are brought to the surface and confronted."[162]

- Every organizational culture will have within itself a social system, that is, a process whereby parts relate to one another in a regularized or patterned way. Whatever happens in one part will affect all other parts. However, how they relate to one another is determined by the culture of the organization.

- Although the church is of divine origin, it is also human; its cultures and social systems can become corrupt and are thus in constant need of purification.[163] A culture of covering up in the church the sexual abuse of minors by clergy and members of religious congregations is a tragic example of systemic corruption.

- Plans to enforce transparency and pastoral account-ability throughout the church will not necessarily ensure that the plans are executed; deep and powerful forces in the church's culture can effectively resist reform. Hence, whistleblowers and the media continue to have a vital role in identifying and revealing cover-ups and calling for reforms.

---

[162]Schein, *Organizational Culture and Leadership*, 306.

[163]See "Dogmatic Constitution on the Church" (*Lumen Gentium*), para. 8.

2

Why Is the Church Prone to Cultural Cover-Ups?

[The potential for abuse of power] is much stronger in hierarchical extremist groups where the leader-follower role and power differentiation are more tangible and stark.
—Michael Hogg and Scott Reid, "Social Identity, Leadership, and Power," in *The Use and Abuse of Power: Multiple Perspectives on the Causes of Corruption,* ed. Annette Y. Lee-Chai and John A. Bargh

When a group first forms, its evolving culture creates a stable, predictable environment. . . . That same group many generations later may find that its culture has become so well embedded, so traditional, that it serves only to reinforce the assumptions and values of the older, more conservative elements of the group.
—Edgar H. Schein, *Organizational Culture and Leadership: A Dynamic View*

[The Church] is much more authoritarian and uniformist than the Church of the Middle Ages ever was.
—Cardinal Walter Kasper, in 1988, cited by Terence L. Nichols, *That All May Be One: Hierarchy and Participation in the Church*

Clericalism is a perversion and is the root of many evils
in the church.
                              —Pope Francis, Opening Address to Synod
                                    on Young People, October 3, 2018

This chapter explains that:
- Pre–Vatican II culture still remains substantially in place.
- Clericalism is a fundamentalist movement.
- Culture change is impossible without appropriate leadership.

The purpose of this chapter is twofold: to identify the multilayered cultural reasons that led the church to conceal, systemically and globally, incidents of sexual abuse among members of the clergy and religious congregations, and *why* it continues to be stubbornly difficult to change the culture.

Since these issues are approached through the lens of cultural anthropology, readers may find it helpful from time to time to refer back to particular axioms listed in chapter 1, for example, the power of culture to mold our behavior in unconscious ways; culture can dull our awareness of this power and its moral consequences (see *Axioms 2, 3, 4, 5*). I am very conscious that theologians and historians will further enlighten what follows with their own expertise; no one discipline has all the answers.

Clericalism Defined

Many forces, including clericalism, colluded to develop cultures of cover-up in the church. Clericalism, which is embraced not only by clerics but also the non-ordained who identify and support its values, is:

the idealisation of the priesthood, and by extension, the idealisation of the Catholic Church. Clericalism is linked to a sense of entitlement, superiority and exclusion, and abuse of power. [It] nurtured ideas that the Catholic Church was autonomous and self-sufficient, and promoted the idea that child abuse by clergy and religious was a matter to be dealt with internally and in secret.[1]

The Gospel emphasizes that all, without distinction, are called by baptism to be disciples of Christ, but clericalism contradicts this by establishing a two-tier class structure: one superior, the clergy; the other inferior, the laity. Since clericalism is at the heart of the crisis in the church, we need to discover its deep-seated cultural supports that made the cover-ups inevitable. Pope Benedict XVI rightly said that "only by examining carefully the many elements that gave rise to the present crisis can a clear-sighted diagnosis of its causes be undertaken and effective remedies be found."[2] What are these elements? Why did they become so entrenched in the church's culture for so long?

A strong culture is characterized by an institution's core values inherent in its mythology being both intensely held and widely shared. And it was because the Catholic Church had such a strong culture "that the avoidance of public scandal, the maintenance of the reputation of the Catholic Church and loyalty to priests and religious largely determined the responses of the Catholic Church authorities when allegations of child sexual abuse arose."[3] Such was the case in the church before Vatican II. The culture still remains. The Australian inquiry concluded that the Catholic Church still has "the internal features of an organisation at high

---

[1]*Royal Commission into Institutional Responses to Child Sexual Abuse: Preface and Executive Summary* (Barton, ACT: Commonwealth of Australia, 2017), 68. Donald Cozzens writes that clericalism is noted for its "authoritarian style of ministerial leadership, a rigidly hierarchical world view and a virtual identification of the holiness and grace of the church with the clerical state and, thereby, with the cleric himself." *Sacred Silence: Denial and the Crisis in the Church* (Collegeville, MD: Liturgical Press, 2003), 118. Len Sperry comments: "Episcopal culture is a variant of clerical culture reflected in the values and behavior associated with bishops and cardinals. The . . . downside [of this culture] is entitlement, arrogance, and a lack of respect and accountability." *Sex, Priestly Ministry, and the Church* (Collegeville, MN: Liturgical Press, 2013), 70.

[2]Pope Benedict XVI, *Pastoral Letter to the Catholics of Ireland* (March 19, 2010), para. 4.

[3]*Final Report of the Royal Commission into Institutional Responses to Child Sexual Abuse* (Barton, ACT: Commonwealth of Australia, 2017), vol.16, bk.1, 36.

risk of its personnel perpetrating criminal child abuse."[4]

A point of painful frustration for Pope Francis is the fact that, despite the council's emphasis on transparency and pastoral accountability, the culture of secrecy and misuse of power still remains deeply entrenched in the church's governance and power structures. The fact that the questions about Cardinal Theodore McCarrick's sexual improprieties remained unexamined for decades reminds us that deep down the power structures still remain firmly in place.[5] Why is this so? The fact is that an offending cardinal can only reach a princely rank if the clerical culture supporting him encourages "those who are complicit by their silence and failure to act."[6] What is there in the clerical culture that "prizes secrecy and loyalty over truth and transparency?[7]" However, before offering an anthropological analysis, I first give a short overview of some inquiries into the abuse crisis in several countries. They all point to the systemic nature of the crisis in which thousands of innocent people have been harmed.

Brief Overview of Global Systemic Patterns

United States

In 1985 Father Gilbert Gauthe, Diocese of Lafayette, was sentenced for the sexual abuse of eleven altar boys. With this case, writes psychologist Marie Keenan, "the floodgates opened in the English-speaking Catholic world, and in the avalanche that followed the publicity surrounding the Gauthe affair, child sexual abuse by clergy came onto the public agenda."[8] The United States Bishops Conference, meeting in 1985, did not agree to a national approach to the issue, but the bishops "limited themselves to a commitment to combat child abuse on an individual basis wher-

[4]Ibid., 258.

[5]See "O'Malley: 'Specific Actions' Needed Now to Address Claims against Cardinal," *National Catholic Reporter*, July 25, 2018.

[6]John Gehring, "Why Is Predatory Behavior of Priests Permitted?" *Commonweal,* July 26, 2018, www.commonwealmagazine.org/change-clerical-culture.

[7]Ibid.

[8]Marie Keenan, *Child Sexual Abuse and the Catholic Church: Gender, Power, and Organizational Culture* (Oxford: Oxford University Press, 2012), 17.

ever it arose."[9] In 1988 the bishops agreed to several guidelines, including that the alleged offender be promptly relieved of ministerial duties and that he comply with all obligations required by civil law. In 2002 the conference approved the creation of a board of lay members—the National Review Board for the Protection of Children and Young People—which published in 2004 a report noting that the Vatican "did not recognize the scope and gravity of the problem facing the Church in the United States despite numerous warning signs; and it rebuffed earlier attempts to reform procedures for removing predator priests."[10]

The year 2002 became a fearful one for Catholics in Boston. Ever more horrific disclosures of sexual abuse by priests were "followed by ever more ghastly revelations of inaction by the church hierarchy."[11] In December of that year the archdiocese released 11,000 pages of records showing that it permitted abusers to continue to work as priests well into the 1990s—"long after the 'reformation' of its ways that Cardinal Bernard Law claimed had taken place."[12] Worse was to follow as other dioceses began to reveal abusers and the hesitancy of bishops and major religious superiors to deal with the situation and adequately compensate and counsel the many victims.

Back in 2002 the American bishops adopted the "Charter for the Protection of Children and Young People" and established the National Review Board of lay members with the task of overseeing compliance by dioceses. Dioceses, since this charter, have made significant advances in implementing the protection

---

[9]Ibid., 18.

[10]The National Review Board for the Protection of Children and Young People, *A Report on the Crisis in the Catholic Church in the United States* (Washington, DC: United States Conference of Catholic Bishops, 2004), 43. In 2004 the John Jay College of Criminal Justice published a research report on the extent of child sexual abuse by Catholic clergy in the United States. It revealed that between 1950 and 2002 there were 11,000 allegations made against 4,392 priests of child sexual abuse in the United States. This constituted approximately 4 percent of the priests who had served during that period. See John Jay College of Criminal Justice, *The Nature and Scope of Sexual Abuse of Minors by Catholic Priests and Deacons in the United States 1950–2002* (Washington, DC: US Conference of Bishops, 2004), 3, 4.

[11]*The Economist*, "Dear Lord, Can It Get any Worse?" December 7, 2002, 37.

[12]Ibid. See also the Investigative Staff of the *Boston Globe*, *Betrayal: The Crisis in the Catholic Church* (Boston: Little, Brown, 2002), passim.

guides, but the charter contained no measures to hold bishops accountable other than "fraternal correction" by fellow bishops. That is, bishops would police themselves. Scarcely a satisfactory method of objective accountability. The Pennsylvania Supreme Court in August 2018 released a sweeping grand jury report on sexual abuse, listing more than 300 accused clergy and detailing a systemic cover-up effort by church leaders over seventy years within the state's eight dioceses.[13]

Canada

In 1989 the media focused on allegations of sexual abuse by religious brothers at an orphanage in Newfoundland that led to nine convictions. In the same year Archbishop Alphonsus Penney, Newfoundland, as a result of allegations and convictions of several priests, established the Winter Commission to examine various allegations of sexual abuse of minors. The commission concluded, inter alia, that clericalism and the patriarchal quality of the church reinforced the belief that the priest "rules by virtue of position alone, and not by virtue of capacity and service."[14] The commission's report noted that the Catholic Church was "crippled by serious weaknesses in personnel, support mechanisms, administrative structures and management" and that "weak organizational structures and poor government within the Archdiocese"[15] had permitted the abuse to continue. As regards the sexual and physical abuse suffered by First Nations boys and girls in residential schools, it was found that religious congregations, managing the schools between 1940 and 1980, were responsible for 68 percent (18,903) of the claims.[16]

---

[13]See Michelle Boorstein, "Acts of Faith," *Washington Post*, August 14, 2018. It is estimated that the Catholic Church in the United States has spent so far US$3.99 billion on clerical abuse settlements. See David Castaldi, Joseph Finn, and Margaret Roylance, "A Step toward Accountability," *Commonweal*, October 30, 2018.

[14]Special Archdiocesan Commission of Enquiry into Sexual Abuse of Children by Members of the Clergy, *The Report of the Archdiocesan Commission of Enquiry into the Sexual Abuse of Children by Members of the Clergy* (Archdiocese of St. John's, Newfoundland, 1990), 93.

[15]Ibid., 139.

[16]Details recorded in *Final Report of the Royal Commission*, 190.

Ireland

Beginning in the 1990s a series of criminal cases and the Irish government's investigations started to uncover incidents of abuse by hundreds of priests and religious. Institutions committed to the care of children were also seen to have seriously neglected their duty to provide appropriate safeguards. The government-sponsored Ryan Report, published in May 2009, showed that the entire system of caring for children in residential schools was gravely faulty. Institutions were more like prisons, it said, and also that "some religious officials encouraged ritual beatings and consistently shielded their orders amid a 'culture of self-serving secrecy', and that government inspectors failed to stop the abuses."[17] Shortly after the Ryan Report came out, the Murphy Report[18] was published in November 2009 detailing sexual abuse scandals in the archdiocese of Dublin. It found that the four archbishops who led Dublin's church from 1940 to 2004 had each mishandled abuse allegations. It also identified at least 320 victims of abuse from an investigation of 46 of the archdiocese's priests. This devastating report into the sexual and physical abuse of children by clergy showed that *"the maintenance of secrecy, the avoidance of scandal, the protection of the reputation of the church and the preservation of its assets was more important than justice for the victims."*[19]

England

In 2000 Cardinal Cormac Murphy-O'Connor, then Archbishop of Westminster, commissioned Lord Nolan to examine and review arrangements made for child protection and the prevention of abuse within the Catholic Church in England and Wales, and

---

[17]Commission of Inquiry into Child Abuse (The Ryan Report) https://en.wikipedia.org/wiki/Commission_to_Inquire_into_Child_Abuse.

[18]See David Quinn, "Sins of the Fathers," *The Tablet*, December 5, 2009, 4–5.

[19]Henry McDonald, www.theguardian.com/world/2009/nov/26/ireland-church-sex-abuse. Italics added. Pope Francis addressing the bishops of Ireland said: "A recurrent theme of my visit . . . has been the Church's need to acknowledge and remedy, with evangelical honesty and courage, past failures—grave sins—with regard to the protection of children and vulnerable adults." *The Tablet*, September 1, 2018, 18.

to make recommendations. The report was published in 2001, and it was a dramatic departure from the past.[20] No longer is the hierarchy to resolve sexual abuse issues of the clergy, it said, as though the church were a perfect self-sufficient society, but instead all allegations of abuse must now be reported to the civil authorities.

In August 2018, an independent inquiry published the reactions to the Nolan report, in the form of a case study, of two leading Benedictine schools.[21] The inquiry repeatedly "reveals [in the schools] a culture of superiority, arrogance and insularity—something that will require a revolution of the heart to dismantle."[22] There were, concluded the inquiry,

> 10 men [at the schools], mostly monks, who were convicted of, or cautioned for, offences involving sexual activity towards children or pornography. . . . The blatant openness of this demonstrates there was a culture of acceptance of abuse. . . . Both [schools] prioritized the monks and their own reputation over the protection of children, maneuvering monks away from the schools in order to avoid scandal.

The report noted that "there was hostility to the Nolan Report . . . for some years after its adoption. [The schools] seemed to take the view that its implementation was neither obligatory nor desirable. *This view appeared to go unchallenged by the wider Catholic Church.*"[23] The case study also illustrates a further tension inherent in monastic cultures (and to a lesser degree in all forms of religious life)—the tension between the role of an abbot as the "father in God" to his monks and the justice demands of the law: "The Benedictine system is based on obedience to an elected abbot, who is the source of all authority . . . a conservative and

---

[20]See also *The McLellan Commission: A Review of the Current Safeguarding Policies, Procedures and Practice within the Catholic Church in Scotland* (2015).

[21]Alexis Jay, Malcom Evans, Ivor Frank, and Drusilla Sharpling, *A Report of the Inquiry Panel: Ampleforth and Downside (English Benedictine Congregation Case Study* (2018), https://www.gov.uk/government/publications.

[22]Catherine Pepinster, "A Gross Betrayal of Trust," *The Tablet*, August 18, 2018, 7.

[23]*A Report of the Inquiry Panel*, 180–81. Italics added.

patriarchal idea of fatherhood. The abbot sees the wellbeing of his monks as his first responsibility. . . . [But] a succession of abbots saw implementation of the . . . protection of child protection policies as a threat to that relationship."[24]

Australia

In 2003 Chris McGillion commented that the

> laity . . . have been primarily affronted by revelations about abusive clergy and the inaction of those in positions of responsibility in bringing the culprits to account. These revelations have eroded the faithful's trust in priests as ministers and patrons and their confidence in bishops as managers, but only slowly, even reluctantly, has the problem of clerical abuse engaged the Church leadership.[25]

However, in 2013, any reluctance on the part of church leadership was to change dramatically with the government's establishment of the five-year Royal Commission into Institutional Responses to Child Sexual Abuse *(2013–18)*. The commission "concluded that there were catastrophic failures of leadership of Catholic Church authorities over many decades."[26]

During the commission's final hearings in February 2017 it was revealed:

> From 1950 to 2010, some 1,265 Catholic priests and religious were the subject of a child sexual abuse claim. These numbers are shocking. . . . The data also reflects on the Church leaders who at times failed to take steps to deal with the abusers, failed to call them to order and failed to deal with them in accordance with the law, and, perhaps

---

[24]"Evils Demand a Fitting Response," Editorial, *The Tablet*, August 18, 2018, 4.

[25]Chris McGillion, "Visions, Revisions and Scandal: The Church in Crisis," in *A Long Way from Rome: Why the Australian Catholic Church Is in Crisis* (Sydney: Allen & Unwin, 2003), 1–2. See also Chris McGillion and Damian Grace, *Reckoning: The Catholic Church and Child Abuse* (Adelaide: ATF Press, 2014), 49–141.

[26]*Final Report of the Royal Commission*, 36.

worse, took steps which had the effect, if not the intent, of enabling them to abuse again. . . . As Catholics, we hang our heads in shame.[27]

The commission's findings provide insights into the cover-up processes of the Catholic Church both locally and globally. The police were not notified, and allegations were dealt with "as matters 'in-house' and out of the public gaze." Tragically, "Few survivors of child sexual abuse . . . described receiving formal responses from the relevant [authorities]. . . . Instead, they were often disbelieved, ignored or punished, and in some cases were further abused."[28] (See *Axiom 14*: Chapter 1.) The inquiry points out that not only was there no accountability to police and civil authorities when allegations were made, but the official internal accountability structures failed to be implemented.

Throughout this period [i.e., particularly before the 1990s], there was a system under canon law for disciplining priests and religious accused of child sexual abuse, the most severe penalty was dismissal. . . . Instead, bishops and religious superiors adopted a range of informal responses. . . . Some perpetrators continued to offend even after there had been multiple responses following initial and successive allegations of child sexual abuse.[29]

Thus, it is rightly said that (see *Axiom 10*, Chapter 1): "Corruption thrives on secrecy."[30] There were even efforts to maintain secrecy at the grassroots of ministries. People were not told why the priest or religious had been moved, nor in some instances was the new parish or school warned of what the perpetrators had done.[31]

---

[27]Francis Sullivan, *Royal Commission into Institutional Responses to Child Sexual Abuse*, Public Hearing: Case Study 50 (February 6, 2017), para. 24714–715. "Of all Catholic priests included in the survey who ministered between 1950 and 2010. . . . 7 percent were alleged perpetrators." Royal Commission, *Final Report of the Royal Commission*, 61.

[28]*Final Report of the Royal Commission*, 61.

[29]Ibid., 37.

[30]Nihal Jayawickrama, "Transparency International: Combating Corruption through Institutional Reform," in *Use and Abuse*, ed. Lee-Chai and Bargh, 290.

[31]See *Final Report of the Royal Commission*, 37.

Reflecting on the organizational and governance structures in the church,[32] the inquiry concluded that "the powers of governance held by individual diocesan bishops and provincials are not subject to adequate checks and balances. There is no separation of powers, and the executive, legislative and judicial aspects of governance are combined in the person of the pope and in diocesan bishops."[33] In consequence, "Diocesan bishops have not been sufficiently accountable to any other body for decision-making in their handling of allegations of child sex abuse or alleged perpetrators." The result is that "the tragic consequence of this lack of accountability have been seen in the failures of those in authority . . . to respond adequately to allegations and occurrences of child sexual abuse." The weakness of unaccountable hierarchical governance structures is evident: they "created a culture of deferential obedience in which poor responses to child sexual abuse went unchallenged."[34] The choice of leaders is also blamed. Some have been chosen "on the basis of their adherence to specific aspects of church doctrine and their commitment to the defence and promotion of the institutional Catholic Church, rather than their capacity for leadership."[35]

Chile

On a visit to Chile in January 2018, Pope Francis dismissed very vocal claims that a bishop he had appointed had concealed the sexual abuse crimes of a local priest. Francis, on return to Rome, became aware he had been mistaken. Having commissioned a lengthy report about the bishop, Francis acted swiftly in calling Chile's thirty-four bishops to Rome to deal with grave charges that this and other cases had been concealed. He accepted the resignations of five bishops and then sent a pastoral letter to

---

[32] As regards the leadership of the Holy See in responding to the inquiry requests in 2014 for information regarding the extent to which Australian clerics accused of child sexual abuse referred to the Holy See, the latter stated that it was "not appropriate to release information about cases where a decision had not yet been reached in a canonical proceeding." Ibid., 117.

[33] Ibid., 44.

[34] Ibid.

[35] Ibid., 45.

Chilean Catholics apologizing for his original refusal to accept the complaints of victims and for the cover-up of sexual abuse scandals in the Chilean church.

The Economist comments: "For decades, [the church in Chile had] treated sexual abuse by priests as a sin rather than a crime, conducting its own investigations without telling government authorities. In some cases, it simply reshuffled clergy implicated in sex crimes to different parishes." This has significantly led to the breakdown of trust in the church. "[The] share of Chileans expressing confidence in the church has collapsed from 76 percent in 1996 to 34 percent in 2017, a decline three times as large as the Latin American average during that period."[36] And 96 percent of Chileans believe that the church concealed and protected priests accused of sexual abuse.[37]

Cultural Models

The aim in the remainder of this chapter is to identify three cultural models of church. This will be done in two stages: first, the explanation of the cultural model from an anthropological perspective; second, the application and implications of the model when it is applied to the church. Culture analysis, as the preceding chapter illustrates, is a challenging task, more particularly if the culture is a long-established and deeply embedded one. Because a culture is such a multifaceted reality authors develop models or typologies to help us grasp what it means.[38] An anthropological model aims to illustrate social reality by highlighting emphases and downplaying details or nuances that might interfere with the clarifying process. Reality is interpreted with a model as a measure; a model is then modified or discarded in light of the

---

[36] "Ghosts from the Past: The Catholic Church Faces New Charges of Covering Up Abuse," *The Economist*, July 28, 2018, 29.

[37] See www.elintransigente.com/mundo/2018/8/7/cuando-todo-un-pais-cree-que-la-iglesia-encubr-los-abuso-sexuales-503981.html#!. In Germany 3,677 people had been abused by clergy between 1946 and 2014; more than half were thirteen or younger. John L. Allen, "Take-Aways on the Latest Twists in the Clerical Abuse Saga," *Crux*, September 18, 2018.

[38] See Pertti J. Pelto and Gretel H. Pelto, *Anthropological Research: The Structure of Inquiry*, 2nd ed. (Cambridge: Cambridge University Press, 1978), 11–12, 254–57.

data that is being reviewed. A culture never perfectly conforms to a model. Moreover, it will in fact have elements of all the models, but one model will be more prominent at a particular time than the others. There is a risk in the use of models. It is often simpler to speak about the tidy model of reality than it is to evaluate reality itself, with its many complexities and contradictions. Remember, a model is merely an aid to interpret reality. It is not set in concrete.[39]

Cultural Models of the Church

The three anthropological models of the church we now examine are:[40]

Model 1: Strong Group/Strong Grid Culture: Pre–Vatican II Church

Model 2: Weak Group/Weak Grid Culture: Vatican II Church

Model 3: Strong Group/Weak Grid Culture: Restorationist Church

The analysis focuses on the *Pre–Vatican II: Strong Group/ Strong Grid* model because it will best help readers understand the pervasive power systems inherent in the pre-council church culture. The roots of the abuse cover-up crisis are primarily to be found here. However, it will be seen that this culture did not fundamentally disappear following the acceptance of the decrees and constitutions of the Vatican II Council, thus illustrating the validity of the axiom: *Culture eats strategies for breakfast* (see *Axiom 1*, Chapter 1).

---

[39]Anthropologist Pierre Bourdieu insists that cultures can never be static and that individuals, though their behavior is constrained by cultures, have the capacity to choose to act differently. See his *Outline of a Theory of Practice* (Cambridge: Cambridge University Press, 1977), 72.

[40]Theologians Avery Dulles, SJ, and Stephen B. Bevans, SVD, identified several models of the church. Though they are theological models, they are also cultural because when they exist in reality they have visible forms: the church as a communion, a community of faith, the people of God, a hierarchical institution, the body of Christ, the spouse of Christ, a proclaimer of the good news, a servant. Each contributes to an integral description of what the church can be, and each has strengths and limitations. See Avery Dulles, *Models of the Church* (Garden City, NY: Image Books, 1978); Stephen B. Bevans, *Models of Contextual Theology* (Maryknoll, NY: Orbis Books, 2002).

In brief, the Pre–Vatican II culture had the following theological qualities:

- The church is a fortress protecting its followers from the inroads of an evil world under the centralized direction of the pope who delegates authority to bishops and from bishops to priests.
- To maintain this unchanging, static, fortress-like culture the faithful must obey detailed rules and regulations as decreed by the hierarchical power structure.
- Bishops are accountable only upward, to the pope, not downward to the people in their diocese, or outward to civil agencies.
- The world is essentially evil and dangerous; theology is theocentric not incarnational.
- Liturgy was in consequence theatrical as directed by ordained specialists; the laity were expected to remain passive; even popular religiosity was to be supervised by the same specialists in case the laity began to question their passive role in the church.
- Evangelization emphasized the salvation of souls with little or no concern for social justice.
- Religious are the spiritual elite, withdrawn from an evil world, with ministries restricted mainly to education, hospitals, and relief for the poor.
- To question or dissent prophetically risked marginalization, even excommunication.

To explain the cultural ramifications of these theological qualities, however, and why they fostered a culture of cover-up in the church, we need to turn to the cultural insights of anthropologist Mary Douglas, one of the most widely read and influential anthropologists of her generation.

Mary Douglas (1921–2007), using a definition of culture similar to the one described in Chapter 1 (see *Axiom 3*),[41] has

---

[41]See Mary Douglas, *Natural Symbols: Explorations in Cosmology* (New York: Pantheon Books, 1970) and *Cultural Bias* (London: Royal Anthropological Institute, 1978).

produced a thought-provoking reflection on the interconnections between social structure, authority/power, morality, ritualism, and cosmology that can aid us in understanding the potentially coercive qualities of cultures.[42] Douglas constructs her reflections on two independently varying social criteria which she terms *grid* and *group*.[43] The *group* variable connotes the degree to which people are controlled in their social interactions by their commitment to a social unit bigger than the individual. For example, the feeling of group identity of *this* particular ship's crew may be weak, because individual members particularly wish to work with different crew members of a ship and may not do so when the ship begins a new journey. In brief, *group* connotes "the pressures of collective organization on the individual."[44] The *grid* variable, in contrast, indicates the restraints on individuals interacting with one another *within* the group. For example, there is a grid that regulates how crew members of a ship should interact. In this case we speak of a *strong grid,* because the rules are unambiguous about how individual crew members must relate to one another and to the captain. They must obey the captain or lose their jobs. Mutiny is out of the question.

Douglas claims that cosmological ideals and the importance of ritual will differ predictably with the extent to which *group* and *grid* are stressed. The social body constrains the way the physical body is seen. Thus if there are tight controls over how people are to dress and act bodily, then there will be a rigidly controlled social group and vice versa. For example, consider the rigid codes of dress for women in Saudi Arabia. In the former Soviet Union, and now in North Korea, the mass festival and military displays of thousands of people uniformly dressed and rigidly marching together mirror the inflexible dictatorial political system of the

---

[42]See Gerald A. Arbuckle, "Theology and Anthropology: Time for Dialogue," *Theological Studies* 47, no. 3 (1986): 437–41.

[43]The *group/grid* models have been used by scripture scholars, for example: Jerome H. Neyrey, *An Ideology of Revolt: John's Christology in Social-Science Perspective* (Philadelphia: Fortress Press, 1988); Leland J. White, "Grid and Group in Matthew's Community: The Righteousness/Honor Code in the Sermon on the Mount," *Semeia* 35 (1986): 61–90.

[44]Richard Fardon, *Mary Douglas: An Intellectual Biography* (London: Routledge, 1999), 115; Richard Stivers, *Evil in Modern Myth and Ritual* (Athens: University of Georgia Press, 1982), 144–47.

country. Obedience is demanded to the social order. No dissent permitted. However, if social control is weak, the body will be at ease, informal, untidy, and sloppy, with loose-fitting clothes and unkempt hair. In Western societies there are generally rules that require office employees to dress with a degree of formality, but this social control ceases when they have leisure time. Thus, the relation of the individual to society differs with the restraints of *grid* and *group*; the more rigid the *grid* and *group* are, the more developed the idea of formal transgression and its dangerous results and the less focus there is on the right of the inner self to be freely expressed.

Model 1: *Strong Group/Strong Grid Culture—Pre-Vatican II Church*

Anthropological Analysis

Examples of cultures approximating in varying degrees the first of Douglas's models,[45] namely the *strong group/strong grid model*, are the Israelites as described in the book of Leviticus;[46] mafia; police; army; trade unions; professional organizations, for example, the legal and medical professions; hospital systems; religious communities; long-established educational institutions;[47] and sports clubs. An extreme example of this type would be the cult surrounding Jim Jones, founder of the Peoples Temple, who was able in November 1978 to entice more than nine hundred members meeting in Guyana to commit mass suicide. The Jonestown commune culture had such a degree of cohesiveness and intensity that it allowed for high control.[48] Of course, cultural

---

[45]Erving Goffman's description of total institutions contains some of the qualities of Douglas's *strong group/strong grid* culture model. He defines a total institution "as a place of residence and work where a large number of like-situated individuals, cut off from the wider society for an appreciable period of time, together lead an enclosed, formally administered round of life." *Asylums: Essays on the Social Situation of Mental Patients and Other Inmates* (London: Penguin, 1991), 15.

[46]See Mary Douglas, *Purity and Danger: An Analysis of the Concepts of Pollution and Taboo* (London: Routledge & Kegan Paul, 1966), 54–72.

[47]C. P. Snow brilliantly describes the tradition-bound administrative governance structure of a Cambridge University college in his novel *The Masters* (Kelly Bray: Stratus Books, 1951).

[48]See Marc Galanter, *Cults: Faith, Healing, and Coercion*, 2nd ed. (New York:

cohesiveness, loyalty, and institutional commitment can lead to positive results, as can be seen in successful companies such as Toshiba and Microsoft, provided such institutions allow room for dissent in order to foster ongoing creativity and survival. However, the constant danger in cultures of this type is that there can be a swing to excessive cohesiveness allowing for no dissent. Cultures that mirror this model expect secrecy and cover-ups to be normal ways of reacting to failures. Let us explore the qualities of this model in further detail.

Obedience to Status Quo. Obedience and conformity are esteemed qualities. Loyalty to the community and its demands is considered to be *the* requirement for membership. People must accept a tradition-based, bureaucratic, hierarchical, and patriarchal system. Myths "legitimize"[49] tribal traditions and the status quo and "hide blatant exertions of power. This enables advantaged individuals to believe that they are entirely deserving of their privileged positions in life and to maintain positive feelings about themselves."[50] (See *Axiom 3,* Chapter 1.)

Role of Hierarchical Leaders. The hierarchical leader's task is to maintain the status quo and guard the tribal boundaries, and for this personal charismatic qualities are not needed. In fact, they may be dangerous in drawing people away from revered traditions to a cult of the leader and set precedents for undermining the status quo of the community. The leader, equipped with secret knowledge, has ritual powers both to impose punishments for disobedience and to cancel them.

In this hierarchical model of authority, which does not allow accountability downward, there is considerable danger of bullying and other abuses of power, such as sexual abuse. The more the cultural status quo is internally or externally threatened, the more detailed rules and sanctions are imposed in the hope that divisive actions will not occur. Leaders vigorously resist change;

Oxford University Press, 1999), 113–21.

[49]See discussion by Emmeline S. Chen and Tom R. Tyler, "Legitimizing Myths and the Psychology of the Advantaged," in *The Use and Abuse of Power,* ed. Lee-Chai and Bargh, 241–61.

[50]Ibid., 246.

dissenting members are openly marginalized as an example to others contemplating dissent. Leaders insist that tribal boundaries are sharply defined and patrolled to preserve the assumed superiority of the "we" group; no dialogue is allowed with "them," the outsiders. To maintain position power (see *Axiom 5*, Chapter 1) and to "save face" with outsiders, hierarchical authorities coercively demand that secrecy and cover-up processes conceal any failures in the system.

Kinship Terminology. Not only are tribal boundaries of the community sharply demarcated, it is also made clear how individuals are to relate to one another within the boundaries. Roles and statuses are clearly defined and maintained. Fictive family or kinship terminology is commonly used to describe how members are to relate to one another, that is, biological kinship is used as a metaphor for membership and the way members are to behave.[51] "Family" members fear to break customs lest the community punish them, for example, by ostracizing, shaming, or ridiculing them. Sociologist Stanley Cohen writes:

> Family members have an astounding capacity to ignore or pretend to ignore what happens in front of their eyes, whether sexual abuse, incest, violence, alcoholism, craziness or plain unhappiness. There is a subterranean level at which everyone knows what is happening, but the surface is a permanent "as if" discourse. The family's distinctive self-image determines which aspects of shared experience can be openly acknowledged and which must remain closed and denied. These rules are governed by the meta-rule that no one must either admit or deny that they exist.[52]

Thus self-regulatory fictive family cultures often fail to ensure that adequate accountability systems are in place and op-

---

[51]When people relate to one another as though they were members of a biological kinship group this extension of the idiom of kinship is called "fictive." For a further explanation see Gerald A. Arbuckle, *Violence, Society, and the Church: A Cultural Approach* (Collegeville, MN: Liturgical Press, 2004), 46–55.

[52]Stanley Cohen, *States of Denial: Knowing about Atrocities and Suffering* (Cambridge: Polity Press, 2001), 64–65.

erative.[53] For example, in the medical profession, where fictive relationships frequently prevail, medical errors that cause harm but are generally preventable are rarely publicized.[54] It has been estimated that as many as 98,000 people die annually as a result of medical errors in hospitals in the United States; more people, for example, die from medication errors than from workplace injuries and twice as many as die in road accidents.[55] Official Australian reports reveal that preventable medical error in hospitals is responsible for 11 percent of all deaths in the country.[56] This was described as "Australia's best-kept secret."[57] In addition to the human suffering due to poor accountability the financial costs are enormous. In Britain it was estimated in 2000 that the costs to the National Health Service (NHS) of hospital-acquired infections amounted to nearly one billion pounds annually.[58] In Australia it was estimated in 1999 that inappropriate medication use resulted in at least 80,000 hospital admissions annually at a cost of about $350 million; approximately half the admissions were considered preventable.[59] The medical profession has been particularly reluctant to acknowledge, and learn from, adverse events. When leaders fail to call "family" members to be accountable for their actions, cronyism or power cliques fill the vacuum.

Under Siege. When cultures or subcultures that approximate this strong group/strong grid model feel particularly threatened by outsiders, their feeling of belonging to a fictive family is in-

---

[53]See Edwin H. Friedman, *Generation to Generation: Family Process in Church and Synagogue* (New York: Guilford Press, 1985), 52–54.

[54]The author in 2008 was appointed by the New South Wales Government, Australia, to an Independent Panel to oversee the reform there of the public health system.

[55]See "Patient Safety: Physician, Heal Thy Systems," *The Economist,* June 30, 2018, 49. Johns Hopkins Medical School puts the number much higher, at 250,000 deaths annually.

[56]See *Best Health*, http://besthealth.com.au/drugs-and-medical-errors-killing-one-of-every-five-australians.

[57]Jeff Richardson as reported by Julia Medew, "Thousands Dying from Preventable Hospital Errors," http://www.theage.com.au/national/thousands-dying-from-preventable-hospital-errors-saysprofessor.

[58]For a detailed analysis see Department of Health, *An Organisation with a Memory* (London: Department of Health, 2000).

[59]See *Best Health*, http://besthealth.

tensified.[60] Failings on the part of the "we" group will be even more actively disguised lest they be publicly shamed by the "out" group.[61] For example, in police forces the combined need to maintain a strong group identity together with the fear of "them" (i.e., the media, the public) can have two serious consequences: first, police personnel can become far more concerned about preserving the system of rules and regulations than about their methods of relating to the public; second, police are tempted to cover up mistakes and corrupt practices in order to maintain the loyalty of "the brotherhood"[62] and public goodwill. If an officer informs on a colleague, he is attacking the "brotherhood," the source of his own identity and support. Similarly, if an officer has been guilty of corruption, he or she hesitates to inform on others lest their own devious operations are revealed.[63] If a member does inform on a colleague, he or she must be immediately ostracized.[64] Or if a member is exposed by outsiders for malpractice, he or she is ostracized and blamed, but the internal system that allows this behavior to occur is not often critiqued.

Rituals of Purity/Pollution. A multiplicity of rituals[65] enforce mythologies of order: they assert who belongs, who has position power, and how that power is to be operated. Initiation rituals, for example, the intensely demanding initiation rituals of the U.S. Marine Corps are formal and lengthy, emphasizing internal

---

[60]See Antonius C. G. Robben and Marcelo M. Suarez-Orozco, eds., *Cultures under Siege: Collective Violence and Trauma* (Cambridge: Cambridge University Press, 2000), 1–41.

[61]See Arbuckle, *Violence, Society, and the Church*, 50–54.

[62]See John Skolnick and John Fyfe, *Above the Law: Police and the Excessive Use of Force* (New York: Free Press, 1994), 80.

[63]See *Commission Report (Mollen Report): Commission to Investigate Allegations of Police Corruption and the Anti-Corruption Procedures of the Police Department* (The City of New York, 1994), 3; Janet B. Chan, *Changing Police Culture: Policing in a Multicultural Society* (Cambridge: Cambridge University Press, 1997), 90–91.

[64]Arbuckle, *Violence, Society, and the Church*, 46, 51.

[65]"Ritual is the repetitive spontaneous or prescribed symbolic use of bodily movement and gesture to express and articulate meaning within a social context in which there is possible or real tension/conflict and a need to resolve or hide it." Gerald Arbuckle, *Culture, Inculturation, and Theologians: A Postmodern Critique* (Collegeville, MN: Liturgical Press, 2010), 83.

and external conversion to maintain the status quo.[66] To break one of the detailed rules is to risk ritual pollution, which leads to expulsion, marginalization, and shaming; the ritual guardians of the community alone can remove the pollution (see *Axiom 15,* Chapter 1). No dissent is permitted. The assumption is that those in position power hold the keys to the perfect system; they alone decree the rules and who may or may not belong. When the status quo is in danger, the more position-power people create new rules and rituals aimed at preventing their loss of power. Those who disagree pollute cultural order and must be expelled.

Bureaucracies Flourish. Bureaucracies flourish in this model because their task, under those in high power positions, is to maintain order through coercion and fear.[67] To a bureaucrat, the world is a world of *measurable* facts to be treated in accordance with preestablished rules, impersonally, without emotional or personal attachment to clients or fellow workers. "The bureaucratic mind is ultimately cynical, for it reduces everything to power,"[68] that is, the power to enforce the status quo and obstruct accountability (see *Axiom 5,* Chapter 1). People are recruited for their ability to be detached and obedient to the status quo.[69] Bureaucracies can thus be self-perpetuating. Organizationally, the overall task of a bureaucracy is divided among different offices, each of which has responsibility for a small section. It is not for people at each level to question their superiors.[70] Their duty was to do what was asked of them was an argument advanced, for example, by soldiers explaining collaboration in atrocities.[71]

---

[66]See Jean S. La Fontaine, *Initiation: Ritual Drama and Secret Knowledge across the World* (Harmondsworth: Penguin, 1985); Gilbert H. Herdt, ed., *Rituals of Manhood: Male Initiation in Papua New Guinea* (Berkeley: University of California Press, 1982).

[67]See Arbuckle, *Violence, Society, and the Church,* 109–12.

[68]Richard Stivers, *The Culture of Cynicism: American Morality in Decline* (Oxford: Blackwell, 1994), 90.

[69]See Charles Wright Mills, *The Sociological Imagination* (New York: Oxford University Press, 1959), 117.

[70]See Howell S. Baum, "How Bureaucracy Discourages Responsibility," in *Organizations on the Couch,* ed. Manfred F. R. Kets de Vries and Associates, (San Francisco: Jossey-Bass, 1991), 264–85.

[71]See Tzvetan Todorov, *Facing the Extremes: Moral Life in the Concentration Camps* (London: Phoenix, 1999), 290, 141–57.

Adolf Eichmann, the Nazi mass murderer, claimed that he was just following bureaucratic orders, a mere "cog in the machine."[72]

By way of example, in hospital bureaucratic cultures there are enormous costs to patients when medical personnel are not called to account by their hierarchical seniors or juniors. In the United States, for example, it has been estimated that about 4,000 wrong-side surgeries are performed annually. Most could be prevented if physicians were called to be accountable to established protocols. Moreover, it is also thought that "many, if not most, of the estimated 100,000 annual deaths from health-care-associated infections in the United States could be prevented by strict adherence to infection-control practices, including hand hygiene."[73] Peter Garling reported of public hospitals in New South Wales that a "sizeable proportion of [clinicians who] trail infection around like sparks in a dry wheat field . . . bring great risk to the patients" simply because they largely "do not practise hand hygiene before and after seeing each patient."[74]

Honor/Shame/Secrecy. An honor/shame dynamic is a powerful coercive and constraining force in this culture model. This quality is characteristic of all cultures although it is more evident in some than others. As explained earlier (see *Axiom 12,* Chapter 1), shame is about one's status as a person or culture; it is about identity. The feeling of shame emerges from the public uncovering of vulnerability; it is the inner feeling of being looked down upon by others. If one's failings or those of the group fail to be hidden, there is enormous shame. This must never happen at all costs. The complementary value of shame is honor. Honor is a person's or a culture's feeling of self-esteem and the public recognition of that evaluation. Honor is the foundation of one's

---

[72]See Hannah Arendt, *Eichmann in Jerusalem* (New York: Viking Press, 1963), 253–56.

[73]Robert M. Watcher and Peter J. Pronovost, "Balancing 'No Blame' with Accountability in Patient Safety," *New England Journal of Medicine* 361, no. 14 (2009): 1402; see also Donald Goldman, "System Failure versus Personal Accountability—The Case for Clean Hands," *New England Journal of Medicine* 355, no. 2 (2006): 121–23.

[74]Peter Garling, *Final Report of the Special Commission of Inquiry: Acute Care Services in NSW Public Hospitals: Overview* (Sydney: NSW State Government, 2008), 16

reputation, of one's social status in the community; as Model 1 is a male-dominated culture model, it is the duty of men to defend the honor of women. There are different methods whereby people assert or uphold honor in society or between cultures, and each may involve the abuse of power.[75] In brief, it is a moral imperative that the honor of oneself and one's cultural group be kept publicly in place. If this demands secrecy or cover-up, so be it.

Application to Pre–Vatican II Church
Siege Mentality. The Catholic Church prior to the council reflected many of the qualities of the strong group/strong grid culture model. Clericalism flourished. Powerful tribal forces combined to protect the church from dangerous secular and religious enemies. The church had to be sheltered, its failings concealed, lest they undermine its identity and power. For example, the church in the United States was considered before 1965 to be "the best organized and most powerful of the nation's subcultures—a source of both alienation and enrichment for those born within it and an object of bafflement or uneasiness for others."[76] *The Economist* reported: "Discrimination against the Catholic minority and strong leadership from Rome encouraged Catholics to create [in the United States] a sort of parallel society in the 19th and 20th centuries."[77] These statements indicate that the strong group/strong grid culture of the American church was highly effective at that time, as it was in many other parts of the world. Membership qualifications were clearly stated; generally one was born into the faith and over time one became inculturated into a very self-contained cultural milieu with its many distinguishing customs and institutions, such as schools, clubs, hospitals, and universities. Certain particular customs, for example, the Friday abstinence, marked one off from "Protestant tribal enemies" across the boundaries.[78]

---

[75]See Arbuckle, *Violence, Society, and the Church*, 79–93; Bruce J. Malina, *The New Testament World: Insights from Cultural Anthropology* (Louisville, KY: Westminster/John Knox Press, 1993), 50–55.

[76]John Cogley, *Catholic America* (New York: Image, 1974), 135.

[77]"Earthly Concerns: The Catholic Church Is as Big as Any Company in America," *The Economist*, August 8, 2012, 18.

[78]See Mary Douglas, *Natural Symbols: Explorations in Cosmology* (New

Anti-Catholic prejudice and discrimination intensified the feeling of being under siege from enemies of the faith. Mark S. Massa, SJ, comments:

> Many Catholics in 1964 lived in a hermetically sealed universe when it came to their faith and religious practices, mistaking the doxology at the end of their prayers ("as it was in the beginning, is now, and will be forever") for a description of the timelessness of their theology and worship. It was this very sense of timelessness and frozen perfection that the historical consciousness of the Catholic sixties assailed and made permanently problematic.[79]

Ritualistic Affirmation. There existed also in the pre–Vatican II culture a complex regulative cosmology and a highly condensed and differentiated ritual and symbolic system about God and the saints; their perceived qualities mirrored the culture's strong group/strong grid qualities. God was presented as the remote Almighty and Unchanging One, Creator/Regulator; Christ as the King, Savior, and Judge of a people who break "the rules." Jesus Christ was rarely described as a compassionate and forgiving companion in life's journey. However, Mary the Mother of God and the saints were depicted as approachable and understanding beings having particular cultic significance in various needs. For example, St. Anthony of Padua was the saint concerned for lost things, in contrast to the stern and remote God the Father and the sacrificing, judging Jesus Christ. In brief, "when the social group grips its members in tight communal bonds, the religion is ritualist,"[80] hierarchical, formal, and legalistic. Morality is more concerned with sexual and private sins than with social issues of justice and human rights.

Hierarchical Power. The hierarchical officials (pope, bishops, and priests) hold considerable position authority and power within the church. Clerics are decreed to be the active and dominant

---

York: Pantheon Books, 1970), 37–72.

[79]Mark S. Massa, *The American Catholic Revolution: How the '60s Changed the Church Forever* (New York: Oxford University Press, 2010), xv–xvi.

[80]Douglas, *Natural Symbols*, 14.

elite in the church, over "a subservient mass"[81] of lay people. The priest is the sacred representative of Christ on earth, therefore set apart from the laity and accountable to his bishop alone. This also has roots in the early centuries of the church, but it grew with increasing strength in the nineteenth and twentieth centuries prior to Vatican II.

> Among. . . [clericalism's] chief manifestations are an authoritarian style of ministerial leadership, a rigidly hierarchical worldview, and a virtual identification of the holiness and grace of the church with the clerical state and, thereby, with the cleric himself.[82]

Associated with the rise of clericalism was the development of the papacy as a centralized monarchical power in the church. With the Peace of Constantine in 313 CE, the political atmosphere became favorable for the church's leadership, and it uncritically acculturated itself to the courtly and hierarchical ways of the imperial system. Such was the beginning of the clerical culture. Theologian Edmund Hill, OP, writes:

> After the Constantinian revolution it was the hierarchically structured church that was seen as participating in the divine mystery. The sense of mystery and sacredness was concentrated on the hierarchy, and the laity became profane, unmysterious, unless they lived under monastic discipline. They also came to participate much less, if indeed at all, in the mission of the church.[83]

---

[81]Russell Shaw, *To Hunt, to Shoot, to Entertain: Clericalism and the Catholic Laity* (San Francisco: Ignatius Press, 1993), 13; Pope Pius X (1903–14) stated in his encyclical *Vehementer Nos*, 1906, that "the one duty of the multitude [i.e., laity] is to allow themselves to be led and, like a docile flock, to follow the pastors," para. 2. In his encyclical *Pascendi Dominici Gregis*, 1917, he condemned the view that "a share in ecclesiastical government should . . . be given to the lower ranks of the clergy and even to the laity and authority should be decentralized," para. 38.

[82]Rod Dreher, "Sins of the Fathers," *National Review*, February 11, 2002, 30, cited by Donald Cozzens, *Sacred Silence: Denial and the Crisis in the Church* (Collegeville, MN: Liturgical Press, 2002), 114.

[83]Edmund Hill, "Church," in *The New Dictionary of Theology*, ed. Joseph A. Komonchak, Mary Collins, and Dermot A. Lane (Collegeville, MN: Liturgical Press, 1987), 198–99. This alienation of the laity has haunted the church to

Bishops now used the power symbols of royalty, such as dress and titles; priests accepted authority over people and downplayed their role as servant leaders within the community of believers.[84] Worship left the home and entered the basilica.[85] Dominican Yves Congar comments that "the liturgy, hitherto sober and content to express the spiritual worship of the faith in acts of acceptance of God's gift and of thanksgiving, now began to develop a splendid ceremonial, many of its elements being borrowed from that of the [Constantinian] Court: processions, sumptuous vestments, gold furnishings and vessels."[86]

Negative aspects of Roman legalism began to have a deep impact on Christian institutions. Sin, for example, which had earlier been thought of as breaking a relationship with the person of Christ and members of the faith community, was now seen in legal terms as fracturing a divine or ecclesiastical law.[87] Over the centuries the church became increasingly portrayed as a *perfect society*,[88] that is, it has all the means for our personal salvation

---

this day, despite the efforts of Pius XI's encyclical advocating the mission of lay apostles but as a participation in the hierarchy's own apostolate, *Ubi Arcano Dei* (December 23, 1922): "Tell your faithful children of the laity that when, united with their pastors and their bishops, they participate in the works of the apostolate . . . the end purpose of which is to make Jesus Christ better known and better loved, then they are more than ever 'a chosen generation, a kingly priesthood, a holy nation, a purchased people,' of whom St. Peter spoke in such laudatory terms (1 Peter 2:9)," para. 58. Pius XII in his encyclical *Mystici Corporis* insisted that the laity no less than the hierarchy has an obligation to the church's total mission. Vatican II goes further. No longer is the church's essence identified with its hierarchical element. The laity has a definite role by baptism in the work of evangelization and sanctification. See "Dogmatic Constitution of the Church" *(Lumen Gentium)*, paras. 7, 32, 34.

[84]See Yves Congar, *Power and Poverty in the Church* (London: Geoffrey Chapman, 1965), 104–10.

[85]See Anscar J. Chupungco, "Liturgy and Inculturation," *East Asian Pastoral Review* 18, no. 3 (1981): 264; Gerald A. Arbuckle, *Earthing the Gospel: An Inculturation Handbook for Pastoral Workers* (Maryknoll, NY: Orbis Books, 1990), 11–12.

[86]Congar, *Power and Poverty*, 116. Centuries later (1090–1153), Pope Eugenius (1145–1153) voiced a rebuke: "When the pope, clad in silk, covered with gold and jewels, rides out on his white horse, escorted by soldiers and servants, he looks more like Constantine's successor than St. Peter's." Cited by Congar, ibid., 125.

[87]See Anscar J. Chupungco, *Cultural Adaptation of the Liturgy* (New York: Paulist, 1982), 7.

[88]Pope Gregory XVI in 1832 wrote in the encyclical *Mirari Vos*: "It is evident

and that of the world. The refusal of the world to listen to the church only confirmed the point that evil resided in the hearts of secular governments and people.

As the essential ritual intermediaries between the laity and Christ, hierarchal officials could threaten not to provide their services, even to the extent of excommunicating people from the body of the church, for example, for not sending one's children to a Catholic school. If the laity dared distort the boundaries,[89] there were powerful symbols to indicate that they had moved to the edge of the group's life and were risking their salvation. Thus for a Catholic to marry a non-Catholic legally within the church the ceremony had to be held in the sacristy, an uncomfortable and impersonal adjunct to the main church building. The culture itself had similar coercive authority and power (see *Axiom 5,* Chapter 1) over individuals; the Catholic community was so strongly bonded that one would not risk breaking the rules lest one become a subject of gossip, shaming, or even worse—expulsion. In such an atmosphere it was natural for justice to be considered in this model primarily as legal justice, which is the emphasis on the rights of the group over the individual.

No Dissent. The culture allowed no room for dissent. Obedience and loyalty to the status quo were to be given without questioning. "Hierarchy, deference, and the rest of the panoply of time-immemorial fealty and obeisance are placed at risk"[90] if dissent is permitted. Coercive fear and the rejection of dissenting

---

how absurd and how insulting to the Church it is to propose a restoration and renewal as being necessary, as if to infer that the Church could be subject to any defect or diminution or any other imperfection of a similar kind." Cited by Luigi Accattoli, *When a Pope Asks for Forgiveness* (New York: Alba House, 1998), 7.

[89]The statement that "outside the Church there is no salvation" (*Extra ecclesiam nulla salus)* was often used by the Church Fathers. When at times it became a "near dogmatic assertion," with little or no qualifications, the boundaries defining the church's identity grew increasingly rigid. "Vatican II authoritatively rejected [this] traditional understanding . . . when it affirmed that those who know neither the gospel nor the church but who seek God with a sincere heart 'may achieve eternal salvation,' (*Lumen Gentium,* par 16)." Adrian Hastings, "Salvation," in *The Oxford Companion to Christian Thought,* ed. Adrian Hastings, Alistair Mason and Hugh Pyper (Oxford: Oxford University Press, 2000), 640.

[90]Peter McDonough, *The Catholic Labyrinth: Power, Apathy, and a Passion for Reform in the American Church* (New York: Oxford University Press, 2013), 291.

voices shaped the entire governance of the church. Thus creative theologians fared poorly in this system, as Yves Congar found to his sadness:

> The present pope [Pius XII] . . . wishes to reduce theologians to commenting on his statements and not daring to think something or undertake something beyond mere commentary. . . . [The] whole history of Rome is about insisting on its own authority and the destruction of everything that cannot be reduced to submission.[91]

Rome became preoccupied with using secrecy as a method of control. For example, theologians could be reported to Rome by anonymous critics; the earliest stage of their investigation would be held in secret, and throughout the process the same people would be the investigators, prosecutors, and judges. Such action has its roots deep in the past. Congar describes the absolutist centralizing movement from the time of Emperor Constantine (d. 337) in this way: "There existed an imperialism which tended to confuse unity and conformity, to impose everywhere the Roman customs and rites, in a word, considering the universal Church as a simple extension of the Church of Rome."[92] During the Middle Ages the subordination of episcopal government to papal control quickened as a way to prevent or weaken lay involvement in ecclesiastical affairs. Pope Gregory VII (1021–85) stated the theory of an absolutist, monarchical view of the papacy:

> [The] pope can be judged by no one; the Roman church has never erred and never will err. . . . [The] Roman church was founded by Christ alone; the pope can depose and restore bishops; he alone can make new laws. . . . He alone can revise his judgments.[93]

---

[91]Yves Congar, "Silenced for Saying Things Rome Didn't Like to Have Said," excerpt of letter written by author to his mother, *National Catholic Reporter*, June 2, 2000, 20.

[92]Yves Congar, "Christianity as Faith and as Culture," *East Asian Pastoral Review* 18, no. 4 (1981): 310.

[93]Cited by Thomas Bokenkotter, *A Concise History of the Catholic Church* (New York: Doubleday, 1979), 112.

By the time of Pope Innocent III (1198–1215), the title Vicar of Christ had been exclusively applied to the pope, though earlier it had been used for both kings and bishops. The idea was that the pope alone represented Christ, but the other bishops were simply vicars or local representatives of the pope. By the early 1500s, "everyone that mattered in the Western Church was crying out for Reformation."[94] But after the Reformation papal authority over the universal church became even stronger. The Council of Trent (1545–63) reaffirmed papal supremacy, further buttressing the pope's hold over the church as a whole. The council reasserted the rights of bishops to control their dioceses, but subject to papal authority.[95] Lay involvement in the church's administration was forbidden. As historian Thomas Bokenkotter comments: "[Trent] left no room for participation of the laity in the administration of the Church. In sum, they bequeathed to modern Catholics a highly authoritarian, centralized structure that was still basically medieval."[96]

Following the definition of papal infallibility at Vatican I, the reverential mystique surrounding the person of the pope increased, so much so that few would be bold enough to criticize his decisions and those of the curial offices.[97] Loyalty to Rome in all things was required. Bishops were seen as vicars of the pope and needed to be chosen for their unquestioning loyalty to him. At the same time as Pius IX (1792–1878) was solidifying his hold over bishops, he was also increasingly isolating the church from the modern world. Earlier, in 1864, Pius had condemned in the document *Syllabus of Errors* a number of contemporary movements such as rationalism and liberalism. He anathematized all who demanded that the Roman pontiff can and should reconcile and adapt himself to progress, liberalism, and modern civilization.[98]

[94]Owen Chadwick, *The Reformation* (Middlesex: Penguin, 1964), 11.

[95]See David J. Stagaman, *Authority in the Church* (Collegeville, MN: Liturgical Press, 1999), 106–10.

[96]Bokenkotter, *Concise History*, 217.

[97]See John R. Quinn, *The Reform of the Papacy* (New York: Crossroad, 1999), 51.

[98]Pius IX began his pontificate sympathetic to the political liberalization developing in Europe, even beginning moderate reforms within the Papal States. But the increasing internal violent disturbances and military threats against the Papal States turned him against liberal political and social movements. See David I. Kertzer, *The Pope Who Would Be King: The Exile of Pius IX and the Emergence*

Following Pius IX, the fears of "modernism," that is, the movement that sought to bring the tradition of Catholic belief into closer relation with the modern world, continued, even intensified, in Rome. Pope St. Pius X "pursued a policy of internal surveillance, punishment, and retaliation unprecedented in its effectiveness," writes historian Father John O'Malley, SJ.[99] The pope commanded that secret vigilance committees be established in every diocese worldwide to report suspected modernists to Rome.[100] Subsequent popes until Vatican II were less severe, but "an ecclesiastical style, not altogether dissimilar in certain particulars to the style of modern totalitarian states, prevailed."[101] Even today the person being investigated is not told of the inquiry until stage thirteen (of eighteen stages); the defendant is unable to choose his defender or even to know his accuser's identity; access to material relating to the allegations against him is denied; no publicity is permitted concerning the proceedings; and there is no right of appeal.

Honor/Shame/Secrecy. The code of family honor in this model, as evidenced in some Mediterranean countries, demands absolute obedience and loyalty of members to patriarchal leaders: "manliness is commonly the key to maintaining honor, that is, the ability to protect the family or group's name and prestige when they are threatened. For women, the primary mark of honor is a sense of shame; that is, a woman has honor as long as she is totally submissive to her husband or guardian."[102] Jesuit historian Father David Schultenover, SJ, argues that Rome became trapped in the Mediterranean model of honor, shame, and patronage, and that theological issues became of secondary importance. Since in the Mediterranean family, "the father's authority is divinely

---

of Modern Europe (New York: Random House, 2018).

[99]John W. O'Malley, "Interpreting Vatican II: A Break from the Past," *Commonweal*, March 9, 2001, 21.

[100]Pius X in his encyclical *Pascendi Dominici Gregis* ("Feeding the Lord's Flock") (September 8, 1907) condemned "modernism" and other beliefs, asserting that Catholic dogma can be changed. For an analysis of the encyclical see Anthony Maher, *The Forgotten Jesuit of Catholic Modernism: George Tyrrell's Prophetic Theology* (Minneapolis: Fortress Press, 2018), 41–48.

[101]O'Malley, "Interpreting Vatican II," 21.

[102]Arbuckle, *Violence, Society, and the Church*, 90.

ordained and virtually absolute, we have a virtual identification of the papacy and the hierarchy with God. With that identification comes divine sanction of hierarchical action and divine condemnation of any contrary action."[103] Women are expected to be submissive in the patriarchal church; those who fail to do so are considered to lack any sense of shame. Moreover, it is the honorable thing for clerics to protect "Mother Church" from being publicly shamed. Consequently since public disclosure of sexual abuse would set the church and clergy up for ridicule and weaken public esteem for the power structures, concealment is seen as the honorable action.

Selection and Formation of Clergy and Religious. Pope Benedict XVI admitted in 2010 that among the causes of sexual abuse of minors by priests and religious are: "inadequate procedures for determining the suitability of candidates for the priesthood and religious life; insufficient human, moral, intellectual and spiritual formation in seminaries and novitiates."[104] The initiation of candidates into the clerical state (and religious life) mirrored in significant ways male initiation rituals of premodern societies, rituals characteristic of strong group/strong grid cultures; seclusion and fear were used to inculcate the clerical mythology. In an isolated monastic atmosphere of unchanging order, candidates for pastoral ministry in the world were taught that the world is evil and to be avoided.[105] The educational process could be summed

---

[103]David G. Schultenover, "The Church as a Mediterranean Family," *America* (October 8, 1994), 13, and *A View from Rome: On the Eve of the Modernist Crisis* (New York: Fordham University Press, 1993), *passim.*

[104]Pope Benedict XVI, "Pastoral Letter to the Catholics of Ireland," March 19, 2010, para. 4.

[105]I was the rector of a major seminary in New Zealand in the late 1970s to train priests of an apostolic congregation. I wrote in the mid-1990s: "The institutional culture, eleven years after Vatican II, was still basically monastic. The rector, by tradition and legislation, held enormous power, but it was fundamentally the power to maintain the *status quo.* Like some medieval Benedictine abbot, he was responsible for the educational side of the seminary but most of his time was taken up overseeing sheep and cattle farms, deciding when grapes should be picked for commercial winemaking, defending property rights. Few had questioned the spending of time on issues which had very little to do with the primary purpose of a seminary for apostolic life." *From Chaos to Mission: Refounding Religious Life Formation* (London: Geoffrey Chapman, 1996), 6.

up in this way: "quasi-indoctrination and voluntary incarceration to foster in candidates for the priesthood and/or religious life submission to the ecclesiastical and pastoral status quo."[106] The world had nothing to offer the church.

Information was handed down from above to be received without question. Conformity to a theological, ecclesiastical, and pastoral status quo was the most esteemed value in a candidate, and testimony to the success of the training program. The fear of punishment, for even the innocent infringement of regulations, was an effective method of instilling conformity in candidates. This stress on keeping even minute rules, under threat of disproportionate punishment, gave candidates a false sense of what was truly sinful. Issues of sexuality and personal development were considered unimportant for the externally conforming clerics. The training encouraged candidates to conceal mistakes and to protect the system at all costs. Donald Cozzens reflects on the impact of this training on future priests:

> In the middle 1960s, the clerical culture in which I lived and worked seemed as immutable as the creed itself. It was neither questioned nor critiqued. That such a culture tended to keep priests emotionally immature and excessively dependent on the approval of their superiors and parishioners was as yet to be understood. . . . In some clerical circles, efforts to retain the pre-conciliar caste are striking. Long-term friends address each other using their ecclesiastical titles and sporting the latest in clerical vesture.[107]

Clerical teachers were chosen chiefly for their known ability to accept and maintain the academic and structural status quo.

Teaching abilities were not necessary because all that was needed was to provide candidates with information already set out in manuals and then to check that it had been adequately received. Seminarians were discouraged from

---

[106]Ibid., 29.

[107]David Cozzens, *Sacred Silence: Denial and the Crisis in the Church* (Collegeville, MN: Liturgical Press, 2002), 114, 116.

reading material beyond the notes distributed to them. Lecturers did not encourage students; in fact, they actively discouraged them from examining their intellectual and emotional responses to the material given them.[108]

Since the church was seen as the perfect society, it was assumed to have all the answers. Creative theologians fared poorly in this system. At the same time, Rome fostered a form of scholastic philosophy, Neo-Scholasticism, which provided the church with a very coherent intellectual framework. Yet this philosophy had one serious disadvantage; namely, it was so self-contained that its supporters saw no need to listen to, or learn from, other philosophies.[109] The social sciences were believed to have nothing to offer, so they were effectively excluded from the seminary curriculum.

After six to seven years of isolation from the real world, clergy were for the most part ill-prepared emotionally and educationally for ministry. Religious clerics who belonged to teaching congregations were often appointed immediately after ordination to teach in schools without any appropriate training and university qualifications. Religious sisters and brothers were even more ill-prepared for this demanding ministry. They were expected to "sink or swim," with little or no training as teachers and support systems. The emotional and spiritual costs to these people were enormous, at times devastating. And in many instances it was unjust to school pupils whose education was put at risk by unprepared teachers.

The Australian Royal Commission into Institutional Responses to Child Sexual Abuse, 2017, severely critiqued the selection, screening, and initial formation of candidates for ministry, for example: "It is apparent that initial formation practices were inadequate in the past, particularly before the 1970s, in relation to the screening of candidates for admission, preparing seminarians and novices to lead a celibate life, and preparing them for the realities of a life in religious or pastoral ministry." The training "occurred

---

[108]Arbuckle, *From Chaos to Mission*, 103–4.

[109]See Kevin Peoples, *Trapped in a Closed World: Catholic Culture and Sexual Abuse* (Mulgrave, Australia: Garratt Publishing, 2017), 75–100.

in segregated, regimented, monastic and clericalist environments, and was based on obedience and conformity." Such formation processes "are likely to have been detrimental to psychosexual maturity, and to have produced clergy and religious who were cognitively rigid. This increased the risk of child sexual abuse."[110] The report also disturbingly noted: "It is clear that inadequate preparation for ministry, loneliness, social isolation, and personal distress related to the difficulties of celibacy have contributed to sexual abuse of children."[111]

Normalization of Cover-Ups. It is true of the Catholic Church that the potential for abuse of power "is much stronger in hierarchical extremist groups where the leader-follower role and power differentiation are more tangible and stark. The potential for abuse of power is much more accentuated in these types of groups."[112] The authority and power of the ritual/administrative leaders are open to considerable exploitation: "creeping infallibility" becomes an approved way for administrative, bureaucratic curial officers, bishops, and priests to avoid having to be accountable for their actions to laity and the church as a whole. And if one is the ritual expert in an unchanging church, then there is little need to cultivate consultative leadership. If one has all the answers before questions are even asked, why listen to others for solutions to problems? Father Avery Dulles, SJ, expresses his concern:

> Without minimizing the charismatic gifts of official leaders [in the church], we may acknowledge that, in a sinful world, those who hold office will commonly be tempted to employ their power in a dominative and manipulative way. They can easily tend to sacrifice other values to the demands of law and order and to misconceive loyalty as if it meant merely passive conformity.[113]

---

[110]*Final Report of the Royal Commission*, 47.

[111]Ibid., 48.

[112]Michael A. Hogg and Scott A. Reid, "Social Identity, Leadership, and Power," in *The Use and Abuse of Power*, ed. Lee-Chai and Bargh, 173.

[113]Avery Dulles, *A Church to Believe In: Discipleship and the Dynamics of Freedom* (New York: Crossroad, 1982), 36–37.

In this church culture there is no built-in public accountability system for hierarchical officials; accountability was expected to be "bottom-up," leaving leaders to function without having to be answerable to their inferiors. In this situation "sinful structures," as defined by Pope St. John Paul II,[114] can so easily develop; structures cease to be the means and become instead the ends of church life. A sinful structure is a social habit, an institutional way of life, a political or economic arrangement, which of its nature causes injustice or leads people knowingly or unknowingly into sinful ways of acting.[115] For example, ecclesiastical officials could live in princely splendor, or construct richly decorated churches, while surrounded by people in immense poverty, simply to maintain the church's status and traditions. It is a culture insensitive to the demands of social justice. A good symbol of this church culture is the "barque of Peter," tossed around by hostile external forces, but safe, internally intact and under the infallible, protective captaining of the pope, the vicar of Christ on earth, assisted by the bishops, priests, and religious.

It is an anthropological truism, and firmly held by Douglas, "that taken-for-granted beliefs, ideas and emotions of a period, place or person [must] never be considered aside from the social circumstances which gave rise to them and then sustained."[116] Given the above description of the multiple cultural forces shaping the pre–Vatican II culture, it is little wonder that cover-ups of the sexual abuse of minors by representatives of the church had become normalized. It was so strongly reinforced by age-old customs that it remained substantially intact even after Vatican II. Our next culture model, as formulated by Douglas, offers insights into the nature of the church's culture as desired by the council.

---

[114]Pope St. John Paul II defines "structures of sin": "The sum total of the negative factors working against a true awareness of the universal *common good*, and the need to further it, gives the impression of creating, in persons and institutions, an obstacle which is difficult to overcome." "On Social Concerns" *(Sollicitudo Rei Socialis)*, para. 36.

[115]See Latin American Bishops, "Puebla Document 1979," ed. John Eagleson and Philip Scharper (Maryknoll, NY: Orbis Books, 1979), 183–84.

[116]Fardon, *Mary Douglas*, 3.

Model 2: Weak Group/Weak Grid Culture—Vatican II Church

Anthropological Analysis

Unlike the preceding culture model, the *weak group/weak grid* model is strongly egalitarian in social relationships and gender, with minimum pressure from structures within and at the boundaries of the group. Martin Buber defines the way in which individuals should interact as the "I-Thou" relationship. This relationship happens when there is mutuality, openness, presence, and directness.[117] The "I" relates to the "Thou" not as something to be studied, measured, or manipulated, but as an irreplaceable presence that responds to the "I" in its individuality. Community members recognize the need for social bonding based on mutuality and interdependence in response to a common vision and mission. Friendships, therefore, are based on the need to work together to realize this, not on the narcissistic wishes of individuals. A feminine aspect is evident in a "heightened awareness of creativity, sensitivity, personal relationships and feelings, personal worth and individual differences."[118]

Generally, communities of this model emerge only under the inspiration of some transformative leader, who denounces the oppressive rigidity of the grid/group traditions or structures of a dominant culture from which escape is sought. Dress codes and rigid rules of conduct based on tradition are considered irrelevant; far more important are the interior conversion and effective commitment of members to the group's mission, vision, and values, resulting in what anthropologically are termed *intentional communities*.[119] In such communities members commit themselves to act together in view of a common vision and mission. The word "intentional" means "deliberate" or "consciously chosen."[120]

---

[117]See Martin Buber, *Between Man and Man* (New York: Routledge, 2002), xii.

[118]Charles Hanley, *Gods of Management: The Changing Work of Organizations* (Sydney: Random House, 1994), 244.

[119]For a fuller description of intentional communities see Gerald A. Arbuckle, *Intentional Faith Communities in Catholic Education* (Strathfield: St. Pauls Publications, 2016), 113–65.

[120]See Bernard J. Lee and Michael Cowan, *Dangerous Memories: House Churches and Our American Story* (Kansas City: Sheed and Ward, 1986), 91.

The group is open to new insights, dialogue, and outsiders (see *Action-Plan 9,* Chapter 6).

Personal identity according to this model comes from an awareness of one's self-worth and potential for change, not from a culture's traditional internal and boundary structures. Religion is highly personalized. A personal relationship to God and to other people who have the same values as oneself is what counts, and traditional rituals are unimportant, unless they reinforce that sense of relationship or emerge out of the events of daily living, in which case they are very simple in structure. The world is inherently good, and if there are problems, they are due to traditional structures that have stifled the good or prevented it from emerging in people's lives. Charity or love, not "depersonalized justice," motivates people's lives. If justice is stressed, it is the pursuit in common action of social justice so that all may benefit. People in this culture model strive to live the call of St. Paul: "Be of the same mind, having the same love, being in full accord and of one mind. . . . Let each of you look, not to your own interests, but to the interests of others" (Phil 2:2–4).

A weak group/weak grid culture is open to considerable innovation, and responsible dissent is welcomed, because both are seen as essential requirements for growth.[121] Concrete examples of this model over time are the early Christian communities in Jerusalem (see the idealized description of these communities in Acts 1:12–14). Scripture scholar Gerd Theissen, writing on the early Palestinian Christian communities, pinpoints their countercultural witness when surrounded by nonbelievers in Christ: "[A] small group of outsiders experimented with a vision of love and reconciliation in a society which had been put out of joint, suffering from an excess of tensions, pressures and forms of aggression, in order to renew this society from within."[122] Other examples are religious movements in their first stage of founding enthusiasm (for example, St. Francis and his early followers), Basic

---

[121]Alexa Clay and Kyra M. Phillips conclude that motivators of creative people are idealism, ambition, curiosity, and stubbornness. *The Misfit Economy: Lessons in Creativity from Pirates, Hackers, Gangsters and Other Informal Entrepreneurs* (New York: Simon & Schuster, 2015).

[122]Gerd Theissen, *Sociology of Early Palestinian Christianity* (Philadelphia: Fortress Press, 1978), 110.

Ecclesial Communities common in the South American church, countercultural communities or communes throughout history (for example, the commune movement in the late 1960s in the West), and new innovative business organizations.[123]

Application to Vatican II Church

This weak group/weak grid culture typology describes the model of the church as desired by Vatican II, a flexible culture model that is constantly adapting to a changing environment. The council recognizes the church as a community of sinners, which requires ongoing purification and renewal. While acknowledging that the church is of divine origin, it asserts that it is also human and vulnerable to all kinds of failings. When the council called the church to share the "joy and hope, the grief and anguish of the men [sic] of our time, especially those who are poor or afflicted in any way,"[124] it destroyed the centuries-long assumption that the church should not become involved in an "evil" world. Historian John O'Malley, SJ, describes the culture shifts in the council: "from commands to invitations, from laws to ideals, from definition to mystery, from threats to persuasion . . . from vertical to horizontal, from exclusion to inclusion . . . from static to ongoing . . . from modification to inner appropriation."[125]

This is a radical shift in thinking, a theological paradigm or mythological shift that would demand equally dramatic cultural, structural, and attitudinal changes at all levels of the church's life. Legalism, clericalism, "a self-centred and elitist complacency, bereft of love"[126] must have no place among the People of God. It is in "the Beatitudes" that the church is to "find a portrait of the Master, which we are called to reflect in our daily lives."[127] Where once the church had sought to remove itself from history, now

---

[123]See case studies in Jessica Livingston, *Founders at Work: Stories of Startups' Early Days* (New York: Apress, 2008).

[124]"Pastoral Constitution on the Church in the Modern World" *(Gaudium et Spes)*, ed. Austin P. Flannery, *Documents of Vatican II* (Grand Rapids, MI: William B. Eerdmans, 1975), para.1.

[125]John W. O'Malley, *What Happened at Vatican II* (Cambridge, MA: Belknap Press of Harvard University Press, 2008), 307.

[126]Pope Francis, Apostolic Exhortation, "Rejoice and Exult" *(Gaudete et Exsultate)* (Strathfield: St. Pauls Publications, 2017), para. 57.

[127]Ibid., para. 63.

following the council it is faced with the evangelical imperative to enter into the lives of people, their cultures, both to give and to be changed by them. The council speaks of this process as a living exchange.

Unfortunately, and tragically, following Vatican II canon law fell into disfavor until the 1990s. Canonist John J. Coughlin notes, "If bishops had fulfilled their duty to abide by the rule of [canon law and its penalties], especially in the cases involving clergy who are serial child abusers, there probably would have been no [sexual abuse and cover-up] crisis." Instead, bishops and major superiors of congregations focused on "the psychological approach to the exclusion of the canonical"[128] with often heartbreaking consequences for survivors of sexual abuse. Many perpetrators returned from their therapeutic treatment only to reoffend. The welfare of the survivors, which should have been the first priority, was not the primary focus.

Ongoing Reformation. The theological paradigm shift is such that the church must continually be involved in reforming itself. Ways of evangelizing and government structures suitable for the maintenance of a fortress church—i.e., a church defensively isolated from the world around it—are totally inadequate for a church committing itself to the task of preaching the Gospel in the world. The world is changing so rapidly that what is pastorally suited for today's needs is inadequate in tomorrow's world. Never will the church be able to claim that it is finally reformed; it must always be in the state of becoming and reforming.

The council, in brief, redefined the church from an inflexibly hierarchical, authoritarian, monarchical, antimodern institution to one that had to be intimately engaged in the world, from a fortress hierarchical church to "the People of God," a pilgrim people openly accountable for their actions at all levels of the church (see *Action Plans 5* and *7*, Chapter 6). The priest's role changes from the representative of Christ to being the represen-

---

[128]John J. Coughlin, "The Clergy Sexual Abuse Crisis and the Spirit of Canon Law," *Boston College Law Review* 44, no. 4 (2003): 997. See also Marie Keenan, *Child Sex Abuse and the Catholic Church: Gender, Power, and Organizational Culture*, 209–14.

tative of the church, "in which the priest is more in communion with and in service of the laity."[129] This is a dramatic change from the pre–Vatican II theological mythology, a change that demands accountability to laity as well as to hierarchical officials.

If the original fervor of this cultural model is to be maintained, however, members must face the challenge to build structures and community identities that do not crush the original enthusiasm. This is not an easy challenge, and it is rarely achieved unless commitment to the ideals of the original founding group is vigorously maintained.[130] Pope St. John XXIII initiated a revolution against ecclesiastical institutionalism to return the Catholic Church to the dynamic virtues of Christ-centered love, justice, and service in a changing world. Pope Francis has the same deliberate aim:

> I invite all Christians . . . to a renewed personal encounter with Jesus Christ. . . . Whenever we make the effort to return to the source and to recover the original freshness of the Gospel, new avenues arise, new paths of creativity open up, with different forms of expression, more eloquent signs and words with new meaning for today's world.[131]

Model 3: Strong Group/Weak Grid Culture: Restorationist Church

Anthropological Analysis

In the *strong group/weak grid* model of culture people have a sense of belonging to *this* group rather than to another, but there is a notable failure to agree about the ways in which individuals are to relate to one another within the group. That is, the *grid* is weak. Internal social cohesion is fragile, and the potential for social conflict is considerable. Fundamentalist movements form in response to people's needs for security and control in a turbulent world. People are suspicious of one another, feeling that others are manipulating the system against them. It is an atmosphere in which witch-hunting or scapegoating flourishes.

---

[129]Marie Keenan, *Child Sex Abuse*, 39.

[130]For examples see Arbuckle, *The Francis Factor*, 193–98.

[131]Pope Francis, Apostolic Exhortation "The Joy of the Gospel" *(Evangelii Gaudium)* (Sydney: St. Pauls Publications, 2013), para. 17.

Restorationism is a quality of many fundamentalist movements that seek to restore society to an imagined utopian past. Fundamentalists find rapid change extremely disturbing and dangerous emotionally. Cultural, economic, social, religious, and personal certitudes are shaken. Consequently, fundamentalists nostalgically and simplistically yearn to return to a golden age, purified of dangerous ideas and practices. They aggressively come together in order to put things right again—according to what they decide are orthodox principles. They turn to emotional and political bullying—and even physical violence at times—to get things back to "normal." History must be reversed. There are numerous contemporary examples: anti-immigrant campaigns, nationalistic movements, Trumpism, Brexit campaigners, neo-capitalists.[132]

Application to Restorationist Church

In retrospect it can be seen that Vatican II's fathers were for the most part blithely unaware of the implications of what they had voted for. The group of documents that emerged from the council "now appears more like placing sticks of dynamite into the foundations of Tridentine Catholicism than simply 'opening the windows' of the church to the world."[133] And the fathers were ill-prepared to lead the radical cultural changes as requested by the council. The council did not establish an appropriate process to implement its mythological changes. To fill the administrative vacuum Paul VI decided in 1967 that the unreformed Roman Curia would be responsible for the implementation of the council's major decrees.[134] Thus the curia quickly moved to bring back the preconciliar mythology. Responsible dissent would be increasingly forbidden by the curia and its supporting hierarchies around the world. The curia had faults characteristic of modern bureaucracies,[135] namely deep-seated resistance to change, lack

---

[132]For a fuller description, and examples, of fundamentalist restorationist movements see Gerald A. Arbuckle, *Fundamentalism at Home and Abroad: Analysis and Pastoral Responses* (Collegeville, MN: Liturgical Press, 2017).

[133]Massa, *American Catholic*, 99.

[134]See O'Malley, *What Happened at Vatican II*, 283; Hans Küng, *Can We Save the Church* (London: William Collins, 2013), 201–5.

[135]See Arbuckle, *Violence, Society, and the Church*, 108–11.

of accountability, departmental silos that refused to collaborate, membership based on like-minded thinking, and "creeping infallibility" in administrative decisions. Year by year the centralized authority of the church gradually encouraged a restorationist pre–Vatican II culture to return, along with its secretive form of governing and a cover-up clericalism.

The mythologies of Vatican II and pre–Vatican II are in increasingly open conflict. Restorationism has become a well-organized attempt to return the church to the cultural ghetto or opposition-to-the-world mythology of the pre–Vatican II times. It is a progressively vociferous movement by people reacting to the theological and cultural turmoil evoked by the council and the modern world at large. Restorationists yearn for a return to the strong grid/strong group culture that dominated the centuries up to the Vatican II Council. Restorationism takes many forms, some fanatically aggressive and others less so. It is marked by degrees of intolerance to any form of opposition; dialogue is rarely possible with individuals or institutions adhering to its beliefs.[136]

Within North America particularly, restorationism is so uncompromising in its statements and criticism of Pope Francis that it amounts to an undeclared schism.[137] Integral to restorationism is a renewed emphasis on clericalism. As in all fundamentalist movements the exponents of clericalism do not agree to dialogue; they have the truth, they assert, so why dialogue? Many restorationists assert that the sexual abuse crisis is due to a "homosexual subculture" in the church, not the clerical culture, which Pope Francis speaks of.[138] Some believe that gays pollute

---

[136]For types of restorationist movements see Arbuckle, *Fundamentalism at Home and Abroad*, 97–124.

[137]See "Catholicism in the US: Vigano and the Political Agenda," Editorial, *The Tablet*, October 27, 2018, 2.

[138]See Ruth Graham, "Conservative Catholics Are Digging for Dirt on American Cardinals" (January 10, 2018). The Australian Royal Commission into Institutional Responses to Child Sexual Abuse rejects the view that there is an automatic connection between homosexual orientation and sexual abuse of children. *Final Report: Preface and Executive Summary* (Barton, ACT: Commonwealth of Australia, 2017), 18; the John Jay College of Criminal Justice, USA, published a report in 2010 which found no statistical evidence that gay priests were more likely to abuse minors. www.usccb.org/issues-and-action/child-and-youth-protection/

the order ordained by God and have no place in the priesthood (see *Axiom 15,* Chapter 1). The return to a rigid, rule-focused seminary routine, together with the exclusion of gays, is what is considered needed by the restorationists; they think that the pre–Vatican II culture would end clerical abuse.

The residual founding mythology of the church as expressed in the documents of Vatican II, not the preconciliar mythology, is struggling to resurface under the leadership of Pope Francis, despite the restorationist opposition. In the face of the intensifying cultural resistance from sections of the curia and others, he struggles to build governance structures to ensure that Vatican II mythology is finally and firmly embedded in the church's culture. He has forthrightly rejected fundamentalist restorationism with its insistence on coercive legalistic rules and the revitalization of clericalism:

> If the Christian is a restorationist, a legalist, if they want everything clear and safe, they will find nothing. . . . Those who today always look for disciplinarian solutions, those who long for an exaggerated doctrinal "security," those who stubbornly try to recover a past that no longer exists—they have a static and inward-directed view of things. . . . God is in every person's life. Even if the life of a person has been a disaster. . . . You must try to seek God in every human life. Although the life of a person is a land full of thorns and weeds, there is always a space in which the good seed can grow. You have to trust God.[139]

A church that fears to be involved in the world becomes a church of defensive rules, a fortress church of the preconciliar type. Francis disparages this. As a cardinal, he had said that the church had become "too wrapped up in itself . . . too navel-gazing . . . 'self-referential'" and this had "made it sick . . . suffering a

---

upload/The-Causes-and-Context-of-Sexual-Abuse-of-Minrs-by-Catholic-Priests-in-the-United-States-1950-2010.

[139]Pope Francis, quoted in Antonio Spadaro, SJ, "A Big Heart Open to God: An interview with Pope Francis," *America*, September 30, 2013, www.america-magazine.org/pope-interview.

'kind of theological narcissism.' "[140] As pope he wrote: "I prefer a Church which is bruised, hurting and dirty because it has been out in the streets, rather than a Church that is unhealthy from being confined and from clinging to its own security."[141] Neither the church nor the evangelizer is to be the focus of our concern, but rather the "center is Jesus Christ, who calls us and sends us forth."[142] The church's primary task is to evangelize, not to protect itself from the sufferings of others, especially people who are poor and vulnerable:

> "Mere administration" can no longer be enough. . . . I dream of a "missionary option," that is, a missionary impulse capable of transforming everything, so that the Church's customs, ways of doing things, times and schedules, language and structures can be suitably channeled for the evangelization of today's world rather than for her self-preservation.[143]

Pope Francis's primary model of the church, therefore, is not hierarchical but the People of God and its spirituality the Beatitudes: "The image of the church I like is that of the holy, faithful people of God. . . . There is no full identity without belonging to a people."[144] And Francis expresses this identity personally by openly proclaiming, "I am a sinner."

Pope Francis, having been criticized by survivors' groups who doubted he fully realized the extent of the sexual abuse of minors and its cover-up in the church, announced the establishment in 2013 of the Pontifical Commission for the Protection of Minors. Its primary task is to propose initiatives that could protect chil-

---

[140]Cardinal Jorge Bergoglio to cardinals meeting in conclave, cited by Paul Vallely, *Pope Francis: Untying the Knots* (London: Bloomsbury, 2013), 155. During the Easter rituals in 2013 Francis warned the clergy against becoming mere "managers" or "antique collectors" obsessed with liturgical niceties, urging them to leave their sacristies to change the secular world. See William Pfaff, "Challenge to the Church," *New York Review*, May 9, 2013, 11.

[141]Pope Francis, "Joy of the Gospel," para. 49.

[142]Pope Francis, quoted by Thomas Reese, "Pope Francis' Ecclesiology Rooted in the Emmaus Story," *National Catholic Reporter* (August 6, 2013), www.ncronline.org/news/spirituality/pope-francis-ecclesiology-rooted-emmaus-story.

[143]Pope Francis, "The Joy of the Gospel," paras. 25, 27.

[144]Pope Francis, quoted by Spadaro, "A Big Heart Open to God."

dren from pedophiles in the church. Any hesitancy in dealing with this issue on the part of Francis was rather dramatically overcome when he discovered the full extent of the problem in Chile. He apologized for his tardiness to the people of Chile: "With shame I must say that we did not know how to listen and react in time." In an earlier letter to Chile's bishops he said: "As far as my role, I acknowledge, and ask you to convey faithfully, that I have made grave errors in assessment and perception of the situation. . . . I ask forgiveness to all those that I offended."[145]

Summary

- Historian Thomas Bokenkotter summarizes the fundamental cause of the contemporary crisis in the church. It is the tension of letting go the long-held classicist view of the church in favor of the historically conscious stance. The former view sees the church as moving through the centuries "more or less unaffected by history." The second approach "acknowledges how much institutions, governing precepts, and basic ideas about religion and morality are shaped by history and therefore how relative they are."[146]
- Vatican II sought to counter the excesses of the classicist view by emphasizing the values of the second position, but restorationists uncompromisingly seek to return the church to the classicist mentality; clericalism, which is at the heart of restorationism, is a contemporary fundamentalist movement.
- Vatican II called for a radical shift in the culture and governance structures of the church, so radical that the term "culture change" inadequately describes what is required. Vatican II invited the People of God to build a profoundly new church with a new culture, not a modification of the pre-council church and its culture.
- The hierarchical church has lacked the necessary leadership for such deep-rooted culture building, as the ongoing global concealment of the sexual abuse scandals illustrate.

---

[145]Pope Francis, *Letter to the Church in Chile*, May 31, 2018.
[146]Bokenkotter, *Concise History*, 401.

Hierarchical leaders are still substantially trapped in a pre–Vatican II culture that is prone to covering up behavior. Yet if the church is to be saved, the required leadership, as described and exemplified by Pope Francis, must emerge.

3

The Grieving Church in Focus

As soon as symbolic action is denied, . . . the flood gates of confusion are opened.

—Mary Douglas, *Natural Symbols: Explorations in Cosmology*

Organizations sometimes have to get into real trouble, however, before they recognize their need for help, and then they often do not seek the right kind of help. Sadly, organizations are no different in this regard from individuals.

—Edgar H. Schein, *Organizational Culture and Leadership*

Indeed, several studies . . . indicate that cultural changes generally are not planned, but accompany sudden, and at times cataclysmic, events.

—W. Gibb Dyer, *Strategies for Managing Change*

This chapter explains that
- Grief intensifies the church's cultural trauma.
- External factors demand church reform.
- Reform calls for refounding the church.

There are two significant catalysts of the contemporary chaos in the church: one is internal to the church itself, namely the efforts begun at Vatican II to return the church to its founding mythology; the second is external, namely the impact on the People of

God of the expressive revolution of the 1960s,[1] and the ongoing revelations of sexual abuse scandals and their cover-up. Paradoxically the public disclosure of these scandals by the media, government inquiries, and the legal courts are able to do what efforts at internal revitalization have been unable to achieve, namely they are forcing the church to admit the institutional evil in its midst. We People of God may complain at times about these external pressures, but without them the church would still be covering up the sexual abuse of minors and vulnerable people. God in faithfulness has humbled us in order that we may re-learn the statutes of scriptural living (Ps 119:71). Marie Keenan is correct:

> In an irony of the current situation, it may well be that the greatest impetus to change in the Catholic Church going forward will turn out to be child sexual abuse by Catholic clergy, and the strength that survivors of abuse have had in challenging the system that failed them.[2]

The preceding chapter described with the aid of three anthropological models the present theological and cultural tensions in the church. Because cultural analysis of change is so complex, the purpose of this chapter is to further deepen our understanding of the chaos in the church since Vatican II by describing and explaining the grieving model of institutional cultural breakdown. The model reveals what happens when leadership is inadequate in cultural disintegration and the grief of people is ignored. Such is the case in the church. The appalling fact is that there are "catastrophic failures of leadership of Catholic Church authorities over many decades,"[3] not just in Australia but globally. The church's hierarchical leaders must choose between either the church retreating into a sect-like existence or refounding. A sect that does not "bear fruit in love of one's neighbor and in justice directed

---

[1]For an explanation of the "expressive revolution" and its impact on religions see Gerald A. Arbuckle, *Catholic Identity or Identities? Refounding Ministries in Chaotic Times* (Collegeville, MN: Liturgical Press, 2015), 53–67.

[2]Marie Keenan, *Child Sexual Abuse and the Catholic Church: Gender, Power, and Organizational Culture* (Oxford: Oxford University Press, 2012), 229.

[3]*Final Report Royal Commission into Institutional Responses to Child Sexual Abuse*, vol. 16, bk. 1 (Barton, ACT: Commonwealth of Australia, 2017), 36.

toward the life of the world is worth nothing," rightly declared Bernhard Häring.[4] If the church retreats into a sect-like existence, the lack of transparency will be further reinforced.

Models of Cultural Change

I begin this section by highlighting insights from models of organizational change created by several management theorists. I then focus on anthropological models of cultural change. As explained in the preceding chapter, a model is a generalized picture, analogy, or explanation of a researcher's observation of complicated realities.

Management Insights

Several theorists emphasize the fact that significant cultural change is not possible unless outside forces break through the culture's rigid defenses and denial. Then to take advantage of the cultural breakdown a new type of leadership is needed. Alan Wilkins and W. Gibb Dyer[5] in their analysis of organizational culture change suggest two varieties of cultures: *morphogenetic* (change-oriented) and *homeostatic* (stability-oriented). The internal organizational systems in a *homeostatic* culture—for example, the church's traditional hierarchical culture—are so rigid that change from within is close to impossible. Significant internal change is possible, they argue, only if there is a grave external environmental crisis that breaks "the tyranny of the old culture."[6] Only from outside can we expect the "astringent appraisal, the rude question. Only from outside can we expect judgments untainted by the loyalty and camaraderie of insiders, undistorted by the comfortable assumptions held within the walls."[7] At the same time, to take advantage of external criticism and cultural disintegration, new and appropriate leadership is essential: "Tam-

---

[4]Bernard Haring, *Evangelization Today* (Notre Dame, IN: Fides Press, 1974), 2.

[5]Alan L. Wilkins and W. Gibb Dyer, "Toward Culturally Sensitive Theories of Culture Change," *Academy of Management Review* 13, no. 4 (October 1988): 522.

[6]Edgar H. Schein, *Organizational Culture and Leadership* (San Francisco: Jossey-Bass, 1987), 321.

[7]John W. Gardner, *On Leadership* (New York: Free Press, 1990), 130.

ing [the] chaos . . . requires a new breed of leaders at every level."[8]

William Dyer further explains in his model of cultural evolution that leaders must take advantage of crises in institutions to build new organizational cultures.[9] He argues that only when there is an emergency and a change in leadership happening almost simultaneously is it possible to have significant cultural change. New leaders must be chosen who can embed new symbols and values into the culture:

> [The] most important decision in culture change concerns the selection of a new leader inasmuch as a new leader who enters an organization during a period of crisis has unique opportunities to transform the organization's culture by bringing and embedding artifacts, perspectives, values, and assumptions into the organization. Leaders do indeed appear to be the creators and transmitters of culture.[10]

Another management specialist, Charles Lundberg, developed what he terms a learning cycle of cultural change.[11] A culture experiences some kind of institutional predicament that causes surprise, he says, which in turn prompts inquiry that may lead to the discovery of some unknown facts making cultural change a possibility. He insists that cultural change is complex because many subcultures with different agendas must be involved; hence, cultural change, no matter how well it is planned, will have uncertain results. Edgar Schein is a little more optimistic about the possible consequences of cultural change. His life-cycle model suggests that institutions pass through several distinct phases: *birth and early growth, organizational midlife,* and *organizational maturity.* Schein asserts that "if we give culture its due, if we

---

[8]Thomas H. Lee, "Turning Doctors into Leaders," *Harvard Business Review* 88, no. 4 (2010): 53.

[9]See W. Gibb Dyer, *Strategies for Managing Change* (Reading: Addison-Wesley, 1984), 162.

[10]William G. Dyer, "The Cycle of Cultural Evolution in Organizations," in *Gaining Control of the Corporate Culture*, ed. R. H. Kilmann, M. J. Saxton, R. Serpa, and Associates (San Francisco: Jossey Bass, 1985), 223.

[11]See C. C. Lundberg, "On the Feasibility of Cultural Intervention in Organizations," in P. J. Frost, L. F. Moore, M. R. Louis, C. C. Lindberg, and J. Martins, eds., *Organizational Culture* (Newbury, CA: Sage, 1985), 169–85.

take an inquiring attitude toward the deciphering of culture, if we respect what culture is and what functions it serves, we will find that it is a potentially friendly animal that can be tamed and made to work for us."[12] But Schein insists that this will not happen unless the right type of leaders emerge to take advantage of the chaos resulting from organizational cultural disintegration.

Anthropological Insights

Unlike management theorists, who are apt to assume that human beings can be managed solely around rational logical ends-means models of organizations, anthropologists emphasize the emotional dynamics of cultures and change (see *Axiom 3,* Chapter 1).

In anthropologist Victor Turner's model of cultural change, life is a course or journey whereby persons move regularly through the processes of two interacting cultures, which he terms *societas* and *liminality.* There are always three stages in the journey model: the exit or separation from the world of "ordinary living" (*societas*), the actual liminal experience itself, and the *reaggregation* into "ordinary living" once more. Each stage may be short or long depending on the circumstances. In the *societas* culture, we all know our statuses and roles in daily living; for example, everyone has a status of some kind: father, mother, doctor, teacher, student, and so forth. With each title there is an expected form of behavior, or role, which gives us a much-needed sense of security and predictability.

However, in the second culture, liminality, statuses and roles cease to be important. Liminality culture is of two kinds: spontaneous and normative or planned. Spontaneous liminality occurs when there is a sudden unplanned breakdown of order; for example, when people together experience a natural disaster, the only thing that matters is survival. Statuses and roles are no longer significant. People are confronted with key questions: Who am I? What is the purpose of life? What should I change?

---

[12]Edgar H. Schein, "How Culture Forms, Develops and Changes," in *Gaining Control of the Corporate Culture,* ed. R. H. Kilmann, M. J. Saxton, R. Serpa, and Associates (San Francisco: Jossey Bass, 1985), 42.

"Liminality," writes Turner, "may be partly described as a stage of reflection,"[13] or put in another way: "Liminality here breaks, as it were, the cake of custom and enfranchises speculation."[14]

A *normative* liminality culture occurs when an event is so structured that it is expected that people are challenged to ask themselves key questions about their life and future. Initiation rituals for new employment are examples of normative liminality. In the midst of the *liminal* experience, people are confronted with a choice point: either ignore the challenge and seek solace nostalgically in past securities, or become paralyzed by the experience, or intimately embrace the founding mythology of the new status. Liminality is "frequently . . . likened to being in the womb, to invisibility, to darkness . . . to wilderness.[15] . . . [People] have no status, insignia, secular clothing, rank, kinship position, nothing to demarcate them structurally from their fellows."[16] The purpose of the liminal stage is symbolically to strip former statuses to the level of social chaos, or "cultural nakedness." Little wonder that this is a time of significant tension and danger. There is no certainty that people in liminality will choose to move forward. As Turner comments: people in liminality must choose to become as it were "a *tabula rasa,* a blank slate" on which is to be inscribed the knowledge and wisdom of all that pertains "to the new status"[17] that they may or may not embrace.

For example, the archetypal experience of cultural disintegration, liminality, and new life for the Israelites is the Exodus. In order to become the People of God they must leave behind their old orderly culture (i.e., *societas*) as slaves in Egypt, but it is a liminal journey fraught with uncertainties: they bicker and fight among themselves, become lost, turn to pagan gods, nostalgically yearn to return to a utopian past. Yet whenever in the midst of the liminal chaos, while under prophetic leadership, they admit their sinfulness and look to the future in the hope

---

[13]Victor Turner, *The Forest of Symbols: Aspects of Ndembu Ritual* (Ithaca, NY: Cornell University Press, 1967), 105.

[14]Victor Turner, *The Ritual Process: Structure and Anti-Structure* (New York: Aldine, 1969), 106.

[15]Ibid., 95.

[16]Turner, *Forest of Symbols,* 99.

[17]Turner, *Ritual Process,* 103.

that they will experience God's action of newness in their lives (Ex 13:21–22).[18] Under the expert leadership of Moses, who repeatedly articulates God's vision for the people, they discover in their repentance and restored trust in God that there can be a new life beyond all human comprehension: "For thus says the Lord, who created the heavens . . . who formed the earth and made it (he did not create it a chaos, he formed it to be inhabited!). . . . I did not say to the offspring of Jacob, 'Seek me in chaos.' I the Lord speak the truth" (Is 45:18–19). When the Israelites enter the promised land they embrace, however shaky, the identities of a new culture (i.e., *societas*).

Today the abuse crisis has cast the church into the fear-evoking chaos of liminality. The church's hierarchical leaders must choose: either remain paralyzed by the chaos or hide in fundamentalist clericalism or courageously embrace the values and culture of Vatican II, thus refounding the church.

The Babylonian exile is the second powerful liminal experience of journeying for the Israelites. Their culture has been reduced to the primeval chaos from which God had originally delivered them. The pivotal symbols of the national culture—Jerusalem, the monarchy, the temple—to which they had become overly attached are destroyed. Yet if the Israelites faithfully repent, they can break through their shattering grief. Jeremiah foretells signs of the nation's refounding (Jer 1:10). God will initiate a new covenant (Jer 31:31). Even in the exile's darkness significant pastoral creativity emerges, for example, the people learn to pray in small, supportive groups without the presence of the temple. And traditional religious practices are updated in light of the changed situation; for example, circumcision becomes no longer so important as an initiation rite, but rather it develops as a new symbol of cultural identity.[19] The besieging of Jerusalem by King Nebuchadnezzar was external force that broke the original Israelite culture and opened the way to creative refounding.

---

[18]See Walter Brueggemann, *Interpretation and Obedience: From Faithful Reading to Faithful Loving* (Minneapolis: Fortress Press, 1991), 317–18.

[19]See Robert P. Carroll, *From Chaos to Covenant: Uses of Prophecy in the Book of Jeremiah* (London: SCM Press, 1981), 31–58.

Grief-Overload Model

Theoretical Background

Cultures commonly experience cyclic regression to chaos, which is the radical breakdown of order, as a troubling and lengthy prelude to a new creation or cultural integration.[20] Cultures, like individuals, can, however, deny in a variety of ways the creative potential in chaos, and escape into an unreal world.[21] To prevent chaos from undermining their way of life, people often resort to new laws or rules, believing that such authoritative action alone will prevent disintegration. Yet more than laws are required; there must be individual and corporate revitalization from within. Unless this happens the onslaught of chaos is inevitable. Even when chaos emerges, there are people who will refuse to admit its existence. They build walls of denial. A culture cannot remain in the escapist denial stage of chaos indefinitely. The more rigid the defense of an untenable position, the more catastrophic and traumatic the smash when it does come. Institutional cultures in chaos and trauma are not a pretty sight; the atmosphere becomes thick with confusion, tensions, polarizations, scapegoating, and low morale. Eventually, the institutional culture either dies or is led to a new stage of adjustment to a world of change.

If the latter, then the process of adjustment is led by innovative leaders or refounding people, but they can do so only if there are a sufficient number of people who have come to hope in the possibility of the new adjustment. Usually it takes a bitter, protracted experience of the confusion or malaise of chaos before some people

---

[20]See Mircea Eliade, *Myth and Reality* (London: Allen and Unwin, 1964), 187–93, and *The Myth of the Eternal Return or Cosmos and History* (Princeton: Princeton University Press, 1965), *passim*. An example of how chaos can evoke creative thinking and action is evident in Britain's decision to withdraw from the European Union. In the midst of significant political and economic chaos, "some of the fundamental ideas that have underpinned Western governments . . . for decades are being questioned. . . . Some of them are promising; others downright dangerous." "Beneath the Chaos of the Brexit Talks, Big Ideas Are Forming," Leader, *The Economist*, September 29, 2018, 18.

[21]This model significantly adapts Anthony F. C. Wallace's model, "Revitalization Movements," *American Anthropologist* 58, no. 2 (1956): 264–81.

begin to yearn for individual and corporate revitalization under the leadership of inventive persons. Charismatic leaders sense this yearning, articulate it, and call people to face the future by drawing strength from their original creation mythology. Such effective leaders, for example, Winston Churchill,[22] Charles de Gaulle,[23] and Lyndon Johnson,[24] are able to do this with consummate skill.

Some innovative individuals, however, can play on people's fears of the unknown and their desire for an instant experience of order and meaning in their lives. They encourage people to withdraw from the world through membership in fundamentalist secular or religious cults or sects that give an unreal and temporary sense of belonging and self-worth. Some cults romanticize an imagined former golden age; they seek to restore old symbols intact, for example the Lefebvre movement and other restorationist movements in the Catholic Church or the Shi'ite Iranian revolution. Millenarian cults, for example, Nazism, and Soviet communism, offer their followers the assurance of an immediate protection from the threatening world of chaos and the promise of an exclusive peace in the future. This model is now further refined.[25]

Stages of Grief Overload

This grief-overload model (Figure 3.1) is based on two main variables that take into account the emotional aspects of culture change and disintegration: the grieving dynamic and leadership.[26] Loss evokes grief (*Axiom 7,* Chapter 1) and the breakdown of even one aspect of a culture can affect every other aspect (*Axiom*

---

[22]See Andrew Roberts, *Churchill: Walking with Destiny* (London: Allen Lane, 2018). Churchill drew heavily on the heroic founding mythology of Britain when leader in World War II.

[23]See Julian Jackson, *A Certain Idea of France: The Life of Charles de Gaulle* (London: Allen Lane, 2018), 770–77.

[24]President Lyndon Johnson, when he pushed for civil rights in the mid-1960s, kept referring to the focus on human rights for all in the American founding mythology. See Laura Tingle, "Follow the Leader," *Quarterly Essay,* no. 71 (2018): 29–30.

[25]See Gerald A. Arbuckle, *Fundamentalism at Home and Abroad: Analysis and Pastoral Responses* (Collegeville, MN: Liturgical Press, 2017), 73–93.

[26]This model updates the one first published by the author in *The Francis Factor and the People of God: New Life for the Church* (Maryknoll, NY: Orbis Books, 2015), 126–98, and *Fundamentalism,* 62–96.

8, Chapter 1): *"The loneliness of mythlessness is the deepest and least assuageable of all.* Unrelated to the past, unconnected with the future, we hang as if in mid-air."[27] If leaders do not allow mourning rituals, that is, rituals that help the bereaved deal with grief,[28] the grief becomes increasingly cumulative and suffocating. An institution then moves inexorably into deepening cultural chaos, trauma, and impasse, concluding with symptoms of chronic paralysis and/or regressive fundamentalist movements. However, if new and skilled leadership manages what is happening appropriately, creative refounding leaders and movements emerge from the impasse (see Chapter 4).

Figure 3.1 Grief-Overload Model

Stage 1: Cultural Consensus

Stage 2: Consensus Threatened—Initial Unease
    a. enthusiasm
    b. grieving

Stage 3: Chaos—Political Reactions
    a. restorationist emphasis
    b. leadership trust weakens
    c. grieving intensifies

Stage 4: Grief Overload—Cultural Trauma
    a. tipping points
    b. reactions, e.g., shame/denial/paralysis
    c. leadership trust disintegrates

Stage 5: Impasse Options
    a. withdrawal
    b. chronic paralysis
    c. pro-active:
        i. escapist: fundamentalist movements
        ii. conversionist: refounding movements

---

[27]Rollo May, *The Cry of Myth* (New York: Delta, 1991), 99. Italics in original.
[28]See ibid., 61.

In *Stage 1* the mythological status quo is generally accepted by people (cultural consensus), but in *Stage 2* internal or external forces threaten to break up the group's mythological consensus. Some people may initially and enthusiastically enjoy the changes, while others begin to fear for their cultural and personal identity/ security. The latter especially begin to grieve the loss of predictabilities. As unease or stress increases, the reaction by those in power is a move to freeze the changes in legislative action, which is seen in *Stage 3*. Chaos is the radical breakdown of order: uncertainty and anxiety replace a world of predictability for people; leaders begin to panic because they fear they will lose power if further changes occur; they try to restore the previous cultural status quo. But it is too late. The turmoil that follows inevitably creates increasing cultural chaos—the result of poor leadership in conflict with the growing aspirations of people for change.

The insights of Alexis de Tocqueville are relevant here.[29] Reflecting on the power of revolutionary forces, he said that dissatisfaction becomes increasingly evident whenever the conditions that give rise to it cease to be seen as inevitable and the possibility for correcting them arises. In these circumstances the momentum cannot be slowed down, even though some of the changes being introduced in the outpouring of enthusiasm may not be the most prudent. For some seven decades the lid had been firmly kept on Soviet society by a ruthless authoritarian elite, but once it became clear that under Mikhail Gorbachev an alternative system was possible then there was no stopping the onrush of political enthusiasm. The breakup of the Soviet Union into nation-states could not be halted. An attempted coup to stop the breakup failed; no matter what the chaos, the people no longer feared the coup's leaders, who belonged to a former age.[30]

In the stage of the culture breakdown, the people's trust in their leaders weakens (and in the fourth stage this trust disintegrates). Trust is "a relationship between one or more persons, which has elements of openness and honesty, and a willingness to accept

---

[29]See Alexis de Tocqueville, *L'Ancien Regime* (Oxford: Oxford University Press, 1904), 182.

[30]See William Taubman, *Gorbachev: His Life and Times* (London: Simon and Schuster, 2017), 574–619.

others based on the opinion that the other party is both capable and dependable."[31] Charles Feltman describes trust as "choosing to risk making something you value vulnerable to another person's actions." And distrust is deciding that "what is important to me is not safe with this person in this situation (or any situation)."[32] No organizational culture, including the church, can maintain morale if trust in its leaders disintegrates. A community's culture is said to be trusting when there is a kind of collective judgment that the people involved will act with honesty in negotiations, and make "a good faith effort to behave in accordance with [their] commitments."[33] Where trust exists, people feel valued, levels of job satisfaction are increased.[34] When trust crumbles, fear takes its place. Katherine Hawley perceptively highlights the central-ity of trust in the maintenance of any community, the church included: "Trust is at the centre of a whole web of concepts: reliability, predictability, expectation, cooperation, goodwill, and—on the dark side—distrust, insincerity, conspiracy, betrayal, and incompetence."[35] When basic trust of members of a group is broken, it is in danger of becoming perverted and replaced by the blind or unquestioning trust characteristic of fundamentalist movements.[36]

Anthropologically a culture is held together, as noted already, by myths, that is, stories that people tell one another (see *Axioms 3* and *4,* Chapter 1). There are always people in cultures who are

---

[31]Rocky J. Dwyer, "Benchmarking as a Process for Demonstrating Organi-zational Trustworthiness?" *Management Decision* 46, no. 8 (2008): 1211–12.

[32]Charles Feltman cited by Brene Brown, *Braving the Wilderness: The Quest for True Belonging and the Courage to Stand Alone* (London: Vermilion, 2017), 38.

[33]Dwyer, "Benchmarking as a Process," 1212. An interesting example of what happens when trust in government breaks down comes from the contemporary United States. In a recent Pew poll only 19 percent of Americans feel they can trust the government always or most of the time. "This erosion of trust eventu-ally will limit the effectiveness of American government; indeed, in many ways it already has." Tyler Cowen, *The Complacent Class: The Self-Defeating Quest for the American Dream* (New York: St. Martin's Press, 2017), 191.

[34]See John Rodwell, Andrew Noblet, Defne Demir, and Peter Steane, "The Impact of the Work Conditions of Allied Health Professionals on Satisfaction, Commitment and Psychological Distress," *Health Care Management Review* 34, no. 3 (2009): 205–93.

[35]Katherine Hawley, *Trust* (Oxford: Oxford University Press, 2012), 3.

[36]See Vamik Volkan, *Blind Trust: Large Groups and Their Leaders in Times of Crisis and Terror* (Charlottesville: Pitchstone, 2004), 14.

officially or unofficially appointed to guard the culture's founding stories and to retell them to generation after generation. As long as they authentically do this, the people will trust them, but if they fail to do so then distrust breaks out; people feel betrayed. For example, many Americans feel betrayed and "justifiably frightened by the tide of racism, anti-Semitism and xenophobia that has swept the country since the election of Donald Trump [as president], whose campaign stoked these views."[37] Since such views run contrary to the values they believe are inherent in the nation's founding story, they no longer trust him.

In *Stage 4* internal or external events become tipping points that push the institution from chaos into emotional overload, which is cultural trauma. People become increasingly disillusioned when the authoritative commands fail to fulfill their hopes and all the cultural and personal disintegration symptoms of chaos further intensify,[38] for example, anger, feeling overwhelmingly shamed in the presence of outsiders, rage, a sense of drifting without purpose, fear, depression, loneliness, paralysis or go-it-alone individualism, scapegoating, even denial that there are problems at all. Cultural order totally disintegrates. People as individuals and their cultures crushingly grieve the loss of the familiar; they unsuccessfully stumble painfully and blindly to find reference points for a new identity or the restoration of the old. As William Shakespeare writes: "Give sorrow words: the grief that does not speak Whispers the o'er-fraught heart, and bids it break."[39] Leaders lose all credibility.

The resulting personal and group upheaval is called *cultural trauma*, yet the very naming of this "disease" can ridicule the immensity of the human tragedy involved. Gorbachev offered

---

[37]Editorial, "Trump Rages, at the Wrong Target," *Times Digest*, November 22, 2016.

[38]From a purely human perspective "chaos" can be a blessing. Management expert Tom Peters writes: "The true objective is to take the chaos as given and learn to thrive on it. The winners of tomorrow will deal proactively with chaos. . . . Chaos and uncertainty are . . . opportunities for the wise." Tom Peters, *Thriving on Chaos: Handbook for a Management Revolution* (New York: Alfred A. Knopf, 1987), xi–xii. Earlier, in 1918, Henry Adams had claimed that "chaos often breeds life, when order breeds habit." Cited by Frederick J. Ruf, *The Creation of Chaos* (Albany: State University of New York Press, 1991), 11.

[39]William Shakespeare, *Macbeth*, IV.iii.209.

dramatic beneficial legislative changes to produce not just personal freedoms but also socioeconomic growth. But legislation alone, without the radical inner conversion of the population, could produce no results. Yet his inability to effect change quickly became a significant tipping point for the people into the cultural trauma that swept him and his successor, Boris Yeltsin, from power. *Trauma* medically is "an objective force that deprives a subject of some part of [*sic*] his normal sovereignty."[40] Sociologist Jürgen Habermas writes that social institutions can also experience trauma which dramatically threatens their identity and the identities of their members.[41] Arnon Bentovim describes psychological trauma: "An event that . . . ruptures the protective layer surrounding the mind with . . . long-lasting consequences for psychic well-being. Helplessness overwhelms, mastery is undermined, defences fail, there is a sense of failure of protection . . . acute mental pain as the memory of the event intrudes and replays itself repeatedly."[42]

Cultural trauma, however, goes beyond individuals and institutions to embrace directly an entire culture.[43] Sociologist Neil Smelser defines cultural trauma as "an invasive and overwhelming event that is believed to undermine or overwhelm one or several ingredients of a culture or the culture as a whole."[44] The founding mythology that emotionally and normatively binds the culture together giving people a sense of collective identity ceases to operate. With their culture shattered, people lose their established sense of belonging. They feel stunned and mythologically rudderless, "subjected to a horrendous event that leaves indelible

---

[40]Jürgen Habermas, *Legitimation Crisis* (Boston: Beacon Press, 1975), 3. See also *Listening to Trauma: Conversations with Leaders in the Theory and Treatment of Catastrophic Experience*, ed. Cathy Caruth (Baltimore: Johns Hopkins University Press, 2014).

[41]See Caruth, *Listening to Trauma*, 1–3.

[42]Arnon Bentovim, *Trauma-Organized Systems: Physical and Sexual Abuse in Families* (London: Karnac, 1992), 24.

[43]See Ron Eyerman, "Cultural Trauma: Emotion and Narration," in *The Oxford Handbook of Cultural Sociology*, ed. Jeffrey Alexander et al. (Oxford: Oxford University Press, 2012), 564–82.

[44]Neil Smelser, "Psychological and Cultural Trauma," in *Cultural Trauma and Collective Behavior*, ed. Jeffrey Alexander et al. (Berkeley: University of California Press, 2004), 38.

[paralysing] marks upon their group consciousness."[45] There is a mythological vacuum; people are no longer able to find an adequate mythological answer to the strains of living.

Stage 5 impasse options can take several forms, such as (1) withdrawal from an institution; (2) chronic paralysis, with traditional leaders at a complete loss to know how to react; or (3) pro-active movements which take the form of *fundamentalist* (escapist) or *conversionist* activities, e.g., refounding movements. Fundamentalists simplistically yearn to return to a comforting utopian past, purified of dangerous ideas and practices.[46] The meaning of refounding will be explained later in this chapter.

Grief-Overload Model Application to Church

Historical Background

The grief-overload model can be applied stage by stage to the global church.[47] The church is in a paralyzing state of unspoken grief, chaos, and trauma. Its hierarchy, priests, and religious—finally, as a consequence of the overwhelmingly tragic findings of the sexual scandals and cover-up—have largely been discredited and demoralized. Lay people feel betrayed, their trust in their religious leaders destroyed. Trust in the church's ministerial leadership has been significantly destroyed. Recall the truism: *Trust crumbles whenever people fail to be transparently consistent in their behavior.* The pattern throughout has been to avoid scandal for the church. Yet justified anger and compassion for the survivors of sexual abuse and cover-ups, but also an ever-increasing sense of shame, have become the daily part of a grieving church.

Vatican II had challenged the church to be ever reforming itself:

---

[45]Jeffrey C. Alexander, "Toward a Theory of Cultural Trauma," in *Cultural Trauma and Collective Behavior,* 1.

[46]For an explanation of fundamentalist movement, see Gerald A. Arbuckle, *Fundamentalism at Home and Abroad: Analysis and Pastoral Responses* (Collegeville, MN: Liturgical Press, 2017), 73–93.

[47]This is an updating of the model first presented in Gerald A. Arbuckle, *The Francis Factor and the People of God: New Life for the Church* (Maryknoll, NY: Orbis Books, 2015), 161–92.

Christ summons the Church, as she goes on her pilgrim way, to the continual reformation of which she always has need, insofar as she is an institution of men and women here on earth. Therefore, if the influence of events of the times has led to deficiencies of conduct, in Church discipline . . . these should be appropriately rectified at the proper moment.[48]

Yet for fifty years the hierarchical church has hidden major governance deficiencies. Spiritual renewal had been encouraged, but not structural reforms. Hierarchical officials would remain firmly in place. The final tipping point into grief overload—cultural trauma—has come with the revelations mainly by outsiders of the cover-ups of the sexual abuse of minors. The church now is glaringly seen to lack the transparency and accountability demanded by the council, a church "more concerned with protecting the reputation of the institution and the clerical profession than in safeguarding real or potential child victims."[49]

Many continue to leave the church in disgust. In Australia it is estimated that the numbers of "disidentifying Catholics" from 2001 to 2011 would amount to just over 200,000 across all age groups above the age of 15.[50] Disidentifying means Australians who used to identify themselves as Catholics, but who no longer do so. More than half of these were between ages 20 and 29 in 2011, but there are signs of disidentification in all age groups, even among the elderly. Robert Dixon estimated that about 60,000 young Catholics ages 15 to 24 did not identify themselves as Catholics in 2001. His estimates "for the period from 2001 to 2011 suggest that the figure for the same age group has risen to about 72,000 or, in other words, that the rate of disidentification has accelerated. It appears that, across all age groups, more than 20,000 Australians *every year* are ceasing to identify themselves as Catholics."[51]

---

[48] "Decree on Ecumenism" (*Unitatis Redintegratio*), in *Documents of Vatican II*, ed. Walter M. Abbott (London: Geoffrey Chapman, 1966), para. 6.

[49] Philip Jenkins, *Pedophiles and Priests: Anatomy of a Contemporary Crisis* (Oxford: Oxford University Press, 1996), 3–4.

[50] The population of Australia is 25 million; the Catholic population is approximately 5 million.

[51] Robert Dixon and Stephen Reid, "The Contemporary Catholic Community: A

In the United States "Catholicism has suffered the greatest net loss in the process of religious change. Many people who leave the Catholic Church do so for religious reasons. . . . For instance, the most common reason for leaving Catholicism cited by former Catholics who have become Protestant is that their spiritual needs were not being met (71 percent). One in ten American adults is a former Catholic."[52] Sociologist Peter McDonough comments: "Many Catholics pick and choose what to accept and reject in the church, when they do not simply opt out and quit. We are in the realm of a nearly deinstitutionalized spirituality. . . . The process of departure and decommitment feels like a safety valve as much as resistance. The net outcome of the drain in membership appears to be a slightly greater residue of conservatism among those who stay on."[53]

Stages of Grief Overload in the Church

Stage 1: Cultural Consensus—Pre–Vatican II
Prior to Vatican II, there was remarkable global cultural consensus among Catholics. Recall that the dominant symbol in the pre–Vatican II church was a fortress, the perfect society, built and constantly reinforced to withstand the attacks of the enemies: Protestants, heretics, and the evils of the Enlightenment. The boundaries of the fortress were sharply marked out and effectively patrolled lest people attempted to break in or out (see Chapter 2).

Stage 2: Consensus Threatened—Initial Unease (1965–67+)
Vatican II significantly changed the theological mythology of the church, creating both enthusiasm among those who yearned for a more Gospel-based church and the beginning of grieving among Catholics who either became disturbed by the changes or felt they were not being implemented with greater speed. When change became possible through the council, the explosion of expectations and anxiety created counterreactions that startled

---

View from the 2011 Census," *Australasian Catholic Record* 90, no. 2 (2013): 145.

[52]The Pew Research Center survey "Faith in Flux": www.pwforum. org/2009/04/27/faith-in-flux.

[53]Peter McDonough, *The Catholic Labyrinth: Power, Apathy, and a Passion for Reform in the American Church* (New York: Oxford University Press, 2013), 289.

Figure 3.2. Grief Overload in the Church

Stage 1: Cultural Consensus

Stage 2: Consensus Threatened—Initial Unease
(1965–67+)
a. enthusiasm
b. initial grieving

Stage 3: Chaos—Political Reactions: (1967+)
a. restorationist emphasis
b. grieving intensifies
c. leadership trust weakens

Stage 4: Grief Overload—Cultural Trauma (1990+)
a. tipping points
i. liturgical impositions
ii. Vatican State dysfunctionality, e.g.,
bank scandal
iii. abuse cover-up crises
b. reactions, e.g., shame/denial/paralysis
c. leadership trust disintegrates

Stage 5: Impasse Options (2000+)
a. withdrawal
b. chronic paralysis
c. pro-active
i. escapist: fundamentalist movements
e.g., restorationism/clericalism
ii. conversionist: refounding movements

all with their intensity and ferocity. It did not help that Vatican II exposed the church to a world which was itself in turmoil—the 1960s expressive cultural revolution. The open polarizations and feuding and the publicity given to priests and religious who departed their ministries left millions of Catholics aware that the council was not an academic concept, but a human drama affecting people's hearts and lives.

Stage 3: Chaos—Political Reactions (1967+)

Rome increasingly reacted in a restorationist manner, causing increasing grief to devoted followers of Vatican II. The curia "tended once more to take over the role of the Church's central government, whereas its proper function is to be a papal instrument."[54] The role of episcopal conferences and the bishops' synods and the collegial development of particular local churches became significantly restricted. The revised Code of Canon Law was promulgated in 1983 and, as Father Ladislas Orsy, SJ, notes, "it offers little or no help for [the] evolution [of particular churches] and we are the poorer for it."[55] The code stresses the power to govern in the church is restricted to those in orders, so that lay women and men do not share this power but must cooperate with the ordained (see Chapter 5). Here was a chance to move the church forward, and the code failed to do so because historically lay people have at times exercised the power to govern and "did participate in important decision-making processes, including synods and Council."[56] In the 1985 Extraordinary Synod called to assess the role of Vatican II, the People of God was removed as the central paradigm in understanding the church. Responsible dissent became increasingly forbidden by Rome. Secrecy shrouded the investigation of academics who questioned the restorationist moves being led by Rome. Moral theologian Father Bernhard Häring, CSSR, sadly wrote in 1990:

> This noisy [restorationist] minority, plagued by neurosis and fear, still lives intellectually and emotionally with the old image of the Church as not just the possessor but the sole possessor of all truths. . . . There is an atmosphere of mutual mistrust: delation by informers, striving for official recognition, and conformity are rewarded. . . . [The Holy Office] wants to use the sanctions of punishment and oaths of absolute loyalty to force the recognition of its monopoly

---

[54]John Wilkins, "Can the Papacy Change?" *The Tablet*, November 7, 1998, 1467.

[55]Ladislas Orsy, "The Revision of Canon Law," in *Modern Catholicism: Vatican II and After*, ed. Adrian Hastings (London: SPCK, 1991), 212.

[56]Ibid. This point is further explained in Chapter 5.

rights in all questions of faith and morals, even as regards non-infallible statements.[57]

Stage 4: Grief Overload—Cultural Trauma (1990+)

As the gap between Vatican II rhetoric and reality widened, the People of God began experiencing more and more the symptoms of accumulated and unarticulated grief, for example, disillusionment, anger, and sadness. Yet denial and suppression of this grief only intensified the despondency and rage in people's hearts. Youthful energy for the mission of Christ became progressively suffocated. Brendan Ryan in 1995 wrote of the mounting frustrations of the laity in Ireland, though he could have been writing of many parts of the church anywhere in the world:

> The church in particular seems to believe it has to give an appearance of absolute unanimity on every issue. . . . The frustration this generates for church members is indescribable. . . . People felt alienated and excluded; they knew that no-one really listened to them and that their active involvement in the church, so much talked about, really meant that more people should become lay readers, distribute communion, and help out with voluntary organisations. . . . Most church-going Catholics have given up on the bishops, who blissfully confuse apathy with acceptance.[58]

The tipping points that evoked grief overload and cultural trauma came as a consequence of several events. The document *Liturgiam Authenticam* (2001) further centralized authority in liturgical matters, contrary to Vatican II's call to leave the reform of liturgy to local bishops. This was followed by the imposition of the frequently unintelligible English translation of the Roman Missal that also maintained its exclusive language. Rome stubbornly refused to listen to widespread complaints from the pews and concerned clergy. These events illustrate the relevance of Eric

---

[57]Bernhard Häring, "The Church I Want," *The Tablet*, July 28, 1990, 944.

[58]Brendan Ryan, *Keeping Us in the Dark: Censorship and Freedom of Information in Ireland* (Dublin: Gill and Macmillan, 1995), 139–40.

Uslaner's description of corruption (see *Axiom 10*, Chapter 1), namely that it "stems from inequality and reinforces it."[59] Rome could ignore the voices of the People of God because the latter had no position power to object, despite the fact that Vatican II had acknowledged their baptismal right to do so (see Chapter 6 for further explanation). Even conservative critic George Weigel could protest that "the People of God are treated as if they were cattle, not sheep to be nourished and shepherded."[60]

John Thavis described in 2013 the bureaucratic dysfunctionality in the Roman Curia:[61] "[A] patchwork of departments, communities and individuals, all loosely bound by a sense of mission but without comprehensive management or rigorous oversight . . . where each agency of the Roman Curia jealously guards its turf, where the little guys and big shots may work at cross-purposes and where slipups and misunderstandings are common."[62] Then came the revelations of the Roman Curia's administrative dysfunctionality in the Vatican Bank scandal.[63]

Then the most catastrophic tipping point of all—the ongoing disclosures of the cover-up of sexual abuse of minors by clergy and religious. Shame and feelings of powerlessness engulf the church. We had been cast down from seemingly "unassailable heights" (Ps 30:6) of religious power and grandeur—all in the space of a short period of time. The People of God hear story after story of victims traumatized by the abuse by clergy and religious and not infrequently made to "feel responsible for inappropriate sexual behavior that is by definition not their fault."[64]

---

[59]Eric Uslaner, *The Historical Roots of Corruption* (Cambridge: Cambridge University Press, 2017), 6.

[60]George Weigel, *Evangelical Catholicism: Deep Reform in the 21st-Century Church* (New York: Basic Books, 2013), 251.

[61]The bishops of New Zealand, in their address to the pope in 1998, reflected the ongoing frustration of many episcopal conferences: "Within the household of the Catholic Church itself, Dicasteries [i.e., Curia] of the Holy See occasionally make norms which impinge on the ministry of bishops with little or no consultation of the episcopate as such. This seems inconsistent." Bishop Peter J. Cullinane, "A Time to Speak Out," *The Tablet*, November 22, 1998, 1589.

[62]John Thavis, *The Vatican Diaries* (London: Penguin, 2013), 5.

[63]See "Vatican Scandals: Muck in the Tiber," *The Economist*, July 6, 2013, 56.

[64]Elizabeth Horst, *Recovering the Lost Self: Shame-Healing for Victims of Clergy Sexual Abuse* (Collegeville, MN: Liturgical Press, 1998), 22.

Stage 5: Impasse Options (2000+)

Reactions to this trauma have led either to further massive departures, chronic paralysis, or proactive efforts: escapism into fundamentalist or conversionist/refounding movements. Given the breakdown of the church's existing culture, it is not surprising that Catholic fundamentalist movements resulted, for example, traditionalist/schismatic; conservative/nonseparatist.[65] Rome, particularly the Roman Curia, in an effort to control what was happening, increasingly sided prior to the election of Pope Francis with conservative fundamentalists.

William Dyer's insight is correct: in cultures of the *strong group/strong grid* type whose mythologies vigorously and defensively resist change, only when there is a major crisis, externally catalyzed, and a change to appropriate leadership almost simultaneously, is it possible to have significant cultural change. Such is the case of the Catholic Church, whose culture has battled against substantial change for centuries. The church's history of cultural cover-ups has finally been exposed by external forces. The church is traumatized. Thus, if the impasse in the church is to be positively resolved, leaders with refounding qualities, for example, Pope Francis, are now required, particularly at the hierarchical level, to move the church forward. These leaders will be so inspired by the original founding experience of the church by Jesus Christ that they will collaboratively shape a new culture adapted to contemporary circumstances. The following chapter is devoted to identifying the type of leadership needed to mold a new, vibrant institutional culture out of the contemporary chaos/trauma in the church, a culture that not only protects innocent children and vulnerable adults but yearns to extend God's love and justice to all.

Summary

- In times of chaos/trauma people lose a sense of control in their lives; it is a dangerous state of ambiguity, instability, conflict, and high stress.

---

[65]For an explanation of these fundamentalist expressions in the church and their growing criticism of the reforms of Pope Francis see Arbuckle, *Fundamentalism at Home and Abroad*, 97–123.

- There are two significant catalysts of the chaos/trauma in the church, one *internal* to the church itself, namely the consequences of the impact of Vatican II and often inadequate hierarchical leadership; the second, *external*, namely the impact on the People of God of the expressive revolution of the 1960s, and the ongoing revelations of global sexual abuse and cover-up scandals.
- The culture of the church has become so affected by the chaos/trauma experience that the People of God feel overwhelmed with unarticulated grief: angry, paralyzed, shamed, and leaderless.
- Yet, paradoxically, the public revelation of the scandals by the media, government inquiries, and the courts are able to do what efforts at internal renewal have been unable to achieve—they are forcing the church to admit institutional evil in its midst.
- If the impasse is to be positively resolved, leaders with refounding qualities are required. They will be so inspired by the original founding experience of the church by Jesus Christ that they will collaboratively begin to shape a new culture adapted to contemporary circumstances. Pope Francis is setting the example for this. The theme of refounding the church will be explained further in the following chapter.

4

Leadership for Refounding
the Church

Taming [the] chaos . . . requires a new breed of leaders at
every level.
—Thomas H. Lee, "Turning Doctors into Leaders"

Leadership and culture management are so central to understanding organizations and making them effective that
we cannot afford to be complacent about them. . . . Culture
is created . . . embedded and strengthened by leaders.
—Edgar H. Schein, *Organizational Culture*
and Leadership

It is from chaos that God created and re-creates. So our
situation does not call for a restoration. . . . The solution
cannot be found in going back, but in refounding.
—John M. Lozano, *New Theology Review*

This chapter explains that:
- Leaders shape and embed an institution's culture.
- The church must refocus on Christ's mission.
- Reform requires refounding leaders.

Incompetent leadership fosters dysfunctional institutional
cultures and obstructs appropriate cultural changes.[1] Tragically,

---

[1]For example, see T. Scott, R. Mannion, H. Davies, and M. Marshall, "Implementing Culture Change in Health Care: Theory and Practice," *International
Journal for Quality in Health Care* 15, no. 2 (2003): 111–18; R. Mannion, H.

poor leadership in the Catholic Church has been the dominant factor in the development and maintenance of a global culture of sexual abuse and cover-up.[2]

The purpose of this chapter, therefore, is to clarify the type of leadership required in the church today, but we immediately face a problem: the definition of leadership, like "culture," is highly contested and there are hundreds of new books on sale daily. Google cites "122 million references to leadership and 35.6 million to public leadership."[3] There are more than 1,500 definitions[4] with even more books on the nature and art of leadership. These books come with many different phrases about leadership such as: "situational leadership,"[5] "hands-on, value-driven,"[6] "heroes of innovation," "rites and rituals of leaders in corporate cultures,"[7] "intrapreneurs,"[8] "transformative and transactional leaders,"[9] "bottom-up leadership,"[10] and "servant leadership."[11]

Servant Leadership

Of course, the theme of "servant leadership" has deep roots in Christian tradition: "For the Son of Man came not to be served but

Davies, and M. Marshall, "Cultural Characteristics of 'High' and 'Low' Performing Hospitals," *Journal of Health Organization and Management* 19, no. 6 (2005): 431–39.

[2]For example, *Royal Commission into Institutional Responses to Child Sexual Abuse: Preface and Executive Summary* (Barton, ACT: Commonwealth of Australia, 2017), 61–63.

[3]Jean Hartley and John Benington, *Leadership for Healthcare* (Bristol, UK: Policy Press, 2010), 3.

[4]See Paul Parkin, *Managing Change in Healthcare: Using Action Research* (London: Sage, 2009), 77.

[5]See Paul Hersey and Ken Blanchard, *Management of Organizational Behavior: Utilizing Human Resources* (Englewood Cliffs, NJ: Prentice-Hall, 1982).

[6]See Tom J. Peters and Robert H. Waterman, *In Search of Excellence: Lessons from America's Best-Run Companies* (New York: Harper & Row, 1982).

[7]See Terrence E. Deal and Allan A. Kennedy, *Corporate Cultures: The Rites and Rituals of Corporate Life* (Reading, MA: Addison-Wesley, 1982).

[8]See Gifford Pinchot, *Intrapreneuring* (New York: Harper & Row, 1985).

[9]See James M. Burns, *Leadership* (New York: Harper Torch, 1978), 149–92.

[10]See "The Shackled Boss," *The Economist*, January 21, 2012, 68.

[11]For development of this model, see Robert K. Greenleaf, *Servant Leadership: A Journey into the Nature of Legitimate Power and Greatness* (New York: Paulist, 1977); Larry C. Spears, ed., *The Power of Servant Leadership: Essays by Robert K. Greenleaf* (San Francisco: Berrett-Koehler, 1998).

to serve, and to give his life as a ransom for many" (Mk 10:45). When the disciples heard that the mother of fellow disciples James and John wanted them to hold key roles in Jesus' coming kingdom they were furious. Jesus reacted by contrasting the leadership style of secular rulers against the style of those called to lead his kingdom: "You know that the rulers of the Gentiles lord it over them, and their great ones are tyrants over them. It will not be so among you; but whoever wishes to be first among you must be your servant, and whoever wishes to be first among you must be your slave" (Mt: 20:25–27). Those who serve must depend on an interior response in those they call to follow. Not coercion, but followership based on the heart commitment; this call to inner conversion is far more challenging to achieve than external behavioral conformity.[12] But the apostles were slow learners. During the Last Supper Jesus reiterates that authority among his followers must be one of service for the building up of faith community: "For who is the greater, the one is at the table or the one serves? Is it not the one at the table? But I am among you as one who serves" (Lk 22:27).

The apostles finally understand. Later in their own teaching they repeat the theme, that authority is to be synonymous with service—the service of listening and persuasion, not exploitation on account of one's status: "Do not lord it over those in your charge, but be an example to your flock" (1 Pet 5:3). It is St. Paul who spells out that only through love can we begin to plumb the astonishing demands that Christian dialogue commits us to: "Love is patient; love is kind; love is not envious or boastful or arrogant or rude. It does not insist on its own way; it is not irritable or resentful; it does not rejoice in wrongdoing, but rejoices in the truth. It bears all things, hopes all things, endures all things" (1 Cor 13:4–7). A leader who dares to be resentful or bullying or covers up the truth is not acting in a Christian way!

All behavior is to be modeled on that of Christ the Servant. It is the purpose that is crucial: the building up of the Christian community, the primary means being listening, example, and persuasion. Speaking of the role of bishops, Vatican II stresses their

---

[12]See Lawrence O. Richards and Clyde Hoeldtke, *A Theology of Church Leadership* (Grand Rapids, MI: Zondervan, 1980), 103–12.

listening or servant quality, saying that they are to "govern the particular Churches assigned to them by their counsels, exhortations and example, but over and above that also by the authority and sacred power which indeed they exercise exclusively for the spiritual development of their flock in truth and holiness, keeping in mind that he who is greater should become as the lesser, and he who is the leader as the servant (cf. Lk 22:26–27)."[13] Pope St. Paul VI takes up the council's repeated emphasis on dialogue as a quality of servant leadership: "Before speaking we must take great care to listen not only to what people say but more especially to what they have in their hearts to say. Only then will we understand them and respect them, and even, as far as possible, agree with them."[14]

From the mass of current literature on leadership and in light of the findings of the previous chapters, what do leaders in the church need to know, by way of summary, before attempting institutional cultural change?

- Life without change is impossible. If institutions are to survive and flourish they require leaders with the appropriate qualities: "The problem for leaders today is that the world changes so quickly, the future becomes far less predictable, the options become exponentially increased, and the way we need to think about those options shifts."[15]
- Leaders must be sensitive to the power of culture (see Chapters 1 and 3): "90 percent of all desired organizational change initiatives fail because organizational culture is not sufficiently taken into account."[16]
- Leaders need to understand the institutional implications of the fact that people, as they belong to cultures, tend more to block creativity and change; they generally prefer

---

[13]"Dogmatic Constitution on the Church" (*Lumen Gentium*), in *Documents of Vatican II*, ed. Austin P. Flannery (Grand Rapids, MI: Eerdmans, 1975), para. 27.

[14]Paul VI, Encyclical: "Paths of the Church" (*Ecclesiam Suam*), in *The Papal Encyclicals: 1958–1981* (Raleigh, NC: Pierian Press, 1966), 153.

[15]Jennifer Garvey Berger and Keith Johnston, *Simple Habits for Complex Times: Powerful Practices for Leaders* (Stanford: Stanford University Press, 2015), 8.

[16]Rasmus Hougaard and Jacqueline Carter, *The Mind of the Leader* (Boston: Harvard Business Review Press, 2018), 161.

the familiarity of order, not the unpredictability of change (see *Axiom 1*, Chapter 1); commonly in existing institutions "personnel are selected and trained to do what was done in the past in the manner in which it was done in the past."[17]

- An authentic leader aims collaboratively to shape and communicate a task-oriented mission and vision which gives focus to the endeavors of others; if the leader fails to do this and to create suitable strategies and accountability structures, the group and their culture become confused, de-energized, and prone to chaos.

- The aims of leadership and management differ. The principal duty of a manager is to avert the complexity of a contemporary organizational culture drifting into total chaos/trauma. A manager's mandate is to minimize risk, but change requires a new system and culture, which in turn necessitates taking risks under wise leadership. Warren Bennis comments: "The manager maintains; the leader develops. . . . The manager relies on control; the leader inspires trust. . . . The manager has his [*sic*] eye on the bottom line; the leader has his eye on the horizon."[18] Understood in this way, we need both leadership and management. Again, Stephen Covey wrote: "Management is doing things right; leadership is doing the right things. Management is efficiency in climbing the ladder of success; leadership determines which ladder is leaning against the right wall."[19]

- Structural change is impossible unless leaders and their followers are committed to the new mythology that inspires the change. That is, structural change alone will not lead to cultural change (see Chapter 6).

- People will be inspired to act if leaders empower them by encouraging their collaboration and by fostering trust

---

[17]Richard Hall, *Organizations: Structures, Processes, and Outcomes*, 6th ed. (Englewood Cliffs, NJ: Prentice Hall, 1972), 190–91.

[18]Warren Bennis, *On Becoming a Leader* (Reading, MA: Addison-Wesley, 1989), 45.

[19]Stephen Covey, *The Seven Habits of Highly Effective People: Powerful Lessons in Personal Change* (New York: Simon & Schuster, 1990), 101.

and respect for their human dignity; this will involve the recognition by leaders of people's talents and the celebration of their achievements.[20]

- Since "Lack of accountability is a fatal flaw of leadership,"[21] leaders must learn how to call people to be accountable for their behavior according to the mission, vision, and strategies they have helped to articulate (see *Action Plans 7* and *8*, Chapter 6).

- Skills for managing cultural resistance to change extend along a continuum from the more *democratic participation*, that is, encouraging people to have some part in shaping the change; through *modeling the change*, that is, demonstrating how change occurs through one's own actions or through explaining to people models of it actually operating elsewhere; *persuasion*, by illustrating the benefits of change; *negotiation*, for example, discovering ways that would accommodate the needs or concerns of those who resist change so that a compromise is reached; to *using the power of one's position to impose the change*, which is not the ideal, but at times this may be necessary.[22]

- Given these qualities a satisfactory working definition of a leader is: *A leader is one who can collaboratively formulate a mission and vision and devise practical methods to achieve these.* It is impossible for one leader, particularly in the contemporary turmoil of the church, to lead effectively alone. This is where teamwork is so crucial in developing and maintaining a proactive culture.[23] Some people will excel in management; others at empowering. But the two most difficult functions for leadership in the church are those of conserving (that is, keeping in touch with the

---

[20]See James M. Kouzes and Barry Z. Posner, *The Leadership Challenge* (San Francisco: Jossey-Bass, 1990), 279–80.

[21]John H. Zenger and Joseph Folkman, *The Handbook for Leaders: 24 Lessons of Extraordinary Leadership* (Maidenhead: McGraw-Hill, 2007), cited by Brian Dive, *The Accountable Leader: Developing Effective Leadership through Managerial Accountability* (London/Philadelphia: Kogan Page, 2008), 50.

[22]See Trudy Upton and Bernard Brooks, *Managing Change in the NHS* (London: Kegan Page, 1995), 101–7; Parkin, *Managing Change in Healthcare*, 155–205.

[23]See Peter Koestenbaum, *Leadership: The Inner Side of Greatness* (San Francisco: Jossey-Bass, 1991), 179–83, 225–26.

founding story) and proacting (that is, being prophetic). That is, remaining in touch with the person and mission of Jesus Christ and how it must be lived in our contemporary society is the most testing task of leadership in the church (see *Action Plan 6*, Chapter 6). Our next step in further clarifying the type of leadership required in the church is to identify the correct leadership style needed.

Leadership Styles

In the Western world three philosophical and sociological movements particularly affect the way people define leadership: modernity, postmodernity, and paramodernity.

In *modernity*, organizations are noted for their order and predictability. Leaders must act rationally because feelings will interfere with rational planning and order. Modernity is a world for men and hierarchical power structures; women are assumed to be too emotional, and it is feared that they will endanger orderly planning and action. In addition to this patriarchy, Social Darwinism is a further dominant influence in modernity and leadership. Individuals and societies are ordained by nature to compete for survival; only the strong will continue, and the weak will die out. Weak individuals and societies must not be provided with help to survive because this would hinder the strong from their just right to keep progressing forward. Market capitalism is founded on the mythology of modernity. It would reduce every aspect of human life to a market transaction: "The thirst for power and possessions knows no limits [in modernity]. In this system, which tends to devour everything which stands in the way of increased profits, whatever is fragile, like the environment, is defenseless before the interests of a deified market, which become the only rule."[24]

Postmodernity[25] rejects the orderliness and assured confidence

---

[24]Pope Francis, "The Joy of the Gospel" (*Evangelii Gaudium*) (Strathfield: St. Pauls Publications, 2013), para. 56.

[25]"Postmodernity" is a highly contested term. See Anthony Giddens, *The Consequences of Modernity* (Cambridge: Polity Press, 1990); Ernest Gellner, *Postmodernism, Reason and Religion* (London: Routledge, 1992), 22; Gerald A.

of modernity. Although postmodern mythology may reject patriarchy and the social elitism of modernity, it contains destructive qualities, such as cynicism, pragmatism, narcissism, and skepticism. It is useless to turn to history for help in understanding the meaning of life because it provides people with a fabricated sense of security or identity as well as a method of achieving power to dominate others. Universal values like compassion, equity, and justice are simply hollow words with no possibility of existence. Human relations are fragmentary and unstable; the self alone has existence, but the real self can never be known. Little wonder that despair is a consequence. In brief, this is a bleak view of humanity, society, and leadership.

Paramodernity is a style of leadership that reacts against the unfounded optimism and rationality of modernity, on the one hand, and, on the other, to the postmodern gloomy and self-destructive view of life. Values such as the need to respect the environment, dialogue, collaboration, compassion, and justice are essential for a society that wishes to respect the innate dignity of the human person. Paramodern leaders recognize that in-depth cultural change cannot occur unless people's rights and feelings are effectively acknowledged, their need to be listened to and heard.[26] Instead of a robot-like universe depicted by the culture of modernity, the world is viewed in terms of relationships between living organisms that are essentially cooperative and characterized by coexistence and interdependence. A change in one relationship affects all others to some degree or other (see *Axiom 8*, Chapter 1).[27] Paramodern leaders also acknowledge that cultural change is never smooth. It is lurching and often erratic; however, when cultural chaos occurs, it can become the launching pad from which new cultures can emerge (see Chapter 3).

Arbuckle, *Violence, Society, and the Church: A Cultural Critique* (Collegeville, MN: Liturgical Press, 2004), 154–62.

[26]Jeanie D. Duck, "Managing Change: The Art of Balancing," in *Harvard Business Review on Change* (Boston: Harvard Business Review, 1996), 66.

[27]For further explanation of these styles, see Gerald A. Arbuckle, *Humanizing Healthcare Reforms* (London/Philadelphia: Jessica Kingsley, 2013), 161–66. Rasmus Hougaard and Jacqueline Carter describe qualities of paramodern leaders and organizational cultures in *The Mind of the Leader* (Boston: Harvard Business Review Press, 2018).

Given these different styles of leadership, which one is required in the church today? If the wrong style is chosen, the chaos/trauma will unnecessarily intensify. Certainly, sensitivity to cultural realities is a must. Just think of the cultural confusion, turmoil, and resistance that the removal of a simple plastic shopping bag caused local shoppers (see *Axiom 5,* Chapter 1). The management failed to realize this, and their cultural insensitivity further exacerbated the community's anger. The church is globally and culturally infinitely more complex than a culture of a supermarket, so cultural skills are even more essential. But more is required, namely the commitment to the mythology and leadership style of paramodernity. We now consider a particular kind of paramodern leadership, namely refounding leadership.

Refounding Movements

> Insanity is doing the same thing again and again but expecting different results.
>
> —Unknown

In refounding movements, under skilled leadership, people begin to reshape their lives and cultures by returning to their mythological institutional founding experience, being so inspired and energized by this experience that they willingly and radically adapt it to present conditions. Refounding movements tackle the roots of institutional malaise by first locking in on the energy of the original founding mythologies (see *Axiom 3,* Chapter 1). A founding or creation myth gives an account of the first beginnings of a culture, and it remains a potential source for reenergizing the culture whenever myth is retold. Anthropologist Bronislaw Malinowski asserts that a founding myth "is not merely a story told but a reality lived . . . a narrative resurrection of a primeval reality."[28] The primeval reality is the revitalizing shock, the archetype, that belongs to sacred time or the time of the beginning that is to be relived here and now. Mircea Eliade believes the founding

---

[28]Bronislaw Malinowski, *Magic, Science and Religion, and Other Essays* (Glencoe, IL: Free Press, 1948), 100, 101.

myth is a "sacred history" and hence "saturated with being . . . and power."[29] Both authors, experts in the study of myths, are speaking of the powerful "eternal" relevance of the dynamism of creation myths for those who accept and re-own them.

By way of examples, recall the abiding power of the Exodus, the founding myth of the Israelite people; whenever they are in deep trouble they recount the myth, and hope and energy are restored, as Psalm 74 so well portrays. The people have been thrown into the Babylonian exile, leaving their sacred symbols of identity destroyed: Jerusalem, the temple, and the kingship. "Your foes have roared within your holy place. . . . And then, with hatchets and hammers, they smashed all its carved word. . . . Yet God my King. . . . You divided the sea by your might. . . . Rise up, O God, plead your cause" (Ps 74:4, 6, 12, 13, 22). Recall also that the founding myth of the United States is rooted in the belief that Americans are forever destined to build the new promised land of peace, plenty, and justice. Writers, orators, and politicians inspire their followers whenever they effusively seek to rearticulate this myth in view of the conditions around them.[30]

Refounding is not synonymous with restorationism. The latter seeks to escape back into the past, avoiding the need, unlike refounding, to grapple creatively with contemporary issues.[31] In rapidly changing and chaotic times refounding is an ongoing process. A refounding insight that is relevant today will not necessarily be so tomorrow. As the world changes, so new needs arise and new refounding intuitions and actions are required. Thus we can never ever say that an institution has been "refounded." This means that there must be an organized sloughing off of the once relevant culture in order to be open to the radically new.[32] But as Chapter 1 explains, the abandonment of inappropriate cultural customs is highly problematic.

---

[29]Mircea Eliade, *The Sacred and the Profane* (New York: Harcourt, 1959), 95.

[30]Gerald A. Arbuckle, *Earthing the Gospel: An Inculturation Handbook for Pastoral Workers* (Maryknoll, NY: Orbis Books, 1990), 38–42.

[31]See Gerald A. Arbuckle, *Fundamentalism at Home and Abroad: Analysis and Pastoral Responses* (Collegeville, MN: Liturgical Press, 2017), 93–95.

[32]See Peter F. Drucker, *Managing in Turbulent Times* (London: Pan Books, 1980), 43–72.

An analogy can help explain the meaning of refounding. Imagine a distant country in which thousands of people are tragically starving due to the corruption of local politicians and their crony supporters. International aid agencies decide to fly emergency food supplies to the country instead of using shipping services—their normal method of aid distribution. By using planes the agencies become involved in renewing their methods of aid to the starving population. Sure, aid is speeded up. But if the agencies decide also to target the roots of the problem of chronic poverty, that is, political corruption, they then become involved in refounding their services. This demands a revolutionary or mega-leap in creative thinking and action.

That is, renewal relates to the symptoms of problems, but refounding goes to their root causes. In October 2018 Sears, at one point the world's largest retailer, filed for bankruptcy.[33] Following the beginning of the online shopping revolution, Sears, like most brick-and-mortar shops, such as Borders, Walmart, and Target, made only attempts at renewal or superficial changes to their business methods.[34] The consequences were disastrous. These once successful retailers failed to make radical changes; in fact, Sears abandoned its mail-order business in 1993. Management had taken over whose primary task was to minimize risk. These retailers lacked the creative imagination and skilled leaders to go to the foundations of their institutional decline. Instead, they made only superficial changes to their traditional retail services with disastrous consequences. Refounding by contrast connotes a radical inventiveness directed at the root causes of problems. In brief, refounding "is not changing what is, but creating what is not."[35] Refounding is not about incremental change but revolutionary change (see *Axiom 9*, Chapter 1).

Refounding people are pained by the widening gap they per-

---

[33]See Rachel Siegel, "Sears Files for Bankruptcy after Years of Turmoil," *Washington Post*, October 15, 2018.

[34]See "Retailers and the Internet: Clicks and Bricks," *The Economist*, February 25, 2012, 14–15.

[35]Tracy Goss, Richard T. Pascale, and Anthony Athos, "The Reinvention Roller Coaster: Risking the Present for a Powerful Future," *Harvard Business Review on Change* (Harvard Business School Press, 1998), 85.

ceive between the founding mythology of an institution and contemporary reality; they have the ability to bridge that gap through dramatic creativity, and they restlessly seek to draw others to help them. In Chapter 3 the examples of Charles de Gaulle, Winston Churchill, and Lyndon Johnson were given—refounding leaders in times of national crises. Refounding persons recognize that people trapped in the utter confusion of cultural chaos urgently yearn to be reinspired by their institutional founding mythology to give them direction and enthusiasm to move forward.

To take another example. Evil though the murderous Stalin was, he, nonetheless, illustrates this key quality of a refounding person—sensitivity to the inspirational power of founding mythologies in times of chaos. On the death of Lenin in 1924 Stalin recognized that the people needed the equivalent of a "tsar." Tsars had ruled Russia ruthlessly for centuries; the people were not used to "party rule" invented by Lenin, so he created the communist equivalent of a tsar. When the Soviet Union disintegrated in 1991, Mikhail Gorbachev hoped to develop, as it were overnight, a democratic system of government, but as he and his successor Yeltsin discovered, the people in the midst of cultural breakdown and trauma rejected them. Without skilled political leadership, sensitive to cultural dynamics, the Russian people were unwilling to make the massive mythological shift from dictatorship to democracy in a short space of time. Democracy could not be established in a mythological vacuum. Gorbachev and Yeltsin lacked cultural sensitivity.[36] Vladimir Putin, however, shrewdly returned to the founding autocratic tsarist mythology of Russia, though modified, that also embraces the Orthodox religion as the springboard to move forward. The covert manipulation of power around one man in the twenty-first-century Kremlin certainly

---

[36]William Taubman comments: "[Gorbachev's] Communist training accustomed him to the idea that society could be drastically transformed overnight. A sworn opponent of Bolshevik-style social engineering, he tried to engineer his own anti-Bolshevik revolution by peaceful, evolutionary means. He trusted the people to embrace self-governance . . . until it turned out that they didn't know how and no longer trusted him." *Gorbachev: His Life and Times* (London: Simon & Schuster, 2017), 691.

resembles those of the Romanov emperors.[37] We can learn from the wisdom of serpents (Mt 10:16)!

Refounding People

Refounding people are deeply distressed to see a gap between an ideal, as articulated in the founding mythology of their institutions, and reality; inspired by the founding mythology, they are impatient to overcome that gap collaboratively through quantum leap creative actions that tackle the roots of problems. They are transforming leaders, that is, they mold and communicate a purpose-oriented vision for community systemic growth, providing a sharply defined focus for the actions of others to empower them to foster their own potential for change.[38]

Refounders are highly creative and intuitive; they are not loners since they know they need other people to work with them as fellow team collaborators. It is highly doubtful that an original founding idea can come from a team, but the application of the idea needs the assistance of others. Collaborators with refounders may be position authority persons, that is "gatekeepers," with the authority officially to approve or block the creative action; they hold the key to refounding because they have the authority to encourage and protect people with creative energy and talent to flourish. Other people may have "nuts and bolts" skills and are willing to collaborate with refounding persons (see *Axiom 5*, Chapter 1). Often position authority persons in an institution are too busy with administration to be refounding persons, but, nonetheless, their role as gatekeepers is a crucial one. Some Examples of refounders include Father Pedro Arrupe, Dr. Christine Brusselmans, and my own mother.

---

[37]See Simon Sebag Montefiore, *The Romanovs: 1613–1918* (London: Weidenfeld & Nicolson, 2016), 655–57. Montefiore comments: "In his Russian exceptionalism, imperialistic pride, domestic conservatism, personal rule and successful international aggression, Putin most resembles Tsar Nicholas I with his policies of Autocracy, Orthodoxy, Nationality." Ibid., 656.

[38]This definition is based on James M. Burns's insights into transforming leadership: *Leadership* (New York: Harper Torch, 1978). See also Archie Brown, *The Myth of the Strong Leader: Political Leadership in the Modern Age* (London: Bodley Head, 2014), 148–93.

Father Pedro Arrupe, SJ, became Jesuit superior general in 1965 during the 31st General Congregation (i.e., Chapter), shortly before the closing of Vatican II. At one point of the Congregation he outlined what he would need for the revitalization of the institute based on the founding mythology of St. Ignatius of Loyola: Jesuits prepared to interact with a world that demanded Gospel responses to "atheism, Marxism, ecumenism, problems of social and international justice"; Jesuits must discover ways to relate the Gospel to cultures, using, where possible, whatever help the human sciences could afford. He warned Jesuits that this mission to the world would demand a radical shift in the congregation's culture: "Adaptation must bear on the structures, works, men, and mentalities. This adaptation is not easy!"[39]

After the Congregation concluded, Fr. Arrupe quickly spelled out what the reform of the congregation must mean, articulating the obstacles to success and the need for a

> "pedagogy" to avoid the dangers of falling into the extremes of unrealizable utopian radicalism and pusillanimous fear which presents those attitudes as impossible for us. . . . The implementation of the [Congregation's] decrees . . . demands of us before everything else a deep and clear affirmation of faith . . . a change of attitudes, of criteria, of ways of thinking, and of the standard and style of life."[40]

He exercised leadership in a "hands-on, value-driven" manner in two ways: through letters to the institute on fundamental issues of refounding, for example, on discernment, on obedience, service, and poverty,[41] which were then followed up by visits, either personally or through his assistants. The source of his refounding strength lay in his deep spiritual life. This strengthened him to face personal suffering, often intensified by substantial opposition at

---

[39]Pedro Arrupe, *One Jesuit's Spiritual Journey: Autobiographical Conversations with Jean-Claude Dietsch* (Anand: Gujarat Sahitya Prakash, 1986), 26.

[40]Pedro Arrupe cited by Thomas P. Faase, *Making the Jesuits More Modern* (Washington, DC: University Press of America, 1981), 337–38.

[41]See Pedro Arrupe, *Challenge to Religious Life Today: An Anthology of Letters and Addresses*, ed. Jerome Aixala (St. Louis: Institute of Jesuit Resources, 1979).

times to his reform movement from fellow Jesuits and even Pope St. John Paul II, and to embrace death with remarkable equanimity and hope. Writing before his retirement and his sickness, he significantly said: "In reality, death . . . is for me one of the most anticipated events."[42]

Dr. Christine Brusselmans, the designer of the Rite of Christian Initiation of Adults (RCIA) after Vatican II, created a refounding vision for evangelizers that recognized the need for contemporary converts to move slowly through the conversion process with and into the ecclesial community. Her deep love of Christ in the Scriptures, and the example of St. Paul, the missionary, taught her that intimate companionship with Christ grows slowly; beginners need to be supported by loving faith communities. The old rite did not fit the restored mythology of initiation, but no one knew how to create the appropriate process. Brusselmans found a way; she was a true refounding person, who developed a vision and strategies for action that are still applicable in many different cultures.

One of the earliest memories of my mother in New Zealand during the Second World War was riding a bicycle along rough country roads in total darkness, sometimes even in heavy rain. The village where we lived was seven miles from a hospital in the nearest town, but because of the shortage of doctors and limited transport facilities people in the village were deprived of medical assistance. My mother as a trained nurse decided on her own initiative to do something about it. She, having vainly tried to interest the hospital authorities in the plight of the villagers, started to visit and nurse needy sick people using her bicycle as the only means of transport then available and offering whatever help she could. She asked nothing in return. Often she was called out during the blackout hours, and off she would go, ignoring the physical dangers of riding in total darkness.

Over time she developed a small group of local people as supporters. I remember listening to a family friend asking my mother why she did this. Her reply was quite simple: "I do this because this is what the Good Samaritan with his compassion and concern for others would have done." My mother continued

---

[42]Arrupe, *One Jesuit's*, 103.

to pester the medical authorities at the hospital for more help, even if this meant riding her bicycle on the lonely road to the hospital to plead her case. She gently but firmly kept reminding officials that public hospitals must exemplify the qualities of the Good Samaritan inherent in the founding story of the New Zealand welfare system: compassion, solidarity, concern for the marginalized. Eventually they assisted her with medicines and in other ways. My mother, as a refounding person, created the opportunity to bridge the gap between the founding myth of health care and the contemporary reality of the hospital's initial lack of concern for rural people.

My mother possessed personal power, but at the same time she had authority to challenge the hospital's officials, not from any formally recognized position, but from her commitment to the mission of the government hospital. Using her personal power, my mother balanced four functions of leadership, namely, the functions of conserving, managing, nurturing or empowering others, and proacting. She exercised a conserving function by passionately identifying with the heart of the founding experience of health care, in her case, the Good Samaritan story and its inherent values. She managed by using her collaborative and conversational style in the manner in which she encouraged others to help. And the latter were empowered to use their skills to support the project. Finally, she was proactive by tackling the roots of the problem, that is, the failure of the hospital to acknowledge the plight of rural people.[43]

Refounding inevitably evokes tensions, even at times risks of schisms, in institutions. Such is the case in the church today, where there is open talk about a possible schism.[44] The radical nature of refounding threatens those who are comfortable with the status quo and fear change. Jesus Christ foretold that his message would inevitably lead to conflicts and divisions: "Do not think I have come to bring peace to the earth; I have not come to bring peace, but a sword. For I have come to set a man against his father . . . and one's foes will be members of one's own household" (Mt

---

[43] Arbuckle, *Humanizing Healthcare*, 172–73.
[44] See Gerald A. Arbuckle, *Fundamentalism at Home and Abroad: Analysis and Pastoral Responses* (Collegeville, MN: Liturgical Press, 2017), 97–124.

10:34, 35, 36). We see this vividly evident, for example, in efforts at refounding religious congregations. Sociologist Sister Patricia Wittberg notes that "all refoundings [in religious congregations] are fraught with schism and controversy."[45] And she quotes Raymond Hostie: "Everywhere the reform [of the Franciscans] unleashed violent internal opposition. The movement . . . split the entire group in two."[46] Reformers may eventually find that the obstacles to revitalization within their own communities are so overwhelming that they have no option but to break away.

Refounding the Church

"Christ," declares Vatican II, "summons the Church, as she goes on her pilgrim way, to that continual *reformation* of which she always has need."[47] The method of reforming the church is the process of refounding. Pope Francis defines the process of refounding the church in this way: "Whenever we make the effort to return to the source and to recover the original freshness of the Gospel, new avenues arise, new paths of creativity open up, with different forms of expression, more eloquent signs and words with new meaning for today's world. Every form of authentic evangelization is always 'new.' "[48] That is, refounding the church is a process in which action-oriented refounding persons, inspired by faith, hope, and love of Jesus Christ and his mission, are able by their leadership to inspire people to act in a collaborative way:

- to identify the pastoral gaps between the Gospel, the church, and world around us;
- to create a new imaginative, prophetic vision of church, based on its founding mission and values;

---

[45]Patricia Wittberg, *Creating a Future for Religious Life: A Sociological Perspective* (New York: Paulist Press, 1991), 31.

[46]Raymond Hostie, translated by Patricia Wittberg from *La Vie et Mort des Ordres Religieux* (Paris: Desclee de Brouwer, 1972), 151.

[47]"Decree on Ecumenism" (*Unitatis Redintegratio*), in *Documents of Vatican II*, ed. Austin P. Flannery (Grand Rapids, MI: William B. Eerdmans, 1975), para. 5. Italics added.

[48]Pope Francis, "The Joy of the Gospel," para. 11.

- to bring this vision into reality through concrete pastoral strategies and their implementation, striking at the theological and cultural realities hindering or obstructing the church's commitment to the mission of Jesus Christ;
- and thus enabling people, with inner faith-based conviction,[49] to foster within themselves, in and through community, their own creative potential for ongoing pastoral cultural changes for the benefit of the People of God, especially the lonely, powerless, and marginalized.

Refounding is primarily a transformative faith journey, in which there are no quick-fixes. Rather it demands that we individually and as institutions enter into a world of Gospel faith and, at times, agonizing darkness and chaos. Seized by the Spirit, refounding people yearn to adapt the founding experience of the church by Christ to the reforming of the church and its ministries. And they invite others to join them in this task. They have a faith-stubbornness and a humility that come from an awareness of their own failings and their utter dependence on God, that ultimately can carry them through the inevitable periods of opposition, rejection, even marginalization within the church. The reforming zeal of refounders comes from a pastorally grounded holiness, says Father Yves Congar, OP, and he quotes Pope Pius XI:

Every true and lasting reform in the last analysis had its point of departure in holiness, in persons who were inflamed and impelled by the love of God and neighbor. . . . By contrast, where the zeal of the reformer did not arise from personal purity, but was the expression and the outburst of passion, it was a source of disturbance rather than illumination, destructive rather than constructive, and more than once the source of distortions more damaging than the evils to which they claimed to bring a remedy.[50]

---

[49]Ibid., para. 189.
[50]Pope Pius XI, Encyclical, *Mit brennender Sorge* (March 14, 1937), *Acta Apostolicae Sedis* (1937), 154, cited by Yves Congar, *True and False Reform in the Church* (Collegeville, MN: Liturgical Press, 2011), 219–20.

Refounding today in the church, in light of the abuse and cover-up crises, calls not only for the reforming of the church's culture, but also for holiness especially in its ministers. And refounding must always be an ongoing process; new needs arise, once effective structures can become over time obstacles to evangelization. It means "keeping [the church's] mission focused on Jesus Christ"[51] and the changing world around us. Jean Vanier's advice to members of L'Arche communities is wise:

> Communities continually need to listen to the Holy Spirit welcoming new challenges. They need to be continually refounded. The essential founding myth remains but the way it is incarnated is called to change. That is where the presence of wise refounders is necessary. They are able to move ahead maintaining and deepening the founding myth, pruning and cutting away things which appeared to be essential in the early years but in reality were not.[52]

Qualities of Refounding Leaders

Contemplation in Action

> We are called to be contemplatives even in the midst of action, and to grow in holiness by responsibly and generously carrying out our proper mission.
>
> —Pope Francis, *Rejoice and Exult*

There is in refounding persons the quality of willing conformity with the mystery of Christ's love: his life, death, and resurrection. And this inevitably means that the authentic refounding person is called to suffer, often intensely, in union with Christ: "The cross remains [for them] the source of [their] growth and sanctification."[53] The road to refounding is a humanly complex

---

[51]Pope Francis, "The Joy of the Gospel," para. 97.

[52]Jean Vanier, *The Founding Myth and the Evolution of Community*, Prophetic Paper 2 (1993), 9.

[53]Pope Francis, "Rejoice and Exult" (*Gaudete et Exsultate*) (Strathfield: St. Pauls Publications, 2018), para. 92.

and a spiritually painful one, for Christ calls us to a more intimate, privileged relationship with himself, which means being invited to share deeply in the purifying experience of his own suffering. What Simeon foretold of Mary, she who assisted at the church's founding, can also be applied to those who are sincerely committed to refounding the church: "and a sword will pierce your own soul too" (Lk 2:35). Refounding people experience the paradox of the Christian life, as Mary did: in the poverty of the cross, through detachment and mortification, they possess all things; in nothing—all things. Those who yearn, or "groan inwardly" (Rom 8:23), for refounding the church instinctively make the prayer of St. Paul their own: "I want to know Christ and the power of his resurrection and the sharing of his sufferings by becoming like him in his death, if somehow I may attain the resurrection from the dead" (Phil 3:10–11).

> To foster a contemplative spirit refounding people will have a love of solitude: Solitude is thus the ability to be alone, to be connected with one's inner self, without the emptiness and yearning of loneliness. Solitude provides the connection with what loneliness yearns for. Solitude is the entering into oneself to know oneself better and thus to learn how best to react positively to the loneliness that has been forced on one. Henri Nouwen describes it this way: "By slowly converting our loneliness into a deep solitude, we create the precious space where we can discover the voice telling us about our inner necessity—that is, our vocation."[54] Loneliness is the yearning to connect. Solitude is the act of connecting with oneself, thus fostering hope that one can connect with others in communion beyond oneself.[55]

It is in contemplative solitude that refounding people are able to identify the agonizing gap between the Gospel message and reality, intuit how the gap can be bridged, and then restlessly move with collaborators to make it happen. There will always be people

---

[54]Henri Nouwen, *Reaching Out* (New York: Doubleday, 1975), 27.
[55]Gerald A. Arbuckle, *Loneliness: Insights for Healing in a Fragmented World* (Maryknoll, NY: Orbis Books, 2018), xviii.

in the church who are accomplished either at contemplating or acting, but all too rarely both.

Prophetic Boldness

Refounding persons, like the prophets of the Old Testament, dare to tell the truth about reality—to name the systemic power of evil.[56] They are God's "whistleblowers" (see *Axiom 14*, Chapter 1). Refounded persons like the prophets will be tempted to escape their burdensome tasks (Jer 20:9), even to fall victim to the people's desires to be flattered with lies to avoid having to spell out the hard, God-centered truths (Is 30:10–11). But they will not be seduced. Evil will be named: "Ah, you who call evil good and good evil, who put darkness for light and light for darkness" (Is 5:20). Walter Brueggemann, when reflecting on the role of these prophets, writes:

> The prophetic antidote to denial is *truth-telling* . . . an act that is sure to provoke resistance and hostility among those in denial, because it requires seeing and knowing and engaging with that which we have refused to see, know, or engage.[57]

Prophets of refounding in the church commonly struggle against the very people who should be supporting them simply because the vision they proclaim of a just world in union with God is felt to be too big, too frightening. Such is the contemporary experience of Pope Francis.[58] To realize their vision people must let go cherished positions of control and power. All this is too disturbing to people set in their ways and who fear the unexpected. When Jesus foretold his suffering in Jerusalem, as the messianic prophets had foretold, Peter would have none of it: "God forbid it, Lord! This must never happen to you" (Mt 16:22). Jesus refused to give in to Peter's fears, and he scolded Peter: "Get behind me, Satan! You are a stumbling block to me; for you are setting your mind

---

[56]See Congar, *True and False Reform*, 215–18.

[57]See Walter Brueggemann, *Disruptive Grace: Reflections on God, Scripture, and the Church* (Minneapolis: Fortress, 2011), 138.

[58]See Pope Francis, "Rejoice and Exult," paras. 129–39.

not on divine things but on human things" (Mt 16:23).

Refounding people, as prophets of the Gospel message, are people of memory and imagination. They constantly and imaginatively recall Christ's mission to the world and its disturbing qualities for the comfortable. For this reason, and following prayerful discernment, they are loyal dissenters. Out of love for the Gospel message, they dissent from structures and pastoral methods that are no longer relevant in the apostolate. For this reason they are often feared and rejected.

Brueggemann speaks of refounding ministry in the church in this way: "*The task of prophetic ministry is to nurture, nourish, and evoke a consciousness and perception alternative to the consciousness and perception of the dominant culture around us.*" He then says: "I suggest that prophetic ministry has to do not primarily with addressing specific public crises but with addressing . . . the dominant crisis that is enduring and resilient, of having our alternative vocation co-opted and domesticated."[59] The dominant crisis in the church is the enduring and resilient presence of pre–Vatican II culture. As long as its power structures, including clericalism, continue, the vision of the People of God, as described in the council, remains domesticated, trapped in a medievalist theological construct. Pope Francis counsels us:

> Jesus himself warns us that the path he proposes goes against the flow, even making us challenge society by the way we live and, as a result, becoming a nuisance. He reminds us how many people have been, and still are, persecuted simply because they struggle for justice. . . . Unless we wish to sink into an obscure mediocrity, let us not long for an easy life, for "whoever would save his life will lose it" (Mt 16:25).[60]

Innovation

The cultural resistance to refounding people can be so considerable that the adage "the new belongs elsewhere" may

---

[59]Walter Brueggemann, *The Prophetic Imagination* (Philadelphia: Fortress Press, 1978), 13. Italics in original.

[60]Pope Francis, "Rejoice and Exult" (*Gaudete et Exsultate*) (Strathfield: St. Pauls Publications, 2018), para. 90.

need to be applied by authority-position people ("institutional gatekeepers") as their contribution to the refounding process.[61] A personal example may help to illustrate this principle. Many years ago I had open heart surgery. In coronary artery disease, progressive obstruction in arteries inhibits the blood flow to the heart. Without surgery death eventually results. Therefore, in order to restore health to the whole body, surgeons skillfully remove healthy veins from other parts of the body and turn them upside down so that they can become new arteries to bypass the diseased arteries. This remarkable bypass operation, through the use of "new structures," that is, the grafted healthy veins that have now become arteries, allows the patient to be, as it were, "refounded." So also in institutions in which there is significant resistance to change. Structures of accountability are built to bypass the resistance points. Innovative people need to be freed from the traditional monolithic structures, the cultural straitjackets of professional boundaries, and the tyranny of customs in the church that have existed for years, if not centuries.

For example, St. Teresa of Avila eventually found that her efforts to reform the Carmelite congregation were in serious danger of collapsing because of opposition within some communities. She was so convinced of this that she sought the aid of King Philip II of Spain to form a separate province, that is to bypass the recalcitrant convents: "I am quite clear that, unless the Discalced are made into a separate province, and that without delay, serious harm will be done: in fact, I believe it will be impossible for them to go on."[62] This does not mean that innovative people are to be protected from all tensions, since tension, passion, and conflict are often the catalysts for creativity. It is rather a question of shielding creative people from emotionally draining conflict that fails to serve the mission. In fact Jesus Christ calls for the application of the principle in pastoral ministry when he says: "Neither is new wine put into old wineskins; otherwise, the skins burst, and the wine is spilled, and the skins are destroyed; but new wine is

---

[61]See Peter Drucker, *Innovation and Entrepreneurship: Practice and Principles* (New York: Harper & Row, 1986), 161–64.

[62]Teresa of Avila, Letter dated July 19, 1575, in *The Letters of Saint Teresa of Jesus*, ed. Allison Peers (Westminster: Newman Press, 1950), 188.

put into fresh wineskins, and so both are preserved" (Mt 9:17). And: "Let the dead bury their own dead, but as for you, go and proclaim the kingdom of God" (Lk 9:60).

Sense of Humor

"Far from being timid, morose, acerbic or melancholy, or putting on a dreary face, the saints," writes Pope Francis, "are joyful and full of good humour. Though completely realistic, they radiate a positive and hopeful spirit."[63] So also refounding persons. They are not "querulous and disillusioned pessimists, 'sourpusses,' "[64] or escapist restorationists. Humor is that sense within us which sets up a kindly contemplation of the incongruities of life. This contemplation reaches a high point when the incongruities being contemplated are one's own stupidities and failings on the one hand and the love and mercy of God toward oneself on the other. A person has a sense of humor, if he or she is able to undertake this contemplation.[65]

The prophets had a sense of humor. Moses, like Jeremiah, tried to escape his prophetic role by pleading his lack of eloquence for the task. God would take no excuses and Moses, recognizing the incongruous situation of attempting to argue with God, submitted and trusted in the power of God to help him in his weakness (Ex 4:10–12). To this day one can hear Moses chuckling to himself over his own foolishness in trying to outsmart God with weak excuses. It was this simultaneous awareness of their own personal weaknesses and their need for God's help in their ministry that sustained the prophets in their times of trial and uncertainties. The ultimate test as to whether or not today's leaders are truly able to acknowledge their own inner inadequacies and need of God will be their ability to laugh at themselves. With this gift, leaders will avoid the arrogance of authoritarianism. Without it they will become dangerous to themselves and to those they claim to serve. Humor helps one to keep things in perspective.

---

[63]Pope Francis, "Rejoice and Exult," para. 122.
[64]Pope Francis, "The Joy of the Gospel," para. 85.
[65]See Gerald A. Arbuckle, *Laughing with God: Humor, Culture, and Transformation* (Collegeville, MN: Liturgical Press, 2008), 1–18.

Jesus Christ, the master, uses humor as his main method of teaching. . . . Human pride, pomposity, selfishness, and avarice are all the objects of the deflating power of humor. Yet Christ is more than the master teacher. He became divine humor incarnate in our midst. Moved by an overwhelming love for us, on the day of his resurrection he triumphed over death. This is the ultimate source of authentic laughter of the heart: "This is the day the Lord has made; let us rejoice and be glad in it" (Ps 118:24).[66]

Creative Imagination

The prophets rejected the distorted culture in which they lived, for they measured it against the vision they knew can and should be realized. Though each prophet called for the same conversion, each directed their words to the particular needs of the time, for example to *this* or *that* group of marginalized people. Each used different imaginative and innovative expressions that the people of their times could readily understand. They broke through the chaos of confusion, of numbness and denial, by pointing out the way the people must go in order to return their culture to God-centered foundations.

The prophets were optimistic people, full of hope, and for this reason they were so imaginatively creative about how the people should return to their pilgrim road in the presence of God. Their exercise of creative imagination was possible, however, only because they were compulsive listeners, that is, they listened to God's covenant requirements and at the same time to the sinfulness and cries of the people and their needs. In summary, the prophets of old—and Jesus followed their example in his own ministry—imaginatively adapted their message to the lives and needs of people without ever lessening its radicalness. Similar imaginative creativity and listening skills will be required in refounding leaders. Brueggemann is right: "The dulled God of the conventional religious tradition will never yield energy for ministry."[67]

---

[66]Ibid., 40–41.
[67]Walter Brueggemann, *Hopeful Imagination: Prophetic Voices in Exile* (Philadelphia: Fortress Press, 1986), 15.

Gift of Lamentation

Pope Francis writes:

> Like the prophet Jonah, we are constantly tempted to flee
> to a safe haven. It can have many names: individualism . . .
> dogmatism, nostalgia, pessimism, hiding behind rules and
> regulations. We can resist leaving behind a familiar and easy
> way of doing things. . . . God is eternal newness. He impels
> us constantly to set out anew, to pass beyond the familiar,
> to the fringes and beyond. . . . Complacency is seductive; it
> tells us there is no point in trying to change things. . . . By
> force of habit we no longer stand up to evil.[68]

Refounding people are future-oriented or hope-filled people, since
they believe their primary task is to challenge the People of God
to let go of whatever is holding them back from moving forward
in love and justice. This is the gift of lamentation or mourning.
"More than bureaucrats and functionaries, the Church needs passionate missionaries, enthusiastic about sharing true life. [They]
surprise us, they confound us, because by their lives they urge us
to abandon a dull and dreary mediocrity."[69]

The art of leading mourning rituals was a special gift of the
prophets, as it is of refounding people in the church (see *Action
Plan 3*, Chapter 6). Jeremiah, for example, grieved over losses at
three levels. He sorrowed over the sight of his own inadequacies
before God; he grieved for and with his people because of their
refusal to change in response to God's call; God and he jointly
grieved over the calamities that were to befall the chosen people
or had already done so. He hoped that through the public sharing of grief the people would acknowledge death and be open to
the new life promised by God. Consequently Jeremiah recounted
with pathos the desperate need for mourning women to rally the
nation to grieve: "Send those who are best at it! . . . Let our eyes
rain tears. . . . For we must leave the country, our homes have
been knocked down!" (Jer 9:16–18).

---

[68]Pope Francis, "Rejoice and Exult," paras. 134, 135, 137.
[69]Ibid., para. 138.

Discernment

St. Paul listed among the important charismata given by the Holy Spirit the discernment of spirits (1 Cor 12:10). The early Christian communities needed to discover whether or not prophetic utterances were of the Spirit of God or demonic spirits. The focus was particularly on leadership and prophecy because Christian communities could be deceived by people who appeared to be good but in fact were not (2 Cor 11:13–15). Pope Francis insists that the gift of discernment is as urgent today as it was in the early Christian communities:

> Without the wisdom of discernment, we can easily become prey to every passing trend. This is all the more important when some novelty presents itself in our lives. Then we have to decide whether it is new wine brought by God or an illusion created by the spirit of this world or the spirit of the devil. At other times, the opposite can happen, when the forces of evil induce us not to change, to leave things as they are, to opt for a rigid resistance to change. . . . "Test everything; hold fast to what is good"(1 Thess 5:21).[70]

In brief, the role and qualities of a refounding person in the church are akin to those found in the prophets of the Old Testament and in the life of Jesus Christ; they are the exemplars of all authentic refounding people down through the centuries. With memory and imagination they call us back to our founding mythology and invite us to join them in refounding the church according to the Gospel message and authentic tradition.[71] There is fire in these people, a Gospel radicality that inspires the converting, disturbs the complacent, the spiritual lethargic, those who deny chaos both inside and outside themselves, and those who compromise with worldly values. They can be feared, like all innovators, because they dare to push back the frontiers of the unknown—chaos, a world of meaninglessness—in the name of Jesus Christ.

---

[70]Pope Francis, "Rejoice and Be Glad," paras. 167–68.
[71]See Congar, *True and False Reform*, 304–7.

Concluding Options

"Life," said Albert Einstein, "is like riding a bicycle. To keep your balance you must keep moving." Without far-reaching cultural changes the church will lose its balance. It will fall by the wayside and become increasingly sect-like, turned in on itself, lifeless, forever trying to cover up its failings from itself and outsiders. Restorationism and clericalism will intensify. Pope Francis writes:

> I dream of a "missionary option," that is, a missionary impulse capable of transforming everything, so that the Church's customs, ways of doing things, times and schedules, language and structures can be suitably channeled for the evangelization of today's world rather than for her self-preservation.[72] . . . There are ecclesial structures which hamper efforts at evangelization.[73]

The previous chapters sharply focus on structures in the church that are not just hampering evangelization but *blocking it!*

This chapter has focused on refounding leadership for reform in the church, responding to the question: *How are we to move forward while removing or bypassing the barriers to refounding the church?* We have three options as we face the challenging future together. Measured by the Gospel, the first two options have no future.

- *Option 1: Nostalgic Escapism.* That is, live in the glorious achievements of the past. But history shows that the more rigid the defense of an untenable position, the more catastrophic the smash when it does come. And the smash has already come. The institutional evil of systemic sexual abuse and cover-ups continues to be globally revealed. No more hiding in nostalgic dreams, says Pope Francis! "Those who stubbornly try to recover a past that no longer exists—they

---

[72]Pope Francis, "The Joy of the Gospel," para. 27.
[73]Ibid., para. 26.

have a static and inward-directed view of things."[74] "More than by fear of going astray," Pope Francis writes, "my hope is that we will be moved by the fear of remaining shut up within structures which give us a false sense of security, within rules which make us harsh judges, within habits which make us feel safe."[75]

- *Option 2: Do Nothing.* This is humanly an attractive option. Then "we become careless, the false promises of evil easily seduce us. . . . [We] choose to remain neutral, satisfied with little. . . . Spiritual corruption is worse than the fall of a sinner, for it is a comfortable and self-satisfied form of blindness. Everything then appears acceptable."[76] Thus, it is so easy, for example, for our universities, schools, hospitals, aged-care facilities, and social services to thoughtlessly coast into becoming basically secular institutions, still showing the crests or symbols of our identities, but no longer sharing in the Christian founding values of these institutions. All that would be left maybe are the words "Saint" or "Catholic" on the entrance signs. My Cambridge University college is Christ College, co-founded by St. John Fisher, but the *only* sign of its Christian founding in the fifteenth century is the word "Christ." Leadership has failed over the centuries. This can happen to us! There can be no watering down of the radical demands of the mission of Christ, if the identity of their institutions is to remain clear. Recall Peter Steinfels, reflecting on the future of Catholic hospitals, when he commented: "It doesn't seem satisfactory to reduce [Catholic identities] to a few codified essentials—that Catholic hospitals abstain from performing abortions, for example. . . . Nor does it seem satisfactory to recast that dimension in elevated but cloudy terms—respect, personal attention . . . so religiously neutral that they might easily apply to the Red Cross Blood Bank as to the Holy Cross Health Clinic."[77]

---

[74]Pope Francis, quoted in Antonio Spadaro, SJ, "A Big Heart Open to God: An Interview with Pope Francis," *America* magazine, September 30, 2013, www.americamagazine.org/pope-interview, 11.

[75]Pope Francis, "The Joy of the Gospel," para. 49.

[76]Pope Francis, "Rejoice and Exult," pars. 162, 163, 165.

[77]Peter Steinfels, *A People Adrift: The Crisis of the Roman Catholic Church*

- *Option 3: Ongoing Refounding.* Refounding, that is, the rearticulation, reowning, and creative reapplication of the founding values of Jesus Christ to contemporary situations, is possible only if we act boldly. If we forget that Jesus Christ is our founder, we will over time weaken the radicality of his message. "Whenever we make the effort to return to the source and to recover the original freshness of the Gospel, new avenues arise, new paths of creativity."[78] "The path of holiness" is the path of refounding for the church, for our ministries, our personal lives. It demands that we keep "our lamps lit" (Lk 12:35) and attentive: "Abstain from every form of evil" (1 Thess 5:22). Refounding the church is ultimately a gift from God, demanding of us a prayerful journey into a world of Gospel faith, ongoing conversion. No amount of *merely* human effort on our part will bring about this refounding, and we should take to heart the advice of the anonymous fourteenth-century author of *The Cloud of Unknowing*:

So set yourself to rest in this darkness as long as you can, always crying out after him whom you love. For if you are to experience him or to see him at all, insofar as it is possible here, it must always be in this cloud.[79]

Summary

- Refounding is not about incremental change; rather it is about creating what does not yet exist, that is, revolutionary cultural change as imperated by Vatican II. It means persisting in the face of pre–Vatican II culture that maintains clerical power and its tragic consequences (see Chapters 1 and 2).
- Refounding people are shocked by the gap between the founding myth and contemporary reality and feel impelled to bridge that gap. The more they recount the story of Jesus Christ, the more the refounders become shocked by the

in America (New York: Simon & Schuster, 2003), 112–13.

[78]Pope Francis, "The Joy of the Gospel," para. 11.

[79]James Walsh, ed., *The Cloud of Unknowing* (New York: Paulist Press, 1981), 121.

gap between Christ's message and the world around them.

- Refounding is primarily a transformative faith journey, in which there are no quick fixes. Rather, it demands that we individually and as institutions enter into a world of Gospel faith and, at times, agonizing darkness and chaos. At the same time, refounding people know that "God is eternal newness. He impels us constantly to set out anew, to pass beyond what is familiar, to the fringes and beyond."[80]

- Karl Rahner is right: "[The] future of the Church cannot be planned ... by the application of generally recognized principles: it needs the courage of ... creative imagination."[81] It needs refounding. The pre–Vatican II culture is not into refounding, but rather management to uphold the status quo.

- The reforming of the church's culture through refounding must always be an ongoing process; new needs arise; once-effective structures can become over time obstacles to Gospel living, the survival and vibrant growth of ministries. Traditional methods of ministry may no longer work; today's responses can become tomorrow's problems. The moment an organization thinks it has satisfactorily refounded itself, signs of cultural sclerosis, dysfunctionality, and even possible corruption are bound to occur.

---

[80]Pope Francis, "Rejoice and Exult," para. 135.

[81]Karl Rahner, *The Shape of the Church to Come* (New York: Seabury Press, 1974), 47.

5

Structural Reform
in the Church

Bishops need to stand back; neither now nor in the past
have they been the most faithful bearers of the Gospel but
have to a great extent failed in their mission.
—David Power, *Love without Calculation*

Anything less than structural reform [in the Church] will be
seen as a crisis weathered rather than a crisis transformed.
—Marie Keenan, *Child Sexual Abuse
and the Catholic Church*

Changing structures without generating new convictions
and attitudes will only ensure that those same structures
will become, sooner or later, corrupt, oppressive and ineffectual.
—Pope Francis, "The Joy of the Gospel"

This chapter explains that:
- Church reforms of governance structures are needed.
- Laity must be involved in governance reforms.
- Theology and history show that laity participation is
  possible.

Refounding "impels us constantly to set out anew, to pass beyond what is familiar, to the fringes and beyond." It means being
aware that "complacency is seductive [because] it tells us that there

is no point in trying to change things; [that] more than bureaucrats and functionaries, the Church needs passionate missionaries, enthusiastic about sharing true life."[1] This was the theme of the last chapter. This chapter focuses on this question: What reforms are necessary to allow lay people to become involved in the church's governance structures? Such involvement inter alia would help make bishops more accountable for their actions. There are no dogmatic or historical reasons against this reform.

Three Levels of Church Governance in Need of Reform

At least three levels of governance in the church need urgent reform: the papacy and curia, national and regional bishops' conferences, and diocesan and parish administrations. As regards the first level, there are two ultimate subjects of authority in the church, namely, the pope alone or the pope with the episcopal college. The pope can freely choose to exercise his universal power personally or collegially: "For the Roman Pontiff, by reason of his office as Vicar of Christ, namely and as pastor over the whole Church, has full, supreme and universal power over the whole Church, a power which he can always exercise unhindered."[2] The pope is accountable to no one but God. Pope St. John Paul II in 1995 requested help in discovering "a way of exercising the primacy which, while in no way renouncing what is essential to its mission, is nonetheless open to a new situation."[3] Pope Francis writes that there has been "little progress in this regard. The papacy and the central structures of the universal Church also need to hear the call to pastoral conversion. . . . Excessive centralisation . . . complicates the Church's life and her missionary outreach."[4] He is seeking to bypass the Roman Curia's resistance to reform by invoking the principle of subsidiarity and the principle "the

---

[1]Pope Francis, "Rejoice and Exult" (*Gaudete et Exsultate*) (Strathfield: St. Pauls Publications, 2018), paras. 135, 137, 138.

[2]"Dogmatic Constitution on the Church" (*Lumen Gentium*), in *Documents of Vatican II*, ed. Austin F. Flannery (Grand Rapids, MI: William B. Eerdmanns, 1975), para. 22.

[3]Encyclical Letter, "May We Be One" (*Ut Unum Sint*) (May 25, 1995), para. 95.

[4]Pope Francis, "The Joy of the Gospel" (*Evangelii Gaudium*) (Strathfield: St. Pauls Publications, 2013), para. 32.

new belongs elsewhere" (see Chapter 4): "If he can't reform it," writes theologian Richard Gaillardetz, "he can at least redirect decision-making away from it and toward synods, episcopal conferences and the local churches,"[5] which he is attempting to do. At the next level down there are national and regional bishops', conferences, diocesan bishops and episcopal councils, councils of diocesan clergy, and diocesan and parochial finance committees; finally, there is the possibility of diocesan pastoral councils, diocesan synods, and parish and deanery councils.[6] A bishop's power "is proper, ordinary and immediate, although its exercise is ultimately controlled by the supreme authority of the Church."[7] The Report of the Anglican-Roman Catholic International Commission (ARCIC III) (2018), *Walking Together on the Way,* notes that lay involvement in governance at these levels is generally confined to the consultative and non-deliberative. In rather understated terms the report says:

> The tendency toward internal/external understanding of clerical distinctiveness means that lay participation in ecclesial governance is generally consultative and non-deliberative, whether in parish councils, diocesan synods, diocesan pastoral councils, or the appointment of bishops and parish priests. . . . [The] current models of governance seem not to give adequate recognition to the anointing of all the baptized and their share in the Good Shepherd's pastoral ministry. . . . Sometimes bishops and parish priests have an authority of governance that is without sufficient checks and balances on the part of those governed.[8]

---

[5]Richard Gaillardetz, "Francis under Fire," *The Tablet,* September 22, 2018, 5. This is a good example of the effectiveness of the principle "the new belongs elsewhere" as described in the preceding chapter.

[6]See Statement of the Anglican–Roman Catholic International Commission (ARCIC III) (2018), *Walking Together on the Way: Learning to Be the Church— Local, Regional, Universal,* July 2, 2018, para. 74.

[7]"Constitution on the Church," para. 27. See Patrick Granfield, *The Limits of the Papacy: Authority and Autonomy in the Church* (New York: Crossroad, 1990), 114–20. There are over four thousand bishops who are personally accountable directly to the pope, but supervision by one man of such a large number is an impossible task.

[8]*Walking Together,* paras. 94, 95.

In the apostolic constitution introducing the new Code of Canon Law, 1983, Pope St. John Paul II emphasizes: "Foremost among the elements which express the true and authentic image of the Church are: the teaching whereby the Church is presented as the People of God and its hierarchical authority as service."[9] The code says: "Flowing from their rebirth in Christ, there is a genuine equality of dignity and action among all of Christ's faithful. Because of this equality they all contribute, each according to his or her own condition and office, to the building up of the Body of Christ" (Can. 208).[10] And "Christ's faithful . . . have the right, indeed at times the duty, in keeping with their knowledge, competence and position, to manifest to the sacred Pastors their views on matters which concern the good of the Church" (Can. 212, para. 3). However, the "tension between the Church as hierarchy and as people of God, between authority as power and authority as service"[11] in practice resolves itself in favor of the Church as hierarchy because "the diocesan bishop is the sole legislator at a diocesan synod" (Can. 466). Presbyteral and pastoral councils have only consultative voting power (see Cans. 500, 514). A bishop can pseudo-consult his priests and laity and thus ignore any form of accountability to the People of God.

In Australia, the Catholic Church has been severely criticized for its lack of accountable governance structures at the diocesan levels. Laity have no effective structures and power to question the actions of their local bishops:

> The powers of governance held by individual diocesan bishops and provincials are not subject to adequate checks and balances. . . . Diocesan bishops have not been sufficiently accountable to any other body for decision-making in their handling of allegations of child sexual abuse or alleged perpetrators. There has been no requirement for their decisions to be made transparent or subject to due

---

[9]John Paul II, Apostolic Constitution (*Sacrae Disciplinae Leges*), *The Code of Canon Law* (London: Collins, 2001), xiv.

[10]Ibid., 35.

[11]Robert J. Willis, "Ministry, Governance, and Relational Growth," in *The Ministry of Governance*, ed. James K. Mallett (Washington, DC: Canon Law Society of America, 1986), 181.

process. The tragic consequences of this lack of accountability have been seen in the failures of those in authority
. . . to respond adequately to allegations and occurrences
of child sexual abuse.[12]

Lay Involvement in Governance Reform

The primary task of *governance* in an organization is to
be the establisher and guardian of the organization's purpose;
management, however, is about the ways and means to achieve
this primary task as set by governance authorities.[13] Laity are
already engaged at managerial levels of dioceses, but there are
two major reasons why the laity must become involved now
in governance reform: theological and contextual. The report
Walking Together on the Way comments:

> While the Second Vatican Council recognized the participa-
> tion of all the baptized in the *tria munera* [i.e., of teaching,
> sanctifying, and leading God's people],[14] and while Roman
> Catholic theology recognizes their role [i.e., that of the
> laity] in discerning teaching through the *sensus fidei*, this
> recognition has not yet fully permeated Roman Catholic
> habits of mind and discourse.[15]

Certainly, inter alia, governance structures urgently need the
management expertise of highly qualified lay people if reforms
are to be professionally led, a point that the Australian report
into Institutional Sexual Abuse of Minors forcefully makes: The
review of governance and management structures of dioceses and
parishes "should draw from the approaches to governance of

---

[12]*Royal Commission into Institutional Responses to Child Sexual Abuse Final
Report*, vol. 16, no. 1 (Barton, ACT: Commonwealth of Australia, 2017), 44.

[13]See Terry Kilmister, *Boards at Work: A New Perspective on Not-for-Profit
Board Governance* (Wellington: NFP Press, 1993), 21, 35–36.

[14]"The Dogmatic Constitution on the Church" (*Lumen Gentium*) states: The
laity, "who by Baptism are incorporated into Christ, are placed in the People of
God, and in their own way share in the priestly, prophetic, and kingly office of
Christ." *Documents of Vatican II*, ed. Austin P. Flannery (Grand Rapids, MI:
William B. Eerdmans, 1975), para. 31.

[15]*Walking Together*, para. 96.

Catholic health, community services and education agencies."[16] Administratively dioceses and parishes are increasingly complex. It is rare for a bishop or priest to have the necessary administrative skills. And laity are needed to help bishops and clergy to be accountable.

But the laity must be involved in more than management, as Karl Rahner argues:

> What is important . . . is the necessity . . . for the collaboration of churchpeople in the life of the Church and the decisions of authority. . . . And today . . . the real efficacy of the Church's ministries (proclamation, administration of the sacraments, government, etc.) depends largely on the free collaboration of churchgoers themselves. This however is not to be expected, unless the people are obviously involved to the greatest possible extent in the decision-making of the institutional Church. . . . Nor is this necessary participation to be expected in practice if it is to be merely informal; it needs *juridical and visible structures* which themselves are not in every case necessarily dependent on the good will of the office-holders strictly so called.[17]

This massive gap between theological rhetoric about the need for effective lay involvement in decision-making at least at parish and diocesan levels and reality *must* now be bridged. This requires changes to canon law.[18] Canonist Ladislas Orsy effectively

---

[16]Recommendation to the Australian Catholic Bishops Conference, no. 16.7. See *Final Report of the Royal Commission,* 73. In Australia, faith-based health care, community, and educational ministries are all subject to government regulations. This helps ensure that these ministries are accountable for their actions.

[17]Karl Rahner, *Concern for the Church* (New York: Crossroad, 1981), 123. Italics added.

[18]The Code of Canon Law at present reads: Can. 129: "Those who are in sacred orders are, in accordance with the provisions of law, capable of the power of governance, which belongs to the Church by divine institution. This power is also the power of jurisdiction (para. 1). Lay members of Christ's faithful can *cooperate* in the exercise of this same power in accordance with the law (para. 2)" (italics added). That is, lay people can cooperate in church governance, but the meaning of "cooperation" is left vague. Canonist Fr. Francis Morrisey, OMI, comments: "In a sense, lay judges are part of the governance structure. Even lay chancellors, as part of the diocesan curia." (Advice received September 11, 2018.)

argues that the canon which restricts the power of governance to those in sacred orders, and allowing the nonordained *only* to cooperate with this governance, has no historical foundations: "Therefore, the restriction can hardly be grounded in dogma. It must be a disciplinary provision, and if so, it can be changed. . . . There is no theological reason why a bishop could not let a qualified person 'participate' in his power to govern provided such a person does not encroach on the exclusive charism that is given by ordination."[19]

New Forms of Lay Ministry

The facts speak volumes about the necessity of involving laity in the governance of the church and in new forms of ministry. With the rapid decline and aging of priests, especially in the Western world, parishes are either being merged or closed. Dioceses are recruiting priests from developing countries, but parishioners are complaining that these priests commonly are unfamiliar with the local cultures, and their ability to preach satisfactorily in English is problematic: "Many Catholics are being led by this situation to ask whether worshipping communities need new forms or models of ministry in order to continue or thrive."[20] Others give up all hope of reform because there are no avenues for them to be heard. Sociologist Peter McDonough comments on the American scene:

> [More] Catholics are leaving the church than are vying for power or doctrinal vindication within it. The real problem for the majority of civilians, those who are neither clerics nor are in the employ of the church, is not fear of retribution but resignation at the uselessness of petitions for reform. . . . Seriously organized activity still requires clerical supervision or a sacerdotal blessing of some sort, titular though it may be.[21]

---

[19]Ladislas Orsy, *Receiving the Council: Theological and Canonical Insights and Debates* (Collegeville, MN: Liturgical Press, 2009), 39, 40.

[20]*Walking Together*, para. 97.

[21]Peter McDonough, *The Catholic Labyrinth: Power, Apathy, and a Passion for Reform in the American Church* (New York: Oxford University Press, 2013), 102. The Pew Research Center concluded in 2015 that 13 percent of all Americans

At the same time as there is a staffing crisis in parishes there is a widespread ongoing laicization of Catholic universities, schools, and health care facilities in the Western world. In a very short period, due to the dramatic decline in religious vocations and the demands for more educational professionalism to meet government requirements, lay people are now overwhelmingly staffing and leading these ministries. Commenting on the United States, McDonough writes: "[With] the removal of religious orders and congregations as sole proprietors . . . [the] colleges and universities took on greater lay faculty and administrators, and their governing boards were manned by trustees from the corporate world."[22] In Australia, Catholic schools form the largest religious educational system in the country, staffed by highly professional lay teachers, though they are ultimately accountable to the hierarchy and parish priests who generally lack expertise to judge what is happening. This lay staff pattern is very much the same for Catholic schools in the United States, Canada, England, and Ireland. In health care, lay involvement at the highest levels is the norm.[23]

Since the early 1990s most health care ministries in Australia and North America are also increasingly governed by lay trustees who head newly formed *public juridic persons* (PJPs) that are ultimately accountable to local bishops or the Holy See. Similarly, an increasing number of schools, originally owned and operated by religious orders, are becoming PJPs. "A public juridic person (PJP) is either an aggregate of persons or of things established by the competent ecclesiastical authority, so that, within limits al-

---

now call themselves "former Catholics." "America's Changing Religious Landscape," www.pewforum.org/2015/5/12/americas-changing-religious-landscape.

[22]McDonough, *The Catholic Labyrinth*, 121–22.

[23]The investment by the Catholic Church in health care services, as in education, is staggering. Where health care services were predominantly staffed by religious, 99 percent are now staffed mainly by highly qualified lay people. In Australia, Catholic services form the largest. nongovernment source of health and aged-care services. In the United States, the Catholic Church owns 11 percent of the hospitals, provides 16 percent of all American community hospital admissions, and employs approximately 800,000 workers. By acute care bed count, three of the ten largest. health care systems in the United States are Catholic, as are seven of the ten largest. nonprofit systems. See Barbra M. Wall, *American Catholic Hospitals: A Century of Changing Markets and Missions* (New Brunswick NJ: Rutgers University Press, 2011), 103–26.

lotted it, it operates in the name of the church, and in accordance with the provision of law, fulfilling the task to it in view of the public good."[24] A PJP has the same degree of "internal governance" as a religious institute, "but it is not part of the Church's governance structure as such."[25] These PJPs are committed to a dual accountability—to the church's hierarchical authorities and to relevant government agencies. The accountability is upward, not downward; that is, there is no structure whereby hierarchical authorities must account to PJPs for their actions.

The speed with which these health care and educational PJPs, under lay trustees, have in the last twenty years developed to replace religious congregations reinforces the urgency for the present clerical governance structures to change in order to admit lay involvement. These ministries are far too important to remain without direct representation in the governance structures of the church. "Whereas at times in the recent past, collaboration came about as a means of supplementing the decline in the number of consecrated persons necessary to carry out activities, *now it is growing out of the need to share responsibility*."[26]

Historical Basis for Lay Involvement

It is relevant to explain further the nature and scriptural foundation of PJPs. A PJP, under lay trustees, formally *sponsors* ministries in the church. What does *sponsorship* mean? Sponsorship is canonical stewardship of a ministry that is carried on in the name of the church. A more pastoral and developmental definition says that sponsorship is simply "the devising of ways to guarantee or ensure that the mission of Christ continues within the church through ministries, in light of rapidly changing circumstances in

---

[24]Catholic Health Association USA, *A Guide to Understanding Public Juridic Persons: In the Catholic Health Ministry* (St. Louis: CHA, 2012), 33. See also Gerald A. Arbuckle, *Healthcare Ministry: Refounding the Mission in Tumultuous Times* (Collegeville, MN: Liturgical Press, 2000), 246–48.

[25]Canonist Fr. Francis Morrisey, OMI. He continues, "[In the Code of Canon Law] references to PJPs are near the beginning (in Book I), and not in the sections of Book II on governance." (Advice received September 11, 2018.)

[26]Congregation for Institutes of Consecrated Life and Societies of Apostolic Life, *Starting Afresh from Christ: A Renewed Commitment to Consecrated Life in the Third Millennium* (May 2000), para. 31. Italics added.

both society and the church."[27] Though the term "sponsorship" is new in the church, sponsorship has in fact been a vital reality in the church's life since apostolic times. *If the early church was flexible within a short space of time in creating governance structures in ministries to respond to evolving pastoral needs, so surely we can today be equally flexible in changing contemporary governance church structures to accommodate new and complex needs.* We look now closely at the experience of the early church as described in the Acts of the Apostles.

Acts is the story of the growth of the church under the impulse of the Holy Spirit (Acts 9:31), and of the ways in which the church became increasingly conscious of its central mission, namely to be "witnesses" of Christ's life and teaching, even "to earth's remotest end" (1:8). The Holy Spirit assumes a central role in the book, initiating and directing missionary activities at key turning points (e.g., Acts 8:26, 29, 39; 10:19; 13:2; 15:28; 16:6–9). It is the Holy Spirit who is causing the church to emerge, inspiring unity and dramatic missionary activity, as new opportunities and challenges develop. And three forms of sponsorship develop in response to changing pastoral needs that eventually called for governance and administrative changes.

The first type of sponsorship was relatively simple. Members of the community in Jerusalem "had all things in common; they would sell their possessions and goods and distribute the proceeds to all, as any had need" (Acts 2:44–45). That is, the community was so small that the needs of those who were destitute were known to all members. So believers dispersed funds readily and *directly* to the needy. But as the community expanded, there had to be changes in the way that poor people could be identified and their needs satisfied. Hence, a new sponsorship structure developed. The apostles received the funds, and they then guaranteed that they reach the poverty-stricken members: "There was not a needy person among them, for as many owned lands or houses sold them and brought the proceeds of what was sold. They laid it at the apostles' feet, and it was distributed to each as any had need" (4:34–35). Now individual donors *indirectly* delivered aid to the poor.

---

[27]This is more fully explained by the author in "Sponsorship's Biblical Roots and Tensions," *Health Progress* 87, no. 5 (2006): 13–16.

But as the community continued to expand and become more culturally diverse, a third type of sponsorship became necessary. People were being neglected. Dissension flared up in the once-peaceful community. Greek-speaking Jewish Christians called Hellenists protested to the apostles that their widows "were being neglected in the daily distribution of food" (Acts 6:1). The Hebrews were blamed, that is, Palestinian Jews who spoke Hebrew or Aramaic, for disregarding the vulnerable widows. In traditional Jewish culture where women depended for their identity, rights, and security on men, widows lived a hazardous life.

What had failed? There had been a fundamental breakdown in governance and administration. A serious gap had developed between the Gospel imperative to aid the poor and the fact that people were being neglected in the Jerusalem community. And apostles had become blind to the problem because they were overworked as leaders of the community (see Acts 6:1). A new administrative structure was needed. The Apostles immediately responded by calling "together the whole community of the disciples" (Acts 6:2). They stated the problem and asked the community for help in responding to it. If they continued to distribute food to needy people in the rapidly expanding community, this would interfere with their primary task of governance and the correct formation of the church according to the teachings of Jesus Christ. "It is not right," they said, "that we should neglect the word of God in order to wait on tables" (6:2).

So they decided to establish a new sponsorship structure. The Apostles asked the assembly to choose "seven men of good standing, full of the Spirit and of wisdom" whom they would then "appoint to this task" of facilitating the mission and ministry of the Twelve (6:3). The apostles could then be freed to devote themselves "to prayer and to serving the Word" (6:4). Seven men were selected according to approved criteria, which was that they had to be men "of good standing, full of the Spirit and of wisdom" (6:5). They were then formally mandated by apostles to lead a new sponsorship model: "They had these men stand before the apostles, who prayed and laid their hands on them" (6:6).[28]

---

[28]Exegetes note there are problems interpreting Acts 6:1–7. Luke Timothy Johnson notes: "There is no obvious connection between the purported role

With this mandate the seven men were officially appointed to a ministry of the church. Luke recorded that the new sponsorship model operated successfully. The community was again living in peace, and the apostles were freed to fulfill their ministerial duties (see 6:7).

Contemporary Lessons

What does this incident from Acts teach us today? It is easy for hierarchical authorities in the church to forget that ultimately it is the mission of Christ that must determine the purpose, governance, and administration of all ministries. This mission is unchangeable, whereas the particularities of rules, disciplines, and procedures are not. The apostles had to be reminded by Hellenists that governance structures had become inadequate, even unjust, because vulnerable people's needs were being neglected. However, the apostles speedily acted to deal with this, and the integrity of the church was restored. So today the church's hierarchies are being vociferously and correctly reminded by the laity that the contemporary governance structures are failing to respond to the sexual abuses by clerics and religious of minors. New administrative and accountability structures are needed that permit the voices of lay people to be listened to *and* heard.

It is true, as theologian Neil Ormerod points out, that certain structural forms of governance are "of divine origin or divinely instituted. . . . [But] there are various details of Church life which no one suggests are of divine origin, such as the existence of the cardinalate or religious orders. Such are clearly of human origin, but useful for the life of the Church."[29] Though the rapidly developing new sponsorship model (PJPs) that is replacing the ministry of religious congregations is not of divine origin, surely

---

of the seven and their actual function. They were supposed to be in charge of community possessions but they turn out to be prophetic preachers. . . . The discrepancy disappears when we remember Luke's consistent habit of using authority over material possessions as symbol for spiritual authority." *The Acts of the Apostles* (Collegeville, MN: Liturgical Press, 1992), 111; Justin Taylor, "Acts of the Apostles," in *The International Bible Commentary*, ed. William Farmer (Collegeville, MN: Liturgical Press, 1998), 1519–20.

[29] Neil Ormerod, "The Knowledge and Authority of Jesus—A Response to Bishop Robinson," *Australasian Catholic Record* 88, no. 1 (2011): 94.

the same reforming rapidity can be directed to contemporary hierarchical governance structures to permit lay involvement to help curtail the abuse of power. And Ormerod adds: "We do not properly train our ministerial candidates in the exercise of power they hold."[30] "This lack of a sense of responsibility is evident not only in matters of sexual abuse, but other areas in parish and diocesan life where power is abused."[31] This abuse of power in all its forms in the present governance and administrative structures must cease. For this lay juridically approved involvement in these structures is necessary.

Laicization of Ministries: Three Challenges

The *first* challenge, and possibly the most difficult, is the need to train clergy to recognize the ministries of lay people and to work closely with them. The *second* challenge is to accept that for theological and contextual reasons laity will now need appropriate juridical status in the governance of the church. But legislation alone will not do it. The *third* task is to determine how best to form lay people in Catholic theology and spirituality both to be involved in governance and to maintain the Catholic ethos in education, health care, and other ministries. Though much is being done already, there can be significant formation gaps. A 2009 study of lay principals in Catholic schools in Australia showed that most felt ill-prepared for their role as the religious leaders of their schools and often felt they were simply "thrown into" administration with little formation, and they have consistently found that they simply do not have the time to read or study.[32] Gerald Grace writes that in England there

is evidence that many candidates for the headship of Catholic schools in England can now talk confidently about achievements in test scores and examinations, business planning and budgets, marketing and public relations, but are relatively

---

[30]Neil Ormerod, "Power and Authority—A Response to Bishop Cullinane," *Australasian Catholic Record* 82, no. 3 (2005): 154–62.

[31]Ormerod, "The Knowledge," 97.

[32]See Angelo Belmonte and Neil Cranston, "The Religious Dimension of Lay Leadership in Catholic Schools," *Catholic Education* 12, no. 3 (2009): 294–319.

inarticulate about the spiritual purpose of Catholic schooling. This is a major contradiction in a system of schools which exists to give the nurture of spirituality a top priority and it demonstrates that the traditional spiritual capital of Catholic school leadership is a declining asset.[33]

Summary

- Vatican II ruled against the centuries-long misconception that the church is an unequal society made up of two ranks, clergy and laity: "Instead the bishops gave priority to faith, baptism, and Christian discipleship (*Lumen Gentium*, paras. 9–17) for establishing our ecclesial identity. They affirmed the necessary equality of all believers (*Lumen Gentium*, para. 32)."[34]

- But what has not changed is the use by hierarchical officials of authority and power to reflect this equality.[35] They are presently accountable for their actions, not to the People of God, but upward to those who gave them their authority. The People of God are ignored, as is evident in the history of sexual abuses and cover-ups. This must change. Hierarchical officials must be accountable to the People of God. For this reform to happen, lay women[36] and men must now become involved in juridical governance structures of the church.

- The "legal barrier contained in Canon 129 that allows the non-clerics to cooperate only with the 'power of

---

[33]Gerald Grace, *Catholic Schools: Mission, Markets and Morality* (London: Routledge, 2002), 237.

[34]Richard R. Gaillardetz, "Power and Authority in the Church: Emerging Issues," in *A Church with Open Doors: Catholic Ecclesiology for the Third Millennium*, ed. Richard R. Gaillardetz and Edward P. Hannenberg (Collegeville, MN: Liturgical Press, 2015), 87.

[35]See John P. Beal, "Something There Is That Doesn't Love a Law: Canon Law and Its Discontents," in *The Crisis of Authority in Catholic Modernity*, ed. Michael J. Lacey and Francis Oakley (New York: Oxford University Press, 2011), 150.

[36]Any reform of governance must. include women. They are involved up to 75 percent in the church's pastoral work. See Paul Collins, *Absolute Power: How the Pope Became the Most. Influential Man in the World* (New York: Public Affairs, 2018), 325.

governance' but not to participate in any way must be removed."[37] There are no theological or historical reasons to prevent laity becoming involved in the governance of the church.

---

[37]Orsy, "Receiving the Council," 44.

6

Refounding the Church

Action Plans and Strategies

More than by fear of going astray, my hope is that we will be moved by the fear of remaining shut up within structures which give us a false sense of security, within rules which make us harsh judges, within habits which make us feel safe, while at our door people are starving and Jesus does not tire of saying to us: "Give them something to eat" (Mark 6:37).

—Pope Francis, "The Joy of the Gospel"

I think we take our eye off the ball if we don't deal with the business of privilege, power and protection of a clerical culture. Those three elements have to be eradicated from the life of the church. Everything else is a sideshow if we do not get at that.

—Cardinal Blase Cupich, cited in Joshua J. McEwee and Heidi Schlumpf, "Exclusive: Cupich says Bishops Must Cede Authority, Allow Lay Oversight of Accusations"

No large institution will overnight transform its paradigm into something entirely different . . . especially not an institution so deeply embedded in human culture as the Roman Catholic Church.

—John W. O'Malley, SJ, *Tradition and Transition*

The barrier to change is not too little caring; it is too much complexity.

—Bill Gates, cited in Tim Hartford,
Why Success Always Starts with Failure

This chapter sets out action plans and strategies relating to:

- the call to hierarchies: conversion
- acknowledgng chaos/trauma
- solidarity: collective mourning and penance
- reacting to shame
- becoming a pilgrim church
- evaluating ministries according to the mission of Jesus Christ
- accountability structures for leaders
- development of collaborative leadership
- intentional faith communities as culture changers
- fostering popular piety
- storytelling and refounding
- formation of priests
- lay formation
- evaluating pastoral care
- pastoral care for survivors

The church is on the brink of seeing whether the global institution will survive and blossom anew or whether it will become a relic of former times. The sexual abuse and cover-up crisis in the institutional church is a culturally systemic problem, ultimately a problem of the misuse of authority and power as previous chapters have indicated. Such evil requires culturally systemic solutions. This chapter addresses these two interrelated issues:

- How is a new culture of nonclericalism, collegiality, and accountability to become embedded in the church so that the mission of Jesus Christ is the paramount central concern?
- What action plans and strategies must be put in place to achieve this aim?

An *action plan* lists what must be done by named individuals and/or collective groups to achieve particular objectives; a *strategy* sets out what *specifically*, that is, in more detail, must be implemented to accomplish the objectives of an action plan.[1] No matter how well formulated the action plans and strategies may be, however, the task of embedding a new culture in the church is a daunting one, even overwhelming, when we consider the startling complexity of the challenges. Not only do we speak of the universal church having a culture, but, at the same time, there are thousands of local churches and communities with their particular histories and cultures to consider. All are being called to embrace a new culture. But as Chapter 1 illustrates, cultural change, even in apparently little things such as ceasing to use plastic bags for shopping in order to protect the environment or insisting that clinicians wash their hands to save the lives of patients, is mighty difficult!

> Changing people and organizations is not an instant affair. It requires an elaborate process of working through—a mourning process of coming to grips with what these changes signify. People who promise quick-fix solutions are playing a delusional game. There is a world of difference between identifying symptoms and analyzing and treating the real nature of a problem.[2]

Chapter 1 explained that there are two requirements for the development of a *new* culture in any institution: visible and invisible structural changes. For invisible structural changes to occur there must be attitudinal conversion to drive the changes. Without this conversion, visible structural changes, such as new laws, will remain mere words. This is what Pope Francis

---

[1] See comments by Andrew Pettigrew, Ewan Ferlie, and Lorna McKee, *Shaping Strategic Change: Making Change in Large Organizations* (London: Sage Publications, 1992), 19–20.

[2] Manfred F. R. Kets de Vries, "Struggling with the Demon: Confronting the Irrationality of Organizations and Executives," in *Organizations of the Couch: Clinical Perspectives on Organizational Behavior and Change*, ed. Manfred F. R. Kets de Vries and Associates (San Francisco: Jossey-Bass, 1991), 381.

means when he writes: "Changing structures without generating new convictions and attitudes will only ensure that those same structures will become, sooner or later, corrupt, oppressive and ineffectual."[3] Therefore, in brief, the existing mythology of an institutional culture, not changes to official rules and policies, will ultimately dictate what one can or cannot do.[4]

Refounding a new church culture requires structural reforms (both visible and invisible) and attitudinal changes (i.e., conversion). And "visible" structural reforms, like laws, have no chance of success unless there is both conversion to the "invisible" structural ecclesial mythology of Vatican II and a revolution in attitudes. This reality has its roots in the fact that by baptism we are *all* called to be missionary disciples of Christ.[5]

The following action plans and strategies for refounding the church are based on the following assumptions about cultural change (see Chapters 1, 3, and 4):

- In-depth cultural change is slow, at times tortuous, unpredictable, and rarely smooth, since it depends on a people's internal acceptance of new mythologies; change responds more to the heart than to the head: "For where your treasure is, there your heart is also" (Mt 6:21) (see *Axiom 1,* Chapter 1).
- Remember in seeking to communicate with cultures that the "message sent" may not be the same as the "message received": "Other people's meanings and interpretations are highly unmanageable"[6] (see *Axiom 2,* Chapter 1).
- Resistance to change is commonly the result of too little concern being given to the *process* of introducing change

---

[3]Pope Francis, "The Joy of the Gospel" (*Evangelii Gaudium*) (Strathfield: St. Pauls Publications, 2013), para. 189.

[4]See Terrence Deal and Allan Kennedy, *The New Corporate Cultures* (London: Orion Books, 1999), 40.

[5]See Richard R. Gaillardetz, *An Unfinished Council: Vatican II, Pope Francis and the Renewal of Catholicism* (Collegeville, MN: Liturgical Press, 2015), 57–60, 87–89.

[6]Mary Jo Hatch, *Organizational Theory: Modern, Symbolic and Postmodern Perspectives* (Oxford: Oxford University Press, 1997), 234.

and not the change itself;[7] cultural change is a complex process, with no quick fixes, no instant solutions.

- Institutional cultural refounding demands that the original creation myth be reowned; if not, the energy for change cannot be sustained (see Chapter 4).

- Cultural change is more likely to happen if position-authority persons, including and especially hierarchical officials in the church, are wholeheartedly prepared to support a refounding project (see Chapter 4).[8]

- Recall the emotional power inherent in cultures: "Leadership is one hundred percent about emotion. . . . Because organizations are people. . . . And people are emotional."[9] (See *Axiom 3,* Chapter 1.)

- Research overwhelmingly shows "that where individuals perceive they will benefit from change and are involved in its implementation, resistance will be reduced";[10] the largest obstacle to success is the failure to involve people authentically.

- Change best begins and is sustained first through small groups of people where experience is shared and trust develops.

The 1971 Synod of Bishops took the theme "Justice in the World," and concluded that "while the Church is bound to give witness to justice, she recognizes that anyone who ventures to speak to people about justice must first be just in their eyes. *Hence we must undertake an examination of the modes of acting and of the possessions and life style found within the Church itself.*"[11] In

---

[7]See Robert A. Paton and James McCalman, *Change Management: A Guide to Effective Implementation,* 2nd ed. (London: Sage, 2000); John W. Hunt, *Managing People at Work: A Manager's Guide to Behavior in Organizations,* 3rd ed. (London: McGraw-Hill, 1992).

[8]See David Buchanan and David Bodley, *The Expertise of the Change Agent* (Hempstead: Prentice Hall, 1992), 14–20.

[9]Tom Peters, cited by Paul Bate, *Strategies for Cultural Change* (Oxford: Butterworth-Heinemann, 1994), 42.

[10]Paul Parkin, *Managing Change in Healthcare: Using Action Research* (London: Sage, 2009), 171.

[11]Second Synod of Bishops, "Justice in the World" (November 30, 1971),

key areas of acting, possessions, and lifestyle this self-examination by many hierarchies has yet to occur. The action plans and strategies set out how this must begin and continue.

Call to Hierarchies: Conversion

Action Plan 1: Since episcopal hierarchies, at all levels in the church, hold position authority to block or foster cultural changes, they must personally and collectively "put their whole [lives] on the line . . . in bearing witness to Jesus Christ";[12] inspired by this universal call to holiness[13] they will wholeheartedly commit themselves to Vatican II's vision of transparency, collegiality, and accountability; if they fail to do so, there can be no refounding of the church.

Explanation

Institutional cultural change is impossible without the strong resolve of its top leaders (see Chapter 4). Yet the strong resolve that the leaders in the church need is impossible without their passionate commitment to holiness. Our founder, Jesus Christ, not only calls his followers to *strive* to be a holy people, but demands, in an authoritative voice, that they *be* holy (Mt 5:48; 1 Cor 1:2). Pope Francis writes: "He wants us to be saints and not to settle for a bland and mediocre existence. . . . 'Be holy, for I am holy' (Lev 11:44; cf. 1 Pet 1:16). . . . [More] than bureaucrats and functionaries, the Church needs passionate missionaries. . . . The saints surprise us, they confound us, because by their lives they urge us to abandon a dull and dreary mediocrity."[14] While there are examples of this conversion among individual bishops, collectively as conferences this has not happened. For this reason

---

para. 40. Italics added.

[12]Pope Francis, "The Joy of the Gospel," para. 24.

[13]See "Dogmatic Constitution on the Church" (*Lumen Gentium*), in *Documents of Vatican II*, ed. Austin P. Flannery (Grand Rapids, MI: William B. Eerdmans, 1975), para. 11.

[14]Pope Francis, "Rejoice and Exult" (*Gaudete et Exsultate*) (Strathfield: St. Pauls Publications, 2018), paras. 1, 10, 138.

clericalism has continued to flourish (see Chapter 2). Father Yves Congar, OP, wrote on the eve of Vatican II:

> *Should not the body of bishops take the initiative by stripping itself voluntarily of all that still remains of external signs of wealth, of the temporal power that is now happily a thing of the past?*. . . From actual poverty thus regained would flow a humility that would make [the church] more responsive to the motions of the Holy Spirit . . . more receptive to the suffering of the world, and more generous in the service of the poor and of peace.[15]

Strategies for Conversion

As an example to the People of God, episcopal conferences will commit themselves to:

- A retreat based on the themes of the Apostolic Exhortation *Rejoice and Exult.*
- Evaluate episcopal lifestyles according to Gospel values of poverty, e.g., all the trappings of monarchical power to cease in the church—such as titles: "My Lord," "Your Grace," "Your Excellence," "Your Eminence"; and dress codes, *capa magna.*
- Identify and support individuals/groups of refounding qualities, be they lay, religious, or cleric.
- Acknowledge frequently and publicly that all the baptized are committed to the ministry of living the Gospel, not only clerics and religious.[16]

---

[15]Yves Congar, *Power and Poverty in the Church* (London: Geoffrey Chapman, 1965), 152–53. Italics added. See also Yves Congar, *True and False Reform in the Church*, trans. Paul Philibert (Collegeville, MN: Liturgical Press, 2011); Anthony Maher, "'The Primacy of the Pastoral': Bridging the Divide between Faith, Theology and Life in the Ecclesiology of Yves Congar," in *Bridging the Divide between Theology and Life*, ed. Anthony Maher (Adelaide: ATF Theology, 2015), 27–48.

[16]"Christian ministry is the public activity of a baptized follower of Jesus Christ [lay or cleric] flowing from the Spirit's charism and an individual personality on behalf of a Christian community to witness to, serve and realize the kingdom of God." Thomas F. O'Meara, "Ministry," in *The New Dictionary of Theology*, ed. Joseph A. Komonchak, Mary Collins, and Dermot A. Lane (Collegeville, MN:

- Petition the Holy See for canonical changes to allow laity to become more juridically present in the governance structures of the church.

Acknowledging Chaos/Trauma

Action Plan 2: Refounding leaders acknowledge that the building of a new culture begins in hope, and will continue, only to the degree that we, as People of God, acknowledge the chaos/trauma in the church, particularly catalyzed by the global scandals.

Explanation

> I sink in deep mire; where there is no foothold;
> I have come into deep waters, and the flood sweeps over me.
> I am weary with my crying; my throat is parched.
> My eyes grow dim with waiting for my God. (Ps 69:2–3)

Walter Brueggemann writes,

> The Bible is much more preoccupied with the threat of chaos than it is with sin and guilt. . . . We have devised ways of forgiveness, of handling sin and guilt, an assurance of pardon. . . . But the storm is not so easy. The storm produces a more elemental, inchoate anxiety, a sense of helplessness. . . . It is bottomless in size and beyond measure in force.[17]

Our church is in chaos. We People of God feel that we are in an ever-increasing storm, with no knowledge of when it will end: "Lord, save us! We are perishing!" (Mt 8:25). Yes, together we anxiously feel this: "If one member suffers, all suffer together with it" (1 Cor 12:26). True, with Pope Francis we "acknowledge once more the suffering endured by many minors due to sexual abuse, and the abuse of power and the abuse of conscience perpetrated by a significant number of clerics and consecrated persons. Crimes

---

Liturgical Press, 1987), 660.

[17]Walter Brueggemann, *Inscribing the Text* (Minneapolis: Fortress Press, 2004), 51.

that inflict deep wounds of pain and powerlessness, primarily among the victims, but also in their family members and in the larger community of believers and nonbelievers alike."[18]

Yes, we acknowledge the abuse that has been perpetrated in the church. But the chaos remains. Let us ponder further this chaos. One of the most formidable images used by God in the scriptures, and repeated by the words and actions of Christ, is that of *chaos*. Chaos and its many synonyms, such as "grave," "wilderness," "sea," connote a state of utter confusion, frightening anxiety, fear, totally lacking in order or predictability; it is the opposite of cosmos.[19] For example, in the Book of Job two mythical figures, Leviathan and Behemoth, symbolize the primordial chaos created by God from which is shaped meaning and order in the world (Job 40:19).[20] Whenever Job is afflicted he comes back, in imitation of these two figures, to God-created chaos and there relearns the apt lesson that humankind without God is powerless. We can do nothing by ourselves to prevent this backward fall occurring. Only God as Creator can finally control chaos and order. As God explains to Job, when God's face is turned away from us and we confront the terrifying force of darkness and uncertainty, then as God's creatures and stewards of the gifts given us, we come into contact once more with the chaos out of which we were shaped and the teachings it symbolizes. That is, we learn anew, if we willingly choose to do so, the very foundations of our being, our own ineffectiveness, and at the same time the saving, the reenergizing authority, forgiveness, and mercy of God in Christ.

To be life-giving, therefore, the wearying and frightening experience of chaos must be openly admitted and personally/corporately accepted. We cannot learn from what is happening *if* we fail to acknowledge and own it. This is what Gospel conversion means. Christ's way to the hope in, and joy of, the resurrection

---

[18]Pope Francis, "Letter to the People of God," (August 20, 2018).

[19]See Bernhard Anderson, *Creation versus Chaos: The Reinterpretation of Mythical Symbolism in the Bible* (New York: Association Press, 1967), 132; Gerald A. Arbuckle, *Catholic Identity or Identities? Refounding Ministries in Chaotic Times* (Collegeville, MN: Liturgical Press, 2015), ix.

[20]See Dermot Cox, *Man's Anger and God's Silence: The Book of Job* (Middlegreen: St. Pauls Publications, 1990), 104.

is only through the austerity of dispossession: "But he emptied himself, taking the form of slave. . . . Therefore God also highly exalted him" (Phil 2:7, 9). St. John of the Cross senses this chaos/ re-creative dynamic:

> When the soul frees itself of all things and attains to emptiness and dispossession concerning them, which is equivalent to what it can do of itself, it is impossible that God fails to do His part by communicating Himself to it, at least silently and secretly. . . . God will enter the soul that is empty, and fill it with divine goods.[21]

Walter Brueggemann explains that for the Israelites the experience of chaos, the antithesis of rest, is often described as "weariness."[22] They are weary when they want to live an ordered life in a way that takes no account of God's plans for them: "This is rest; give rest to the weary." But they were condemned to remain weary because "they would not hear" him (Is 28:12). Only God's powerful intervening action or that of God's mediator can take away the feeling of chaotic weariness: "These texts play upon an old mythological pattern of chaos and creation."[23] The lesson for us is: we People of God must co-operate, admitting the chaos we are in: "May fasting and prayer open our eyes to the hushed pain felt by children, young people and the disabled."[24] Only then is this the result: "Blessed are those who trust in the Lord. . . . They shall be like a tree planted by water, sending out its roots by the stream" (Jer 17:7–8).

We see in the New Testament also that God allows chaos to develop as a prelude for people to respond with creative acts of faith and hope. Thus, the two disciples on the road to Emmaus, symbols of countless others who had come to know Jesus in the

---

[21]St. John of the Cross, "Living Flame," in *The Collected Works of St. John of the Cross*, trans. Kieran Kavanaugh and Otilio Rodriguez (Washington, DC: ICS Publications, 1979), para. 3.46.

[22]See Walter Brueggemann, "Weariness, Exile and Chaos: A Motif in Royal Theology," *Catholic Biblical Quarterly* 34 (1972): 19–38; and "Kingship and Chaos: A Study in Tenth Century Theology," *Catholic Biblical Quarterly* 33 (1971): 317–32.

[23]Brueggemann, "Weariness, Exile, and Chaos," 29.

[24]Pope Francis, "Letter to the People of God" (August 20, 2018).

years of his public ministry, are thrown into a state of chaotic confusion and desolation, because the security they had sought was not what Jesus had promised. They are downcast: "But we had hoped that he was the one to redeem Israel" (Lk 24:21). They had failed to comprehend that Christ should enter into the darkness and shame of the tomb so that they might themselves be led out of chaos (Lk 24:26). They had yet to learn that God's love is overwhelming; new and dynamic life will emerge out of the chaos, provided they in hope "believe all that the prophets have declared" (Lk 24:25). The message is: be truthful, acknowledge sinfulness, repent and trust in the power of Jesus Christ. In the present humiliatingly painful chaos we can rediscover that we are humanly powerless without God's abiding love and help: "The Church . . . at once holy and always in need of purification [must follow] constantly the path of penance and renewal."[25] Indeed, the first recorded words of Jesus when beginning his public ministry are: "The time is fulfilled and the kingdom of God has come near, repent and believe in the good news" (Mk 1:15).

Strategies for Acknowledging Chaos/Trauma

- Hierarchies need to admit that the institutional church has allowed immeasurable suffering to the survivors of sexual abuse to occur, distress made worse by covering up this tragedy; as Pope Francis writes, these actions are "objectively in contradiction to the Gospel [causing] harm to many people."[26]
- Hierarchies need publicly to acknowledge "that it is the Church in its totality, in its life, its doctrines, its catechisms, its witness and structures, that is invited to purification, to a remembering and a healing of memories."[27]
- Confronted with the chaos, church leaders "need to

---

[25]"Dogmatic Constitution on the Church," para. 8.

[26]Garry Wills, "The Vatican Regrets," *National Catholic Reporter*, May 25, 2000, 19.

[27]David Power, *Love without Calculation: A Reflection on Divine Kenosis* (New York: Crossword, 2005), 87.

brood" as "the Spirit of God brooded over the face of the deep" (Gen 1:2).[28] Stephen Croft, reflecting on this text, comments that brooding implies that leaders need to be courageous in order "to dwell with and within the chaos, to explore [its] complexity and to attempt to understand the context well." And "to brood means to love." The more "the people [are] within [the chaos the more they] will need love and care and commitment from those entrusted with leadership."[29]

Solidarity: Collective Mourning and Penance

Action Plan 3: Repentance calls for collective mourning.

Knowing how to mourn with others: that is holiness.[30]

Today we are challenged as the People of God to take on the pain of our brothers and sisters wounded in their flesh and spirit.[31]

Explanation

We People of God are overwhelmed with unarticulated grief from two sources: grief from the church's lost opportunities to build a church of collegiality and transparency as specified by Vatican II and grief from discovering the global scandals of sexual abuse of minors and their concealment (see Chapter 3).

Grief or grieving is the internal experiences of sadness, sorrow, anger, loneliness, anguish, confusion, shame, guilt, and fear as a consequence of experiencing loss. The term *mourning*, on the other hand, refers to formal or informal

---

[28]King James Version.

[29]Steven Croft, *The Gift of Leadership According to the Scriptures* (Norwich: Canterbury Press, 2016), 60–61.

[30]Pope Francis, "Rejoice and Exult" (*Gaudete et Exsultate*) (Strathfield: St. Pauls Publications, 2018), para. 76.

[31]Pope Francis, *Letter to the People of God.*

rituals and internal processes of transformation that the bereaved undertakes to deal with grieving. Grieving is very much an automatic reaction to loss, but mourning requires a decision to relate to grief in constructive ways, that is, a willingness to acknowledge publicly that grief has occurred, to let it go, and then to be open to the world ahead.[32]

One mourns the passing of the old attachments and prepares for new ones.[33] "Healing," wrote Henri Nouwen, "means, first of all, the creation of an empty, but friendly space where those who suffer can tell their story to someone who can listen with real attention."[34] The scriptures are a plentiful source for mourning or lamentation rituals that provide friendly faith-based spaces for people to tell their stories of loss. Did not Jesus on the cross agonizingly and so publicly complain to the Father in the words of the lament Psalm 22: "My God, my God, why have you forsaken me?" (Mt 27:46).

The lament psalms teach us how to complain prayerfully in the midst of our overwhelming sadness, our anger, shame, and feelings of betrayal and abandonment. Our loud faith-based laments become rituals of mourning through which our griefs can be abandoned and we can again look to the future in hope. Not to complain, as the scriptures teach us, means that we will continue to be haunted, suffocated, by our sorrows. We will be destroyed, overwhelmed, by the unspoken anguish of our powerlessness. Ponder the public lament of the Israelites as they agonizingly view the destruction of the pivotal symbol of God's presence, the temple. Desolation reigns supreme. God gets all the blame, but once their sadness has been so dramatically proclaimed and put aside, the Israelites discover space within their hearts for a hopeful trust in God:

---

[32]Gerald A. Arbuckle, *The Francis Factor and the People of God: New Life for the Church* (Maryknoll, NY: Orbis Books, 2015), 61–62.

[33]John Bowlby defines healthy mourning as "the successful effort of an individual to accept both that a change has occurred in the external world and that he is [thus] required to make corresponding changes in his internal, representational world and to reorganize, and perhaps to reorient, his attachment behavior accordingly." *Attachment and Loss,* vol. 3, *Loss* (New York: Basic Books, 1980), 18.

[34]Henri Nouwen, *Reaching Out* (London: Collins, 1976), 88.

O God, why do you cast us off forever?
Why does your anger smoke against the sheep of your
pasture? . . .
Your foes have roared within your holy place. . . .
with hatchets and hammers, they smashed all its carved
work. . . .
Rise up, O God, plead your cause; remember how the
impious
scoff at you all the day long. (Ps 74:1, 4, 6, 22)

To lament, however, demands that we struggle to put aside our denials of loss. Walter Brueggemann comments:

Such a denial and cover-up . . . is an odd inclination for passionate Bible users, given the large number of psalms that are songs of lament, protest, and complaint about the incoherence that is experienced in the world. At least it is clear that a church that goes on singing "happy songs" in the face of raw reality is doing something very different from what the Bible itself does.[35]

Nor does lament mean we forget the tragedies of the survivors of abuse. Theologian Robert Schreiter reminds us that "to urge the forgetting of painful memories and events is to either trivialize the events themselves . . . or to trivialize the victim (you are not significant enough to have been offended that much)."[36] The forgetting that we are called to in rituals of mourning is "an overcoming of anger and resentment, being freed from the entanglements of those emotions and their capacity to keep us bound to an event."[37]

Strategies for Collective Mourning and Penance

- Hierarchical persons need to initiate liturgical services acknowledging the evils of sexual abuse and cover-ups

---

[35]Walter Brueggemann, *The Message of the Psalms* (Minneapolis: Augsburg, 1984), 51–52.

[36]Robert Schreiter, *The Ministry of Reconciliation: Spirituality and Strategies* (Maryknoll, NY: Orbis Books, 2000), 66.

[37]Ibid., 67.

that have occurred and begging God's forgiveness; this
needs to be done in ways that allow participants to express
their personal and collective grief at what has occurred;
this can be done in various ways, for example, dedicating
special services in Advent and/or Lent.[38]

• Individual dioceses or conferences of bishops need to establish Truth, Justice, and Healing Commissions with the
task, inter alia: to receive complaints from alleged victims
of sexual abuse of minors; to assist in lasting healing for
survivors of abuse; to identify any systemic institutional
failures that have blocked or hindered the protection of minors; and to sponsor research into best practice procedures,
policies, and structures for the protection of minors.[39]

Reacting to Shame

Action Plan 4: *Since the issue of individual and collective shame,
resulting from revelations of sexual abuse and cover-up, must
be addressed in the refounding process, leaders will within
mourning rituals provide space for people to ponder scriptural
reference of shame to aid healing.*

Explanation

To be shamed is to be labeled as something contaminated, and,
therefore, denied a respected status in society (see *Axiom 12,*
Chapter 1). It is unfortunate that though shame is "a defining

---

[38]For a fuller explanation of Scripture-based mourning see Gerald A. Arbuckle,
The Francis Factor and the People of God: New Life for the Church (Maryknoll,
NY: Orbis Books, 2015), 59–124.

[39]This description is based on the model of the council initiated by the Australian Catholic Bishops Conference, 2014, to liaise with the government-sponsored
Royal Commission into Institutional Responses to Child Abuse. The council
consisted of twelve people, with expertise spanning such fields as child sexual
abuse, trauma, mental illness, suicide, psycho-sexual disorders, education, public
administration, law, and governance. The majority of council members were lay,
two of its members were bishops, and one of its members was a religious sister.
Three of the council members were either themselves victims of abuse or had
immediate family members who were victims. The CEO was a lay person. *Issues
Paper,* no. 6 (August 11, 2014), 2, 5.

aspect of human existence," it is "rarely addressed in churches and ministry."[40] Shame is about our status as people or who we are; it is about the loss of identity and the need to recover and feel we again belong to a community of faith and that, despite its sinfulness, the church is still loved by Jesus Christ: "Healing and release from shame does not come simply from sermons or discipleship programs, but from community."[41] People need space to ponder biblical examples that give meaning to their own experiences in a church overwhelmed with shame. In the New Testament we see Jesus Christ repeatedly relating to people who feel shamed in society; he goes out of his way to identify with them by showing his love for them so that in the process they are released from feeling shamed. The ultimate act of identifying with those who feel shamed is Christ's death and resurrection, because there he takes on our shame that we may with him be one with his resurrection (Phil 5–11).

Strategies for Reacting to Shame

No one who believes in him will be put to shame. (Rom 10:11)

Scriptural reflections and homilies can be built around many instances where Jesus heals shame by love:

- There is a woman, shamed by society, who is healed of persistent bleeding (Lk 8:43–48); not only is she physically healed, but by touching her, Jesus declares she is once more no longer excluded by society. Her dignity is restored.
- Christ also deliberately associates with other people who feel shamed by society: tax collectors (Lk 19:1–10), lepers (Lk 5:12–16), blind people (Mk 10:46–52).
- And he relates parables in which he identifies with the shamed: the parable of the unexpected guests (Lk 14:15–24).

---

[40]Jayson Georges and Mark D. Baker, *Ministering in Honor-Shame Cultures* (Downers Grove, IL: InterVarsity, 2016), 28.
[41]Ibid., 235.

- In the parable of the prodigal son, the father welcomes back his shamed son (Lk 15:11–32).

Becoming a Pilgrim Church

Action Plan 5: Refounding leaders work to replace the "Fortress Model" of the church with the "Pilgrim Model," in which a listening church commits itself to the preferential option for the poor.

Explanation

On earth, still as pilgrims in a strange land, following in trial and in oppression the paths he trod, we are associated with his sufferings as the body with its head, suffering with him, that with him we may be glorified.[42]

The fortress model dims or camouflages the presence of Christ and the pervading influence of the Gospel in the life of the church. Acceptance of a culture of cover-up is the consequence. The pilgrimage model faded in importance as an image of the church in post-Reformation times because the institutional church now emphasized "a static ontology of grace, clearly defined structures of the supernatural organism, and an ahistorical approach to spiritual life as a primarily interior relation to God."[43] Vatican II, with its call to Christians to enter into dialogue with a changing world, again returned to the ancient pilgrimage theme: we are a sinful pilgrim people "united in Christ and guided by the Holy Spirit, press onwards towards the kingdom of the Father."[44] Since the church is the People of God, a community of disciples on pilgrimage in history, the pilgrimage model is the best suited to guide the People of God through the contemporary chaos of the church.

---

[42]"Dogmatic Constitution on the Church," para. 7.

[43]Richard Byrne, "Journey: Growth and Development in Spiritual Life," in *The New Dictionary of Catholic Spirituality*, ed. Michael Downey (Collegeville, MN: Liturgical Press, 1993), 565.

[44]"Pastoral Constitution on the Church in the Modern World," in *Documents of Vatican II*, ed. Austin P. Flannery (Grand Rapids, MI: William W. Eerdmans, 1975), para. 1.

Pilgrimage or journey is a fundamental paradigm of the conversion process in the Scriptures, for example, the Exodus. The biblical God is not a distant divinity "frozen into an immobile and inaccessible splendour. . . . [God] is a pilgrim God—alive, creative, resourceful. If God is the first Pilgrim, then faith consists essentially in imitating, in following, in walking in God's footsteps: it receives from God both its dynamism and its direction."[45] The paschal mystery of our salvation is Christ's pilgrimage, and he calls us to the same journey with all its radical demands. "Thomas said, 'Lord, we do not know where we are going, so how can we know the way?' Jesus said: 'I am the Way; I am truth and Life. No one can come to the Father except through me' " (Jn 9:5–6).

Pilgrims become *listening* people, critically attentive to their cultural environment, and they discover that listening builds relationships and trust. Pilgrims yearn to listen to what the Spirit is wanting of them. This means they must first be prepared to listen to themselves—their inner fears, motives, intuitions, their ongoing need for redemption, the sufferings of those around them. Refounding leaders as pilgrims are listening people who want to understand what others feel and think. This requires periods of stillness, silence, a love of learning, and solitude.[46]

Today the People of God have been forced by scandals and abuse of power in the church into a position of growing powerlessness in society. Authentic pilgrims consent to this poverty of influence by uniting themselves with the *kenosis,* the self-giving, of Christ (Phil 2:5, 7, 8).[47] In his teaching and lifestyle Jesus proclaims that people who are poor are to be privileged "heirs of the kingdom" (Jas 2:5). He is to be the Messiah of the poor, "He has sent me to . . . let the oppressed go free" (Lk 4:18). After an ambiguous reaction on the part of his listeners (Lk 4:22), Jesus reiterates by way of examples taken from the lives of the

---

[45]John of Taize, *A New Testament: The Way of the Lord* (Washington, DC: Pastoral Press, 1990), 10.

[46]See Gerald A. Arbuckle, *Loneliness: Insights for Healing in a Fragmented World* (Maryknoll, NY: Orbis Books, 2018), xvi–xviii, 17–24, 210–12; Pope Francis, "Rejoice and Exult" (*Gaudete et Exsultate*) (Strathfield: St. Pauls Publications, 2018), paras. 29, 31.

[47]See David Power, *Love without Calculation: A Reflection on Divine Kenosis* (New York: Crossword, 2005), 5–23.

prophets Elijah (1 Kings 17:17–24) and Elisha (2 Kings 5:1–19), that his mission is preferentially directed toward those who are underprivileged and marginalized. By identifying with Christ the Poor One, people become true pilgrims. Through "penance and prayer" they open their eyes and hearts "to other people's sufferings and to overcome the thirst for power and possessions that are so often the root of those evils."[48]

There is an initiatory quality to a pilgrimage; "a 'pilgrim' is an initiate, entering into a deeper level of existence" than he or she has known before.[49] In the journey of life we are all initiates called by God to enter into an ever-deepening experience of faith and conversion, at a level never before reached by us. Pilgrimages are not only initiatory events, they are also mourning rituals in which pilgrims must, with the grace of God, let go of all that holds them back from achieving their goal (see *Action Plan 3*). Pilgrimages are also "faith levelers"; that is, in the pilgrimage model of the church, pope, bishops, priests, and lay people are on the same level in their journey of faith. Ranks become irrelevant.

Strategies for Becoming a Pilgrim Church

- Lifestyles and accommodation for cardinals, bishops, priests, and religious need to be evaluated according to the "preferential option for the poor."
- "In the interests of child safety and improved institutional responses to child sexual abuse [Catholic Bishops Conferences] should request the Holy See to: (a) publish criteria for the selection of bishops, including relating to the promotion of child safety; (b) establish a transparent process for appointing bishops which includes the direct participation of lay people."[50]
- Pope Francis is calling for a *listening church,* the contrary of clericalism; the art of listening is necessary if the

---

[48]Ibid.

[49]See Victor Turner and Edith Turner, *Image and Pilgrimages in Christian Culture* (Oxford: Basil Blackwell, 1978), 8.

[50]*Final Report of the Royal Commission into Institutional Responses to Child Sexual Abuse* (Barton, ACT: Commonwealth of Australia, 2017), vol. 16, bk.1. Recommendation to the Australian Catholic Bishops Conference, no. 16.8, 73.

People of God are "to arrive at the roots that allowed such atrocities to occur and be perpetuated and thus find solutions to the abuse scandal, not merely with containment strategies—essential but insufficient—but with the [commitment] to take on the problems in [their] complexity."[51]

Evaluating Ministries According to the Mission of Jesus Christ

Action Plan 6: Since the founding mission of the church is the mission of Jesus Christ, refounding leaders will evaluate their ministries according to his mission.

Mission, vision, and values are the building blocks of organizational culture. If people are to be expected to creatively adapt to change, they must understand [these blocks].
                                    —William J. Duncan et al.[52]

Explanation

The fundamental origin of the Catholic identities of our ministries and institutions is Jesus Christ and his mission according to the Catholic tradition (Eph 2:19–22). As we reflect on our founding roots, we see that the fundamental challenge to being church is to become disciples of Jesus Christ of Nazareth, that is alive and announcing his vision of the kingdom where the poor have an honored place. The church is in deep trouble because it has lost touch with its primary task, its mission, the same founding mission that the Father gave the Son, the mission to go out and bring the Good News to all (Mk 16:14–18). The punishment for failure to define and implement an institution's mission is confusion and chaos, the blurring of its values, and the inability to evaluate task performance.[53]

Pope Francis reminds us: "The center is Jesus Christ, who calls

---

[51]Pope Francis, "Letter to the Church in Chile" (2018).

[52]W. Jack Duncan, Peter M. Ginter, and Linda E. Swayne, *Strategic Management of Health Care Organizations* (Oxford: Blackwell, 1995), 465.

[53]See comments by A. K. Rice, *The Enterprise and Its Environment* (London: Tavistock, 1963), 190.

us and sends us."[54] It is his story of educating that we must ultimately build upon. It is his story that needs to be repeatedly retold in refreshingly new ways "so that the Church's customs, ways of doing thing, times and schedules, language and structures can be suitably channeled for evangelization."[55] Jesus Christ, and his mission, is the one who ennobles us, gives meaning to human life, and is *the* model for all Christian evangelization and leadership. Certainly, we may be adhering to all the dogmas, ethical principles, and social teachings of the church, but what ultimately will make our ministries *unique* are our efforts to be Jesus the truthful, compassionate, and merciful one. Without this relationship to Christ our ministries have no reason to exist. In brief, Jesus Christ is the primary founder and source of Catholic identities of our ministries. Particular saints, initiators of religious congregations of existing ministries, and institutions are secondary founders.[56]

Strategies for Evaluating Ministries

- The driver in institutional cultural change is leadership that focuses on mission, vision, values. Therefore, refounding leaders of church's ministries, building on the foundational mission of Jesus Christ, must be able to articulate and communicate the particular mission, vision, and values of these ministries that have been collaboratively formulated. The mission and vision statements of these ministries must be realistic and adhered to.

- A *mission statement,* which will contain the values of a ministry, will distinguish it from all others of its type by asking and answering the questions: "Who are we?" and "What do we do?" The statement must be sufficiently inspirational, and grounded in reality,[57] to empower

---

[54]Pope Francis, quoted by Thomas Reese, "Pope Francis' Ecclesiology Rooted in the Emmaus Story," *National Catholic Reporter*, August 6, 2013, www.ncronline.org/news/spirituality/pope-francis-ecclesiology-rooted-emmaus-story.

[55]Ibid., para. 27.

[56]Arbuckle, *Catholic Identity or Identities?* 121–42.

[57]*The Economist*, when reflecting on mission statements in the business world, warns that "the danger is that, by aiming to inspire, firms produce pious platitudes instead. . . . The best statements are short and describe the business in a way that customers and employees can understand and appreciate." "When Visions and Values Descend into Verbiage," *The Economist*, August 4, 2018, 46.

people to act. *Values*, contained in a mission statement, are action-oriented priorities, which are "basic convictions that one specific way of acting or end-state is personally or socially preferable to another."[58]

- A *vision statement*, in contrast, is a mental passage from the known to the unknown, creating the future from a mass of existing facts, hopes, dreams, dangers, and opportunities. A vision statement articulates everyone's agreed-upon destination in response to the question: "What do we want this ministry to look like within a set period of time? A realistic vision statement must be sharply focused. Otherwise, strategic planning to realize the vision will be fuzzy. If there is no clear vision, the group becomes confused and de-energized. "Where there is no vision, the people perish" (Prov 29:18).[59] A *strategy* is a plan for the use of resources in order to implement in concrete terms a group's mission and vision.[60]

Accountability Structures for Leaders

Action Plan 7: The refounding of the church demands that appropriate and operative accountable structures are established at all governance levels; only in this way will the church's focus on its mission be maintained, the rights of children and vulnerable adults protected, and trust again develop.

Explanation

Lack of accountability is a fatal flaw of leadership.[61]

Clericalism . . . leads to an exclusion in the ecclesial body that supports and helps to perpetuate many of the evils that we

---

[58]Gerald A. Arbuckle, *Healthcare Ministry: Refounding the Mission in Tumultuous Times* (Collegeville, MN: Liturgical Press, 2000), 153.

[59]King James Version.

[60]See Arbuckle, *Healthcare Ministry*, 152–53.

[61]John H. Zenger and Joseph Folkman, *The Handbook for Leaders: 24 Lessons of Extraordinary Leadership* (Maidenhead: McGraw-Hill, 2007), cited by Brian Dive, in *The Accountable Leader: Developing Effective Leadership through Managerial Accountability* (London/Philadelphia: Kogan Page, 2008), 50.

are condemning today.... Without the active participation of all our Church's members, everything being done to uproot the culture of abuse ... will not be successful in generating the necessary dynamics for sound and realistic change.[62]

Urgency

As this book shows all too sadly, hierarchical and congregational leaders have failed dismally to be accountable for their actions.[63] Cover-ups and other abuses of power have been allowed to occur because people have neglected to be accountable for what is happening. What is true of the Australian scene would commonly be the case globally: "*The powers of governance held by individual bishops and provincials are not subject to adequate checks and balances.... There has been no requirement for their decisions to be made transparent or subject to due process.*"[64] And as long as the pre–Vatican II culture model remains, clergy and religious will continue to behave with "deferential obedience"[65] toward their bishops and religious provincial superiors. The commission adds this significant conclusion: "The exclusion of lay people and women from leadership positions ... may have contributed to inadequate responses to child sexual abuse."[66]

How, therefore, are "adequate checks and balances" to be created so that bishops, priests, and religious superiors are made accountable for their actions? Jason Blakely suggests: "Overcoming clericalism means creating open, transparent and equal relationships between priests and laity. Such a community is willing to allow moral correction of priests by laity. Such a community is open and willing to learn from all its members."[67] Yet to achieve such a refounding culture of mutual accountability

---

[62]Pope Francis, *Letter to the People of God* (August 20, 2018).

[63]When accountability systems fail, it opens the door for internal power struggles and cronyism. In cronyism a person with political and/or economic power appoints family members or friends to key positions. Rumors and the grapevine become the only information channels. See Gerald A. Arbuckle, *Violence, Society, and the Church: A Cultural Approach* (Collegeville, MN: Liturgical Press, 2004), 47–48.

[64]*Final Report of the Royal Commission*, 44. Italics added.

[65]Ibid.

[66]Ibid.

[67]Jason Blakely, "Sexual Abuse and the Culture of Clericalism," www.americamagazine.org/faith/2018/08/23/sexual-abuse-and-culture-clericalism.

will require not only conversion but also the establishment of appropriate governance structures that give shared power to the laity (see Chapter 5).

One further contemporary problem making accountability to the People of God unworkable is the size of mega-dioceses. For example, the New York archdiocese has 2.8 million Catholics and 296 parishes, plus schools and other ministries; the Melbourne archdiocese, Australia, has 1.3 million Catholics and 216 parishes, hospitals, schools, and other ministries. Pope Francis calls evangelizers to "take on the 'smell of the sheep.'" Then "the sheep are willing to hear their voice."[68] In these situations, even with the assistance of auxiliary bishops, the gap between bishop and people is intolerably large. Bishops cannot take on the "smell of the sheep." And the risk of becoming involved in "mere administration"[69] is an inevitable possibility.

Defining Accountability

The term "accountability" describes a relationship in which one party has the duty, contractual or otherwise, to account to another for their performance of certain actions. Accountability is the right use of power. Brian Dive, an experienced international manager and consultant, writes:

> An accountable organization is one in which the responsibilities of the individuals who work in it are clearly defined, understood, and not overlapping. Those individuals are answerable, and what they must answer for is aligned to the purpose of the organization. In an accountable organization people . . . know they will be given the means to carry out the objectives they have agreed to. They also know what the consequences will be for not completing the tasks and assignments they have agreed to complete.[70]

Dive continues with this warning: "The problem is that most organizations do not know how to make sure this [accountabil-

---

[68]Pope Francis, "The Joy of the Gospel," para. 24.
[69]Ibid., para. 25
[70]Dive, *The Accountable Leader*, 32.

ity] happens. They are not sure how to hold leaders to account, or indeed what leadership means for different jobs throughout an organization."[71] Consequently, individuals and groups often surrender their autonomy, responsibility, and decision making to their group and leaders, with tragic consequences. Clericalism encourages this surrendering.

Clarifying Roles

The lack of clarity of roles in institutions is "a major source of conflict between people . . . making it easy for people, when its suits them, to arrogate authority to themselves, or to deny accountability and to pass the buck."[72] *Role* is "defined or taken up as a person identifies the aim of the system they belong to, takes ownership of that aim as a member of the system, and chooses the action and personal behaviour which from their position best contributes to achieving the aim."[73] It is the task of the leader to call people regularly to be accountable for their behavior as demanded by the roles they have accepted. At the same time a leader will ensure that the principle of subsidiarity is to be respected.[74] It is an abuse of power if this is not happening. In a dysfunctional and toxic culture, such as a clerical culture, roles remain unclarified and accountability neglected. However, not only subordinates are to be accountable for their actions. Leaders must also be.[75] When mutual accountability does not exist, energy that should be directed to refounding projects is dissipated in the resulting confusions and conflicts. Because the process of

---

[71]Ibid., 50.

[72]Elliott Jaques, *Requisite Organization* (Arlington, VA: Cason Hall, 1996), 76.

[73]Bruce Reed, *An Exploration of Role as Used in the Grubb Institute* (London: Grubb Institute, 2001), 2; John Newton, "'I've Never Thought of That Before': Organisational Role Analysis and Systems Development," *Social Analysis* 7 (2005): 67–79.

[74]The principle of subsidiarity means that whatever people are able to do for themselves ought not to be removed from their competence and taken over by other people. Decisions should not be made at higher levels if they can be effectively made lower down. For a fuller analysis of the foundations of the principle see Pontifical Council for Justice and Peace, *Compendium of the Social Doctrine of the Church* (Vatican: Libreria Editrice Vaticana, 2004), 104–7.

[75]See Chris Lowney, *Everyone Leads: How to Revitalize the Catholic Church* (Lanham, MD: Rowman & Littlefield, 2017), 97–112.

establishing and evaluating roles and accountability structures is complicated, wise leaders will seek professional advice to do so.[76] This is *not* the task of amateurs.

Jesus recognized the need for his disciples to be accountable for their pastoral actions. "He called the Twelve together and gave them power and authority . . . and sent them out to proclaim the kingdom of God and to heal" (Lk 9:1–2). On their return Jesus drew them aside "and they told Jesus all they had done" (Lk 9:10). Jesus at times would take an incident where the disciples had failed to understand their missionary task, using it as an occasion for pastoral learning. For example, when the disciples were confused about the meaning of their leadership role, Jesus took the opportunity to explain to them the nature of servant leadership in his kingdom (Lk 9:46–48) (see Chapter 4).

Strategies for Developing an Accountability Culture

- All by reason of their baptism have the right *and* obligation to call the entire church to be accountable to Vatican II values of transparency and collegiality. No one needs permission to do this, but it needs to be done with "the love, joy, peace, patience, kindness, goodness, trustfulness, gentleness and self-control" that Paul speaks of to the Galatians (Gal 5:22).
- Aided by professional advisers skilled in organizational accountability, leaders at all levels of the church will ensure that roles are clarified and establish effectively operative accountability structures that respect the principle of subsidiarity.
- Since the meaningful and direct consultation with, and participation of, lay people in the appointment of bishops, as well as greater transparency in that process, would make bishops more accountable and responsive to the lay people, conferences of bishops will "request the Holy See

---

[76]*The Final Report of the Royal Commission* states: "The Australian Catholic Bishops Conference and Catholic Religious Australia should establish a mechanism to ensure that diocesan bishops and religious superiors draw upon broad-ranging professional advice in their decision-making." Recommendation no. 16.22, 76.

[to] amend the appointment process of bishops."[77]

- Conferences of bishops will request that the Holy See amend canon law "so that offences related to child sexual abuse [be] framed as crimes against the child rather than 'delicts' against morals or a breach of the obligation to observe celibacy."[78]

- Dioceses will adopt authoritative constitutions, written with the assistance of lay women and men, outlining the roles, powers, and responsibilities of lay people, priests, religious brothers and sisters, and bishops.

- Diocesan synods will be held every five years in which lay people will have governance authority to participate, formulate, and evaluate progress in developing a new culture of collegiality and transparency at diocesan and parish levels.[79]

- Since a "policy, which protects whistleblowing done in good faith, can . . . be a protection against further abuse, . . . a policy for the protection of whistleblowing should be adopted immediately"[80] in dioceses (see Chapter 5).

- Conferences of bishops should consider requesting the Holy See to divide mega-dioceses into smaller ones in order to make accountability to the People of God a more reasonable possibility.

Development of Collaborative Leadership

Action Plan 8: Refounding leaders will cultivate a collaborative style of leadership since in the refounding process this is a central driver in cultural change and one important guarantee of transparency in decision-making.

---

[77]Ibid., Recommendation 16.8, 73.

[78]Ibid., Recommendation 16.9, 73.

[79]See William S. Cossen, "The Real Reason the Catholic Church Remains Plagued by Abuse Scandals," *Washington Post*, August 23, 2018. Historian Cossen describes the efforts of John England (1786–1841), first bishop of the Diocese of Charleston, SC, USA, to bring together clergy and lay people in regular conventions to assist in directing the development of local churches. While England's "proposal offered broader lay engagement, it did not offer authentic empowerment."

[80]*The McLellan Commission: A Review of the Current Safeguarding Policies, Procedures and Practice within the Catholic Church in Scotland* (2015), para. 4.26.

When change is driven from the top of the organization— without significant across-the-board participation—it is a recipe for failure...Participation empowers the vision.[81]

Explanation

A pivotal driver in cultural change is *collaborative leadership*. People are likely to resist change for these reasons: loss of what is known and tried or concern over personal loss. Changes substitute ambiguity and uncertainty for the familiar. (See *Axioms 1* and *7*, Chapter 1.) People will commonly enthusiastically accept change if its purpose and effects are well known in advance. If not, they will resist. Hence, the more people are involved in a collaborative way in change, the more they will be able to understand why the change is desired or necessary; if they are left out of the change process, their feelings of uncertainty intensify. Paul Parkin, a writer on change management, commented that the "'great man' theory of the single charismatic leader, developed from Nietzsche's conception of 'superman' so beloved by politicians and the head-hunter industry, is outdated and a mistake."[82] The collaborative approach also means that all ministerial team members will need to share in decision-making processes.[83] They may do this in one of several ways; for example, discussion leads to consensus or a majority vote or the team leader decides after consultation with other members. If circumstances permit, the preference is for the first option, namely full participation in decision making through consensus.

Strategies for Developing Collaborative Leadership

- Each newly appointed bishop will be expected to undergo leadership formation, with periodic refresher programs,

---

[81]James Belasco, *Teaching the Elephant to Dance* (New York: Penguin, 1990), 220.

[82]Parkin, *Managing Change*, 94.

[83]Since research shows it takes on average sixty ideas before one innovation is initiated, the most practical course a manager can take to encourage leadership and creativity in ministries is to foster a culture of trust and ease of communication. The more that trust and openness are encouraged, the more people are willing to articulate their ideas for evaluation and experimentation. See Simon Majaro, "Creativity in the Search for Strategy," in *The Financial Times Handbook of Management*, ed. Stuart Crainer (London: Pitman, 1995), 165.

that will include methods of consultation, accountability structures, organizational cultural analysis, subsidiarity, promotion of child protection.

- "Each religious institute . . . [will] ensure that its religious leaders are provided with leadership training, both before and after their appointment,"[84] that will include methods of consultation, accountability structures, organizational cultural analysis, subsidiarity, promotion of child protection, succession planning.

Intentional Faith Communities as Culture Changers

Action Plan 9: Since small, intentional mission-driven communities are agents of culture change, refounding leaders will foster their growth in parishes and other faith-based institutions, e.g., schools, health care, and community services.[85]

Growth in holiness is a journey in community, side by side with others. . . . A community that cherishes the little details of love, whose members care for one another and create an open and evangelizing environment, is a place where the risen Lord is present.[86]

Explanation

It is highly significant that the apostles formed small communities whose practice exemplified true sociality in a pagan world. Their unity of belief and practice accounts for the astonishing expansion of Christianity in early times. There are lessons here for today. Secularist pressures on our faith-based institutions such as health care, schools, and community services are intensifying. These institutions face an uncertain future regarding their identity and viability: Can the priority that needs to be given to the mission be reconciled with the realities of competition from big

---

[84]*Final Report of the Royal Commission*, Recommendation 16.36, 44.

[85]For a fuller explanation of intentional faith communities and their development see Gerald A. Arbuckle, *Intentional Faith Communities in Catholic Education* (Strathfield: St. Pauls Publications, 2017), 139–65.

[86]Pope Francis, "Rejoice and Exult," paras. 141, 145.

business, increasing costs, and government requirements?[87] And, for example, can the founding story of Catholic health care, as articulated in the Good Samaritan parable, continue to inspire institutions now that the original carriers of the story are in rapid decline? Similar questions are raised about the future of Catholic schools. Kathleen Engebretson, reflecting on her Australian experience of Catholic schools in Australia, and this would be the pattern in most ministries today, observes that there "are many individuals prepared to work in Catholic schools and to claim that they support its ethos." However, there are few who "are prepared to create and animate the ethos of the institution instead of just supporting it, who are passionate about the religious and cultural riches of the Church."[88]

Faced with these challenges, how is refounding to occur in these ministries? All organizations begin "as small groups and continue to function in part through various small groups within them."[89] The way to revitalize a parish, a school, or health care culture is through small faith-committed intentional communities: "For when two or three are gathered in my name, I am there among them" (Mt 18:20). Theologians Bernard Lee and Michael Cowan write, "An intentional Christian community is a relatively small group of persons committed to ongoing conversation and shared action along four distinguishable but interrelated dimensions."[90] The four dimensions are (1) people maintain a high degree of mutuality in their relationships; (2) they critique the world in which they live from the standpoint of gospel values; (3) they cultivate and sustain "lively connections with other persons, communities and movements of similar purpose," and (4) "they attend faithfully to the Christian character of their community's life."[91] The word "intentional" means "deliberate" or "consciously chosen."[92]

---

[87]See Richard A. McCormick, "The End of Catholic Hospitals?" *America*, July 4, 1998, 5–11.

[88]Kathleen Engebretson, *Catholic Schools and the Future of the Church* (London: Bloomsbury, 2014), 38.

[89]Edgar H. Schein, *Organizatonal Culture and Leadership* (San Francisco: Jossey-Bass, 1987), 188.

[90]Bernard J. Lee and Michael A. Cowan, *Dangerous Memories: House Churches and Our American Story* (Kansas City: Sheed & Ward, 1986), 91.

[91]Ibid., 92.

[92]Ibid., 91.

I suggest the following working definition: An intentional community is a group of people who feel the need to be supported in their ministries, for example, education, health care, and social services, and willingly commit themselves to develop a gospel-centered intimacy to be expressed in shared faith, ongoing conversation, and shared action for mission. A title for these small communities could be "Reflection for Action Groups" (RFAG). The availability of committed people to form these core faith communities will be limited in most contemporary ministries. These are the essential signs that an RFAG is effectively operating:

1. Sharing, that is, participants freely talk about God and about life experiences reflecting on these in light of scripture and tradition. They are *not* discussion groups, for members focus on their experience of Jesus Christ in their lives and educational ministry.
2. Learning, that is, participants in order to share their experience in light of scripture and tradition willingly undertake to learn more about the scriptures and the other foundations of Catholic identities on which the [ministry's] mission is based.
3. Core communities (RFAG) provide mutual support for their members who want to grow in the love for, and commitment to, Jesus Christ, the primary founder of the ministry.
4. The mission of core communities (RFAG) is to work for compassion, justice, reconciliation, and peace within the ministry's culture and the wider society.
5. Members cultivate a passionate commitment to the purpose of the communities and believe that their individual actions will help realize this purpose.
6. Members are willing to make a commitment for at least one year.[93]

Strategies for Developing Intentional Faith Communities

Refounding people will openly invite members of their ministry to form core communities for mission (RFAG); people should not feel in any way coerced to join; included in the invitation will be an

---

[93]Arbuckle, *Intentional Faith Communities*, 205.

explanation of fundamental qualities of core communities; when leaders have been selected by members they will need training in how to lead the communities.

Fostering Popular Piety

Action Plan 10: Movements of popular piety are to be encouraged; they inspire "active evangelizing power,"[94] *refusing to be dominated by clericalism.*

Explanation

Popular devotion is one of the few places where the People of God is sovereign removed from the influence of that clericalism that seeks to always control and stop the anointing of God on his people. Learning from popular piety is to learn to enter into a new kind of relationship of listening and spirituality that demands a lot of respect and does not lend itself to quick and simplistic readings since popular piety "reflects a thirst for God that only the poor and simple can know."[95]

Popular piety or religiosity refers to beliefs and practices relating to supernatural powers that exist *independently* of, or are not officially sanctioned by, ecclesiastical authorities. At the unofficial level of the church, movements of popular piety flourish, often in small intentional faith communities. Recognizing the need for all kinds of mediators or agents to intercede for them in a threatening world, it is not surprising that devotions to Our Lady and the saints are so important in popular piety.[96] It is called *popular* because it is thought that this form of religion belongs to the "masses" or working class only, as opposed to the educated elite. But this description is too restrictive because people of all classes find spiritual sustenance in popular piety.

Church officials, however, have frequently disparaged popu-

---

[94]Pope Francis, "The Joy of the Gospel," para. 126.

[95]Paul VI, *Evangelii Nuntiandi,* para. 48.

[96]See descriptions: Thomas Bamat and Jean-Paul Wiest, eds., *Popular Catholicism in a World Church* (Maryknoll, NY: Orbis Books, 1999); Michael R. Candelaria, *Popular Religion and Liberation: The Dilemma of Liberation Theology* (Albany: State University of New York Press, 1990), 1–38.

lar religiosity and seek either to destroy or domesticate it, often without success. Sociologist Bernice Martin claims that one reason for the rapid rise of Pentecostalism in South America is the disparaging of popular piety by "the educated international opinion-formers" following Vatican II who consider it to be in "dubious aesthetic taste and obsolete theological fashion."[97]

> This over-intellectualized Catholicism has offended many of the poor, who found the plain washed church interiors, the weakening of pious respect for Mary, the expulsion of the colorful devotions, and the removal of the statues of their favorite saints too much to take.[98]

Yet the Latin American Episcopate is more positive in their approach. They write that at "its core the religiosity of the people is a storehouse of values that offers the answers of Christian wisdom to the great questions of life. . . . It creatively combines the divine and the human, Christ and Mary, spirit and body, communion and institution . . . intelligence and emotion."[99]

Strategies for Fostering Popular Piety

At the heart of popular piety is the quality of child-like simplicity. It is an unambiguous loving trust in God and an undivided commitment to do God's will (Luke 11:34; Matt 6:24). Consequently refounding people will frequently ponder the implications —for themselves personally and for their faith communities—of these words of Jesus Christ when he called a child to join the disciples: "Truly I tell you, unless you change and become like children, you will never enter the kingdom of heaven. Whoever

---

[97]Bernice Martin, "From Pre- to Postmodernity in Latin America: The Case of Pentecostalism," in *Pentecostalism: The World Their Parish*, ed. David Martin (Oxford: Blackwell, 2002), 124–25.

[98]Gerald A. Arbuckle, *Culture, Inculturation, and Theologians: A Postmodern Critique* (Collegeville, MN: Liturgical Press, 2010), 135.

[99]"Final Document of the Third General Conference of the Latin American Episcopate, Puebla," in *Puebla and Beyond*, ed. John Eagleson and Philip Scharper (Maryknoll, NY: Orbis Books, 1979), 184–85. See also *Encountering Christ in Harmony: A Pastoral Response to Our Asian and Pacific Island Brothers and Sisters* (Washington, DC: United States Conference of Catholic Bishops, 2018), 24–26.

becomes humble like this child is the greatest in the kingdom of heaven. Whoever welcomes one such child in my name welcomes me" (Matt 18:3-5).

Storytelling and Refounding

Action Plan 11: *Refounding people recognize that storytelling can be a catalyst for cultural change.*[100]

Explanation

Stories catch people's attention. They bypass the normal defenses and engage people's feelings, their hearts. Listeners begin to see that they also can act to change their cultural environment as people were able to do in the narratives. Tom Peters's observation supports this: "[The] best leaders, especially in chaotic conditions . . . , almost without exception and at every level, are master users of stories and symbols."[101] Michael Kaye, a leading Australian expert on communications, comments:

> One reason for an organization gradually dying is a failure to renew itself through a healthy story-telling culture. A lot of organizations which fall apart have become demythologized. They have no way of knowing how to move forward because only the old stories and myths of past success continue to be recirculated. When there is no new thinking in the organization new stories are not generated. . . . If knowledge is power, then storytelling is an empowering agent.[102]

For example, in Fiji the traditional culture that emphasizes group harmony, cohesiveness, togetherness, stability, patriarchalism, and hierarchical authority, makes it extremely difficult, if not

---

[100]See Arbuckle, *Catholic Identity or Identities?* 173–225, and "To Teach and Heal as Jesus Did," *Health Progress: Journal of the Catholic Health Association of the United States* 96, no. 1 (2015): 25–33.

[101]Tom Peters, *Thriving on Chaos: Handbook for a Management Revolution* (London: Pan, 1989), 418.

[102]Michael Kaye, *Myth-Makers and Story-Tellers* (Sydney: Business & Professional Publishing, 1996), 123.

at times impossible, for individuals to develop their own sense of personal autonomy and initiative. The fear of being mocked, gossiped about, and shamed informally enforces conformity to the group's norms. It is a *strong group/strong grid* culture (see Chapter 2). Father Michael McVerry, SM, principal of the Tutu Training Centre, has developed an internationally esteemed, nonformal rural educational process that involves trainees at all stages of planning and implementation.[103] He believes "that people feel a commitment to a decision in proportion to the extent that they feel they have participated in making it."[104] The process is based on storytelling. McVerry is himself a brilliant storyteller, and this encourages trainees to articulate and share their stories of how they have failed and succeeded in confidently developing personal autonomy and changing their traditional culture in the process. Listeners when hearing the narratives of others begin to make sense of their own experiences of change and feel encouraged to share them with others. "Being listened to, whether for five or fifty minutes, can feel a great gift, being listened to and heard an even greater one."[105]

Storytelling is the inductive method that Jesus Christ as teacher used.[106] He knew that abstract principles about the need to change behavior are easier to grasp when viewed through the lens of a well-chosen story or parable. The parables are fictitious stories that Jesus tells in order to explain his teachings about personal and cultural change. In fact, a large part of the teachings of Jesus is conveyed through the numerous parables.[107] They are about ordinary individuals and everyday incidents but are told in a way that people in every age can identify with. Parables, like all symbols, have multiple meanings. The writers of the Gospels illustrate this.

---

[103]For a fuller explanation see Arbuckle, *Catholic Identity or Identities?* 227–45; also Paul Ricoeur's (1913–2005) authoritative analysis of the significance of narrative in human experience. *Time and Narrative,* vols. 1–3, trans. Kathleen M. Blamey and David Pellauer (Chicago: University of Chicago Press, 1984, 1985, 1988).

[104]Malcolm Knowles, Edwood F. Holton, and Richard Swanson, *The Adult Learner* (Oxford: Butterworth-Heinemann, 2011), 264.

[105]Anne Long, *Listening* (London: Darton, Longman, and Todd, 1990), 35.

[106]See Arbuckle, *Catholic Identity or Identities?* 121–42, 173–225.

[107]About one-third of the documented sayings of Jesus in the Synoptic Gospels are in the form of parables. See Brad H. Young, *The Parables: Jewish Tradition and Christian Interpretation* (Peabody, MA: Hendrickson, 1998), 7.

For Matthew (Mt 18:12–14), the Lost Sheep functions to exhort church leaders to care for the weak in the community; in Luke, it justifies Jesus' mission to the lost (Lk 15:4–7).[108] The parables of Jesus Christ and incidents in his life and/or in the Old Testament, for example, can again be discussion starters or springboards for people to craft their own meaning systems and discover that they can contribute to a new culture in the church, no matter the obstacles. Merely rational arguments about why the church must change sound flat and inane. Recall that culture is primarily about affective belonging and communication (see *Axiom 3*, Chapter 1).

Strategies for Storytelling

- Since the art of storytelling is so crucial in faith development, pastors and teachers in parishes, schools, and colleges need to be professionally formed in this skill.
- Since the future of the church depends more and more on people who are qualified, not only in the knowledge of the scriptures, but also in their ability to communicate this information to others in an inspiring manner, dioceses, colleges, and religious congregations need to sponsor laity to develop these dual gifts.

Formation of Priests

Action Plan 12: Given the rapid decline of vocations to the priesthood and the abuse crisis among priests it is urgent that existing recruitment policies and formation programs be assessed.[109]

---

[108]See Charles W. Hedrick, *Many Things in Parables* (Louisville: Westminster John Knox Press, 2004), 100–104.

[109]*Final Report of the Royal Commission* called the Catholic Church "to review . . . current models of initial formation to ensure that they promote pastoral effectiveness (including in relation to child safety and pastoral responses to victims and survivors) and protect against the development of clerical attitudes." Recommendation 16.24, 76. Also: The Australian Bishops Conference "should further develop, regularly evaluate and continually improve, their processes for selecting, screening and training of candidates for the clergy and religious life, and their processes of ongoing formation, support and supervision." Recommendation 16.20, ibid., 75, 76.

Explanation

The church must face two key issues regarding the future of the priesthood. First, in the Western world vocations to the priesthood are in rapid decline; a vanishing priesthood means for Catholics a dying sacramental life.[110] Second, the sexual scandals point to an urgency to develop formation processes that prevent clericalism. As regards the first issue—the rapid decline in the number of priests—inter alia there is a need to review the wisdom of maintaining a diocesan celibate clergy.[111] Karl Rahner comments: "It is not as if . . . the norms for selecting priests (e.g., the law of celibacy, exclusion of women from the priesthood . . .) had *necessarily* to be laid down by Rome for the whole Church. In these and similar matters Rome could leave a great deal to the particular churches."[112]

Regarding the second issue, namely, priestly and religious formation, the Australian inquiry into the sexual abuse of minors expressed grave concern about the current "processes for selecting, screening and training of candidates, and their processes of ongoing formation, support and supervision of clergy and religious."[113] The inquiry added that "there should be a national review of current models of initial formation to ensure that they promote pastoral effectiveness (including in relation to child safety and pastoral responses to victims and survivors) and *protect against the development of clericalist attitudes.*"[114] The inquiry

---

[110]See Richard A. Schoenherr, *Goodbye Father: The Celibate Male Priesthood and the Future of the Catholic Church* (Oxford: Oxford University Press, 2002), xxx.

[111]*Final Report of the Royal Commission* concluded that "based on research . . . there is an elevated risk of child sexual abuse where compulsorily celibate male clergy or religious have privileged access to children in certain types of Catholic institutions, including schools, residential institutions and parishes. For many Catholic clergy and religious, celibacy is implicated in emotional isolation, loneliness, depression and mental illness," 71.

[112]Karl Rahner, *Concern for the Church (Theological Investigations*, vol. 20) (New York: Crossroad, 1981), 121–22. Theologian Gerald O'Collins, SJ, believes that the present argument to exclude women from the priesthood is inadequate: "If limiting priestly ordination to men is to be recognised as an unchangeable truth of Catholic faith, it needs a more effective defence than this." "Still Open to Doubt," *The Tablet*, June 9, 2018, 11.

[113]*Final Report of the Royal Commission*, Recommendation 16.20, 75.

[114]Ibid., Recommendation 16.14, 76. Italics added.

sees a definite link between contemporary seminary/religious life formation processes and clericalism.

The seminary system of priestly formation has its origins in the Council of Trent (1545–1563) which, in reaction to existing abuses and the Protestant Reformation, sought to reform clerical training. The type of formation adopted by the council can be termed the Institutional/Conformity Model.[115] It was based on the classicist view of the church, namely, that the church could move through the centuries unaffected by changes in society. All the truths needed for life are to be found in the Catholic Church; society is divinely ordered to be hierarchical and patriarchal. Thus the priest's identity is essentially a cultic one and the conveyor of dogmatic truths to laity. Since the world is evil, priestly formation needs to be isolated from society (see Chapter 2). Although there have been modifications to the model since Vatican II, the emphasis in priestly training on separation from the world has generally continued, thus favoring clericalist and elitist attitudes.

With Vatican II's openness to the world, the identity of the priest changed accordingly:

> Priests exercise, within the limits of their authority, the office of Christ, the shepherd and head. They assemble the family of God as a community fired with a single ideal, they lead it through Christ, in the Spirit, to the Father. All the elements essential to an appropriate priestly spirituality are present here: animating spirit or dynamism, identity, context, activity, and goal.[116]

Hence, there must be radical changes to the traditional model of formation.[117] Since the priest's primary ministry is pastoral, priests must be formed within the world, not in isolation. By leading a

---

[115]See Gerald A. Arbuckle, *From Chaos to Mission: Refounding Religious Life Formation* (London: Geoffrey Chapman, 1985), 102–7.

[116]Robert M. Schwartz, *Servant Leaders of the People of God: An Ecclesial Spirituality for American Priests* (New York: Paulist Press, 1989), 212–13.

[117]See Katarina Schuth, "Assessing the Education of Priests and Lay Ministers: Content and Consequences," in *The Crisis of Authority in Catholic Modernity*, ed. Michael J. Lacey and Francis Oakley (New York: Oxford University Press, 2011), 317–47.

community of faith by preaching and sacramental ministry, the priest is called to help the whole community deepen the quality of its gospel life and its worship.[118] As this is the mission of the priest, candidates must exemplify leadership and personal qualities adequate to this task. Also, there must be evidence to support the well-founded hope candidates will be able to contribute to the refounding of the church.

Strategies for the Selection and Training of Priests

- Individual conferences of bishops need to petition the Holy See to allow voluntary celibacy for diocesan clergy.[119]
- Candidates for priesthood and religious life should not be accepted until:
  - they have been psychologically screened and assessed by a professional team, the majority of whom are lay people;
  - they have obtained a university degree or trade certificate;
  - they are committed to life-long learning;
  - they have proved themselves willing and able to be involved in refounding ministries.
- Theological training is to take place in institutions alongside lay students, and the process of formation is to be based on the "oscillation principle," i.e., candidates while not living in separate institutions will at set times in the year come together for specialized personal formation in priestly life.

---

[118]See "Decree on the Ministry and Life of Priests" (*Presbyterorum Ordinis*), *Documents of Vatican II*, para. 2.

[119]*The Final Report of the Royal Commission* recommended: "The Australian Catholic Bishops Conference should request the Holy See to consider introducing voluntary celibacy for diocesan clergy." Recommendation 16.18, 75. And "whether or how existing models of religious life could be modified to facilitate alternative forms of association, shorter terms of celibate commitment, and/or voluntary celibacy (where that is consistent with the form of association that has been chosen)." Recommendation 16.19, 75. The Australian Catholic Bishops Conference agreed that the Holy See should be informed of these recommendations. See *Australian Catholic Bishops Conference and Catholic Religious Australia's Response to the Royal Commission* (August 31, 2018), 16–17.

- An adult learning methodology based on experience will be used in theological training of candidates.
- Formators of candidates are to be chosen for their personal integrity and well-proven professional skills in pastoral theology, spirituality, and the social sciences.
- Candidates must have regular periods in pastoral ministries, particularly ministries that relate to people who are poor.
- Once ordained, priests must have regular pastoral supervision and regular professional updating workshops, including regular updating workshops on the protection of minors and vulnerable persons.
- No priest from another country should be incardinated in a diocese unless:
  - professionally screened;
  - fluent in the local language, with the ability to speak and preach clearly;
  - trained to be culturally sensitive to local needs;
  - fully briefed on the laws and regulations relating to the protection of minors and vulnerable persons.

Lay Formation

Action Plan 13: Since many of the church's key ministries are now led by lay people, it is essential, if a new culture of church is to emerge and be sustained, that they be not only professionally competent, but be profoundly knowledgeable of, and formed in, the founding mythologies of their ministries according to the Catholic tradition.

Explanation

Lay leaders in our ministries face significant challenges and need consequently to be well formed in the church's theology and social teaching. The church's educational, health care institutions, and social services are committed to articulate the mission of Jesus Christ to the contemporary world, but they face uncertain futures. Their ability to maintain the primary emphasis on the mission as the driving force in all decision making is increasingly threatened by cultural, economic, and political forces (see *Action Plan 9*).[120] They are in constant danger of "forgetting that the most important measure of success is the achievement of mission-related objectives, not [their] financial wealth or stability."[121] What Basil Mott, Dean of Health Studies, University of New Hampshire, wrote in 1986 still remains relevant today: "I speak of such . . . tough talk as strategy, tactics, market penetration, and product realignment-jargon that depicts a world of winners and losers, a macho world that is like war." This is scarcely "a language that evokes the values of serving and caring for human beings."[122] For example, the values of faith-based health care, as they emerge in the Good Samaritan story, are fundamentally opposed to this kind of patriarchal and competitive management language. Well-researched strategies and targets are needed, but they must always be prepared and implemented in the context of the mission of holistic healing.

Strategies for Lay Ministries

- Only people who are who prepared to be attitudinally and operationally deeply imbued by the mission and values of a ministry should be appointed to key positions in that ministry.
- It is urgent that diocesan and religious congregations direct resources to adult education to train lay people in theology and social teachings of the church so that they are well prepared to participate as leaders in ministries, including governance levels, of the church.[123]

---

[120]See Arbuckle, *Healthcare Ministry*, xi–xxiii; Leonard J. Nelson, *Diagnosis Critical: The Urgent Threats Confronting Catholic Health Care* (Huntington, IN: Our Sunday Visitor, 2009), 9–22, 79–130.

[121]J. Gregory Dees, "Enterprising Nonprofits," in *Harvard Business Review on Nonprofits* (Boston: Harvard Business School Publishing, 1999), 164.

[122]Basil J. Mott, "Whither the Soul of Health Care?" in *The For-Profit Hospital*, ed. Richard M. F. Southby and Warren Greenberg (Columbus, OH: Battelle Press, 1986), 144.

[123]Peter Drucker's comments are relevant here: "[Few] service institutions attempt to think through the changed circumstances in which they operate. Most believe that all that is required is to run harder and raise more money. Precisely because results in service institutions are not easily measured, there is need for organized abandonment. There is need for a systematic withdrawal of resources of money, but above all, people—from yesterday's efforts." *Managing in Turbulent Times* (London: Pan Books, 1982), 46.

Evaluating Pastoral Care

Action Plan 14: Bishops,[124] *priests,*[125] *congregational superiors,*[126] *and lay leaders, in their pastoral care of the People of God in this abuse crisis, must recommit themselves to the mission of teaching, sanctifying, and governing.*

Explanation

Vatican II defines the pastoral ministry of bishops in collaboration with their priests as that of teaching, sanctifying, and governing. This ministry is one, not three; all aspects must be motivated and undertaken in a Gospel manner.

> If circumstances at times require that one of these three aspects be given greater prominence, the other two are never to be separated or disregarded, lest the inner unity of the entire ministry be weakened in any way. . . . Hence the bishop, by virtue of his very ministry, is responsible in a special way for the growth of holiness of all his faithful.[127]

And:

> Above all, upon the bishop rests the heavy responsibility for the sanctity of his priests. Hence, he should exercise the greatest care on behalf of the continual formation of his priests. He should gladly listen to them, indeed, consult them, and have discussions with them about those matters

---

[124]See *Documents of Vatican II*, ed. Austin P. Flannery (Grand Rapids, MI: William B. Eerdmans, 1975). "The Dogmatic Constitution on the Church" (*Lumen Gentium*), paras. 25–27; "Decree on the Bishops' Pastoral Office" (*Christus Dominus*), paras. 12–20.

[125]See *Vatican II Documents*, "Decree on the Ministry of Priests" (*Presbyterorum Ordinis*), paras. 4–6.

[126]See *Vatican II Documents,* "The Dogmatic Constitution on the Church" (*Lumen Gentium*), para. 43; "Decree on Renewal of Religious Life" (*Perfectae Caritatis*), paras. 1, 2.

[127]Sacred Congregation for Religious and for Secular Institutes, and Sacred Congregation for Bishops, *Directives for the Mutual Relations between Bishops and Religious in the Church* (Homebush: St. Paul Publication, 1978), para. 7.

which concern the necessities of pastoral work and the welfare of the diocese.[128]

It is an act of spiritual abuse, theological scandal (see *Axiom 13*, Chapter 1), if a bishop or his priests culpably fail to provide pastoral care according to Gospel values. Thus the clerical sexual abuse is not only an emotional and psychological abuse of survivors, it is also an act of spiritual abuse because they are denied Gospel guidance and above all example. Moreover, the knowing assignment of priests to situations where sexual abuse is most likely to occur may not only be criminal but the spiritual abuse of the victims *and* the perpetrators. Pope Francis speaks of "spiritual corruption." It "is worse than the fall of a sinner, for it is a comfortable and self-satisfied form of blindness."[129] Canon law does not minimize the seriousness of failures in this ministry: "A person who, through culpable negligence, unlawfully and with harm to another, performs or omits an act of ecclesiastical power or ministry or office, is to be punished with a just penalty" (Can. 1389, para. 2).

Likewise, lay leaders of ministries and religious congregational leaders also have the same pastoral ministry of teaching, sanctifying, and governing. For example, congregational leaders "must carry on a veritable *spiritual direction*" of their communities. "They must foster perfection in what concerns the increase of charity according to the end of [their institutes]. . . . As to the *office of governing,* superiors must render the service of ordering the life of the community, of organizing the members of the institute."[130] As is the case with bishops, culpable failure in any aspect of this ministry is an act of spiritual abuse because people have the right to be treated with respect and according to Gospel values. Thus a congregational leader who fails to govern according to a congregation's constitutions and statutes spiritually abuses individual members and/or communities; not only are members and communities left disempowered, their dignity affronted, but

---

[128]"Decree on the Ministry of Priests," para. 7.
[129]Pope Francis, "Rejoice and Exult" (*Gaudete et Exsultate*) (Strathfield: St. Pauls Publications, 2018), para. 165.
[130]Ibid., para. 13.

the neglect affects their quality of ministry to the faithful they are called to serve. Such are the ripple effects of spiritual abuse.

Strategies for Evaluating Pastoral Care

- As the pastoral care of his priests is the first responsibility of a bishop, each diocese must annually evaluate, according to collaboratively approved criteria, how this role obligation is being fulfilled; the evaluation is to be undertaken by a committee consisting of an equal number of lay people and clerics.
- In religious congregations of pontifical rite and diocesan congregations it is the duty of congregational leaders and bishops respectively to assess the effectiveness of roles and accountability; if superiors or leaders of communities are failing to be accountable to their constitutions and statutes, they must be counseled and, if necessary, replaced.

Pastoral Care of Survivors

Action Plan 15: The church and religious congregations have an obligation in justice to ensure the survivors of sexual abuse are offered appropriate short- and long-term pastoral care.

Explanation

The Australian inquiry into the sexual abuse of minors concluded: "The most common impact of child abuse is on the survivor's mental health. The impacts include: depression, anxiety and post-traumatic stress disorder; other symptoms of mental distress such as nightmares and sleeping difficulties; and emotional issues such as feelings of shame, guilt and low self-esteem." Further distressing consequences included "difficulties with trust and intimacy, lack of confidence with parenting and relationships," the development of "addictions after using alcohol or other drugs to manage the psychological trauma of abuse."[131]

---

[131]*Final Report of the Royal Commission*, 16.

A study of clergy-enacted sexual abuse shows that the abuse "can catastrophically alter the trajectory of psychosocial, sexual, and spiritual development [of survivors]."[132] Even the retelling of their story can plunge survivors into profound grief.[133] When family members and others refuse to believe that abuse has occurred, it adds to the sufferings of survivors. The ripple effects—for example, shame, disillusionment, breakdown of trust—extend also beyond survivors, affecting family members, friends, staffs of institutions, and the wider community (see Chapter 3).[134] These ripple consequences "can be long-lasting and may affect future generations."[135]

Christian pastoral care "has one fundamental aim: to help people to know love, both as something to be received and something to give."[136] Its particular functions "are healing, sustaining, reconciling, guiding and nurturing."[137] As regards the pastoral care of the survivors of sexual abuse, the Australian inquiry warns: "Inappropriate and damaging responses by institutions can not only place children at risk, they can leave victims and their families feeling betrayed by the institutions they trusted. This can result in re-traumatisation and a fear and distrust of institutions."[138]

Strategies for Pastoral Care of Survivors

- Jesus teaches by word and example that the most important form of pastoral care is to listen, a quality open to all. Consider the story of Bartimaeus. He is "sitting at the side of the road" (Mk 10:46). In this one statement we see why society has rejected him. He is a beggar as well as being blind; for no

---

[132]Jason M. Fogler, Jillian C. Shipherd, Erin Rowe, Jennifer Jensen, and Stephanie Clarke, "A Theoretical Foundation for Understanding Clergy-Perpetrated Sexual Abuse," *Journal of Child Sexual Abuse* 17 (2008): 330.

[133]See Judith L. Herman, *Trauma and Recovery: From Domestic Abuse to Political Terror* (London: Pandora, 1992), 175–95.

[134]See "'Ripple Effects' of Sexual Assault," Australian Government/Australian Institute of Family Studies, ACSSA Issues No. 7 (June 2007): 1–11.

[135]*Final Report of the Royal Commission*, 17.

[136]Alistair V. Campbell, *Paid to Care?* (London: SPCK, 1985), 1.

[137]Stephen Pattison, *Pastoral Care and Liberation Theology* (Cambridge: Cambridge University Press, 1994), 14.

[138]*Final Report of the Royal Commission*, 17.

reason of his own, both factors render him ritually dirty and socially shamed. The words "sitting at the side of the road" symbolically describe this social exclusion and stigmatization. Survivors of sexual abuse are most often made to feel the same sense of shame and exclusion. As one abused survivor says: "I feel dirty, and responsible for what happened to me as a child. I have isolated myself . . . hidden my true feelings. The loneliness I have experienced is overwhelming."[139]

Jesus is traveling by, and Bartimaeus cries out for healing. The crowd does its best to silence and further shame him, "but he only shouted the louder" (Mk 10:48). This is a culture of violence, an abuse of power—the dehumanizing of people—and no one questions it. Jesus will have none of this fundamentalist and violent poppycock. He calls Bartimaeus to his side and tenderly asks him what he wishes: "Rabunni, let me see again!" (Mk 10:51). Jesus actually listens to a poor person, contrary to the culture of his time. This is the message of Bartimaeus: let me again be an acknowledged member of society, with a sense of pride and responsibility. By speaking directly to Bartimaeus—a social nonperson—Jesus breaks through the shame and the political, economic, and cultural barriers that ensnare the blind man. By defying these stigmatizing and discriminating barriers, Jesus allows Bartimaeus to find again his ability to be and act like a human person with dignity.

Jesus by his attitude and action reassures Bartimaeus that he is a person of dignity and therefore to be respected. He empowers Bartimaeus no longer to accept the cultural stigma demanding poor persons must remain silent and excluded. Jesus actually asks Bartimaeus what he would like: "What do you want me to do for you?" (Mk 10:51). Jesus having been himself rebuffed by society, even threatened already with death, knows from personal experience the fears and loneliness of Bartimaeus. Jesus is thus able to reach out to Bartimaeus and compassionately touch his inner anguish of social isolation and loneliness. Bartimaeus feels that Jesus understands and is empowered confidently to act with courage in the face of the crowd's rejection. Once healed, Barti-

---

[139]Cited by Royal Commission, ibid., 15.

maeus is no longer marginalized. He has the right to walk again freely "along the road."

There are two critical strategies from this incident, first, the vital need: to listen to *and* hear survivors' stories because authentic empathy is the effort to understand the suffering of the survivor as he or she experiences it; second, the importance of creating communities where survivors feel welcome and trusted.

- It is urgent that dioceses and other institutions establish services that provide long-term pastoral care for survivors. Financial compensation and payments for a set number of counseling sessions may be insufficient to respond to the needs of survivors.
- Pastoral care needs to be extended to those who, in addition to survivors, are affected by sexual abuse, for example, family members, communities, the wrongly accused, and the perpetrators themselves.
- People who are accused of sexual abuse must have their rights protected. They are innocent until proven guilty. If guilty they also have the Gospel right to pastoral care.

Summary

For Jesus, it is not enough for his followers to hear what he says. They must act on what he is teaching them! "But the one who hears and does not act is like a man who built a house on the ground without a foundation. When the river burst against it, immediately it fell, and great was the ruin of that house" (Lk 6:49).

The lesson of the story is as valid today as in the time of Jesus. Reforming the church through refounding demands rock-hard foundations: *ongoing* radical structural reforms inspired by profound *conversion* to the person and mission of Jesus Christ: "Let us run with perseverance the race that is set before us, looking to Jesus the pioneer and perfecter of our faith" (Heb 12:1–2). Then we will genuinely be like the wise person "building a house, who dug deeply and laid on rock; when a flood arose, the river burst against that house but could not shake it, because it had been well built" (Lk 6:48). However, if we attempt refounding without authentic foundations, future generations will rightly mock and bemoan our stupidities. But the challenges presented in this book's chapters are clear to the wise. The anthropological evidence is overwhelming. There is no room for cover-up. Yet the more we become truly pilgrim people, the more we will rediscover the inner power of God's energizing love: "For to me, living is Christ and dying is gain" (Phil 1:21). This is the wisdom that ultimately motivates people committed to refounding the church.

Index